PSYCHOLOGY IN SPORTS COACHING

Some of the most effective coaches understand the fundamentals of sport psychology, which include interacting effectively with athletes, creating the optimal environment, assessing the psychological needs of their athletes, and even providing them with the mental training required to maximise performance.

Fully revised and updated, the second edition of *Psychology in Sports Coaching: Theory and Practice* clearly and accessibly introduces the principles and practice of sports psychology in the context of the coaching process. Drawing on the very latest research and theory, the book introduces the psychological tools and techniques that coaches can use to get the best performances out of their athletes.

Including six new chapters on applying self-determination principles in coaching, creating the optimal motivational climate, increasing motivation, developing anti-doping attitudes, promoting challenge states, and mindfulness-based stress reduction training, the book also offers step-by-step guidance on key topics such as:

- Assessing the needs of athletes
- Facilitating awareness through goal-setting and performance profiling
- Working with special populations, including children and injured athletes
- Building team cohesion
- Maximising relationships and socially supporting athletes
- Teaching mental skills such as imagery and coping
- Building mental toughness and confidence.

Every chapter contains useful features to aid learning and understanding, including in-depth case studies, critical thinking questions, clear and concise summaries, and practice exam questions. *Psychology in Sports Coaching: Theory and Practice* is essential reading for any student of sports coaching or any practising coach looking to extend and develop their skills, and useful applied reading for students of sport psychology.

Adam R. Nicholls is a Reader in the Department of Sport, Health, and Exercise Science at the University of Hull, UK. He teaches a variety of modules relating to sport psychology and incorporating sport psychology within coaching practice. His primary research is related to stress, appraisal, and coping among athletes, which is reflected in his publications. Recently he developed an interest in attitudes towards doping, particularly among adolescent athletes and coaches. This work is funded by the World Anti-Doping Agency, the International Olympic Committee, and the European Commission: Education, Audiovisual and Culture Executive Agency. He is a chartered psychologist and Associate Fellow of the British Psychological Society. He is also a Registered Sport and Exercise Psychologist with the Health and Care Professions Council. He currently serves as an Associate Editor for *Frontiers in Psychology*, and sits on the editorial board for the *International Journal of Sport Psychology*.

"The domain of sport psychology is often underplayed in terms of coach education and development, however many of the topics highlighted in this book represent key knowledge areas that can help us as coaches to address the genuine needs of athletes. By understanding more in the field of psychology, we can help to create both relationships and environments that allow us to support individuals to achieve their potential in the sports that they play."

— *Andy Rock, Academy Director, Bath Rugby, UK*

"Dr Nicholls' text showcases an excellent array of applied psychological perspectives in the specialist domain of sport coaching. The updated chapters are truly reflective of the emerging conceptualisation of sport coaching and offer coaches, students, administrators and academics alike a realistic glimpse into the potential for enhancing our understanding of the uses of psychology in making a difference to coaching processes and practice."

— *Professor David Morley, Professor of Youth Sport & Physical Activity and Head of the Academy of Sport & Physical Activity, Sheffield Hallam University, UK*

"This second edition of *Psychology in Sports Coaching: Theory and Practice* provides practical insight and guidance for coaches and athletes in a sporting environment. The applied nature of this book is why it is such an important read and resource for coaches and athletes alike."

— *Dr Colin Sanctuary, Head of Physical Development, Newcastle Knights RL, Australia*

PSYCHOLOGY IN SPORTS COACHING

Theory and Practice

Second Edition

Adam R. Nicholls

Routledge
Taylor & Francis Group

LONDON AND NEW YORK

Second edition published 2017
by Routledge
2 Park Square, Milton Park, Abingdon, Oxon, OX14 4RN

and by Routledge
711 Third Avenue, New York, NY 10017

Routledge is an imprint of the Taylor & Francis Group, an informa business

First edition published by Routledge 2013

British Library Cataloguing in Publication Data
A catalogue record for this book is available from the British Library

Library of Congress Cataloging in Publication Data
A catalog record for this book has been requested

ISBN: 978-1-138-70186-1 (hbk)
ISBN: 978-1-138-70187-8 (pbk)
ISBN: 978-1-315-20383-6 (ebk)

Typeset in Bembo
by HWA Text and Data Management, London

Printed and bound by CPI Group (UK) Ltd, Croydon, CR0 4YY

To Lawson

May you always try your hardest and enjoy everything you do. Be content with whatever happens in the knowledge that you have given your all.

Love always, Dad.

CONTENTS

List of figures   x
List of tables   xi

Introduction   1

PART I
Providing sport psychology training as a coach   **7**

1   Do's and don'ts for coaches who provide sport psychology to
    their athletes: ethics, referrals, and the HCPC   9

PART II
Identifying the psychological needs of athletes   **13**

2   Conducting intake interviews   15

3   Using questionnaires to assess the needs of athletes   23

PART III
Facilitating awareness among athletes   **31**

4   Goal setting   33

5   Performance profiling   43

PART IV
Coaching different populations: how to support the needs of different athletes   53

6 Coaching children   55

7 Coaching adolescents   61

8 Coaching adults   70

9 Coaching athletes with learning disabilities   79

10 Providing psychological support to an injured athlete   91

PART V
Relationships, support, and influence within coaching practice   103

11 The coach–athlete relationship   105

12 Understanding and building team cohesion   113

13 Supporting athletes socially   122

14 Enhancing motivation among athletes   130

15 Creating the optimal motivational climate   139

16 Applying self-determination theory and research to enhance coaching practice   148

17 Promoting anti-doping attitudes among athletes   157

PART VI
Developing mental skills among athletes   169

18 Mental imagery   171

19 Mental toughness training   183

20 Maximising sport-confidence   194

21 Coping effectiveness training   207

22 Enhancing challenge states and minimising threat states
    among athletes   220

23 Mindfulness-based stress reduction training   231

24 Preventing choking under pressure in sport   239

    References   *247*
    Index   *275*

FIGURES

5.1	Completed performance profile	47
5.2	Team performance profile	48
5.3	April performance profile	50
12.1	Team cohesion in sport	114
16.1	Self-determined motivation continuum	149
17.1	An adapted version of Donovan's SDCM	159
17.2	Adapted version of the SDCM-AA	163
20.1	Confidence performance profile	201
21.1	Symptoms of stress	213
21.2	Demand and coping evaluation	214
22.1	Cardiac activity associated with challenge and threat states	222
22.2	Vascular resistance associated with challenge and threat states	222
22.3	Achievement goals in sport	225
23.1	The axioms of mindfulness	232
23.2	The benefits of mindfulness training	233
24.1	The physical symptoms associated with choking	240
24.2	The psychological symptoms associated with choking	240

TABLES

3.1	Questionnaires widely used within the sport literature	26
5.1	Physical, technical, tactical, and psychological characteristics	45
5.2	Example of completed table of important qualities	46
12.1	Factors that influence task and social cohesion	115
17.1	Threats associated with enforcement	160
17.2	Threats to health associated with PEDs	160
17.3	The possible health consequences of doping	165
20.1	Important attributes to be confident about	198
20.2	Qualities and meanings	199
20.3	Sources of sport confidence	200
21.1	Stressor controllability	216

INTRODUCTION

The second edition of this book has specifically been written to help students studying coaching to understand the psychological principles of coaching to maximise coaching effectiveness. The purpose of this introduction is to explain:

- Overview of changes for the second edition
- Sports coaching: it's purpose, what it is, and how it differs from teaching
- What sport psychology is and isn't and its synergy with coaching
- Contexts in which coaches and sport psychologists work together
- Contexts in which coaches might prefer not to work with a sport psychologist
- The benefits of incorporating psychology within coaching
- Psychology and an athlete's ability
- The structure and contents of this book
- How to get the most out of this book
- Chapter features.

Overview of changes for the second edition

The second edition of this book contains six new chapters:

- Enhancing motivation among athletes (Chapter 14)
- Creating the optimal motivational climate (Chapter 15)
- Applying self-determination theory and research to enhance coaching practice (Chapter 16)
- Promoting anti-doping attitudes among athletes (Chapter 17)
- Creating challenge states and minimising threat states among athletes (Chapter 22)
- Mindfulness-based stress reduction training (Chapter 23).

In addition to these new chapters, the other chapters are all updated so that they include the latest theory and research. Furthermore, the second edition also includes case study questions.

Sports coaching: its purpose, what it is, and how it differs from teaching

According to Lyle (2011), the purpose of sports coaching is to improve the performance of an athlete or sports team. Providing a definition of sports coaching that fully encapsulates what it is, can be somewhat problematic and goes much beyond this introduction. There are a number of extensive commentaries regarding what sports coaching is and how it can be conceptualised (Cushion, 2007a, 2007b; Lyle, 2007).

For the purposes of this book, sports coaching refers to the process in which a person or people attempt to improve the sporting performance of an athlete or team in competition, by manipulating the behaviour and creating practice environments that facilitate improvement. This person, or people, are often given the title of "coach", and perform a multitude of roles (Lyle, 2011). Indeed, Lyle (2011) stated that the coach provides technical advice to his or her athlete or team with the sole purpose of helping the athlete or team achieve better performances and thus results when competing. In addition to providing technical support, Côté and Gilbert (2009) also suggested that sports coaches provide leadership, motivation, and education to their athletes. Although the primary role of coaches who engage in sports coaching is performance enhancement, sports coaching also has the potential to enhance the psychological well-being of athletes by making sport a positive experience for athletes (Côté et al., 2010).

Coaching is different from teaching. Sports coaching refers to the process of preparing an athlete or team to perform within a sports competition, whereas teaching refers to developing a person's skills not for competitive purposes (Lyle, 2011). As such, sports coaching is primarily concerned with performance enhancement within competitive sport.

The synergy of coaching with sport psychology

Unlike sport psychology, coaching is not primarily concerned with maximising psychological well-being. However, coaching has the potential to improve well-being by creating positive experiences for athletes (Côté et al., 2010). As such, coaching and sport psychology complement each other nicely, so it could be argued that one of the roles a coach should play should involve an element of psychology, to enhance performance above and beyond what technical training drills may achieve alone.

Some coaches may be sceptical of sport psychology, partly due to the negative attention that this discipline receives or a coach's negative experiences of sport psychology. There are many unqualified individuals working in professional sport who pose as sport psychologists. These individuals will not be sufficiently trained to provide an adequate service and may cause more harm than good. Such individuals may give coaches and athletes unrealistic expectations regarding what sport psychology can achieve.

It is important that coaches realise that sport psychology is not an instant cure for the problems an athlete may be encountering. As stated by Nicholls and Callard (2012), teaching an athlete mental skills is not like waving a magic wand in front of his or her face, that will instantly transform the athlete or team into world beaters. However, sport psychology involves teaching athletes a variety of mental skills, which when practised can help athletes improve their performance and boost mental well-being.

Contexts in which coaches and sport psychologists work together

Coaches and sport psychologists may work together when athletes from individual sports such as tennis or golf employ both a coach and a sport psychologist. In other circumstances, coaches may employ the sport psychologist to work with their team. Generally, a coach would employ a sport psychologist when he or she feels that the athlete or team are suffering from psychological problems (e.g. anxiety) that are having a negative impact on performance or feels that performance can be enhanced through the implementation of psychological techniques. The sport psychologist would work with the athlete or team to help them with anxiety, which could then result in performance being increased when the full effects of the sport psychology sessions are observed.

Additionally, coaches might work exclusively with sport psychologists, so the sport psychologist does not have any contact with the athletes, but provides information to the coach who relays that on. For example, the sport psychologist might help the coach with matters such as how to provide more effective instructions, feedback, and communication strategies. There are a number of sport psychologists who work exclusively in this capacity. As such, there are many contexts in which coaches and sport psychologists may work alongside one another.

Contexts in which coaches might prefer not to work with a sport psychologist

Although coaches can employ sport psychologists themselves to help their athletes, there may be some instances in which coaches are reluctant to introduce a sport psychologist to his or her team or athlete. For example, a coach may be reticent to hire a sport psychologist if he or she has just started coaching an athlete or team, because the coach may feel that the sport psychologist could in some ways undermine his or her relationship with the team or athletes. Some athletes might not feel comfortable talking about their feelings or problems with sport psychologists who they do not know, and would prefer to speak to their coach. In these instances, coaches might prefer not to employ a sport psychologist, even though the team or athlete could benefit from mental training. In these instances, coaches could provide psychological training themselves and incorporate psychology within their coaching.

The benefits of incorporating psychology within coaching

Coaches invest lots of time learning about how to improve the technical skills of their players or athletes through many different drills, how to improve the fitness or conditioning of their players, and how they can teach different tactics or strategies to enhance performance. Perhaps less time is spent learning and understanding how a coach can apply psychological principles within their coaching. Using psychology in coaching is something that has been, on the whole, ignored in many coaching manuals. This is a shame because there are so many athletes that could benefit from being taught different psychological skills. For example, there are many athletes who perform well in training, but struggle to transfer their performance to competition settings. Physiologically or technically the athlete has not changed, but perhaps these athletes struggle psychologically and could benefit from a coach providing them with some psychological training.

Incorporating psychology within coaching enables the coach to become more effective by improving the quality of his or her coaching, which will have numerous benefits for players including increased enjoyment and performance.

Psychology and an athlete's ability

Psychology is not just for elite athletes, and athletes at all levels ranging from beginners to Olympic champions can potentially benefit from psychology. Therefore, those who coach club level tennis players to those who coach international rugby union teams can help their players by incorporating psychology within their coaching and some of the principles advocated in this book.

The structure and contents of this book

This book has been written for students who study coaching, and who want to learn more about applying sport psychology principles to coaching. This book provides the reader with an understanding of how coaches can apply psychological principles to their coaching to maximise the enjoyment, learning, and performance of the athletes that are coached. The book is presented in six parts:

Part I: Providing sport psychology training as a coach

This part of the book provides a brief introduction to what sport psychology is, and what it isn't, and provides information on how coaches provide psychological training to their athletes. In particular, it covers information on the ethical implications of coaches providing psychological training, the referral process, and the regulation of sport psychologists, which is a protected term.

Part II: Identifying the psychological needs of athletes

This part of the book provides information on the techniques that coaches can use to assess the needs of their athletes, and to establish which mental skills training interventions to deliver. As such, it provides information on how coaches can conduct needs analysis interviews (Chapter 2) and use questionnaires (Chapter 3). Some athletes may prefer to talk more than other athletes, whereas others may prefer writing their answers down in the form of questionnaires.

Part III: Facilitating awareness

In this part, information is provided on how the coach can assess what the athlete would like to achieve in his or her sport through helping the athlete set different goals in (Chapter 4) and performance standards that the player wants to achieve through performance profiling (Chapter 5).

Part IV: Coaching different populations: How to support the needs of different athletes

This part of the book provides information on considering the needs of the athlete and how this should influence coaching sessions. There are chapters on coaching children (Chapter 6), adolescents (Chapter 7), adults (Chapter 8), athletes with learning disabilities (Chapter 9), and providing psychological support to injured athletes (Chapter 10). These chapters provide information on the different learning styles and needs of these athletes. Furthermore, information on how to provide effective feedback, instruction, reduce dropout rates, help athletes through the injury process, and coaching behaviour are other factors that are considered within Part IV.

Part V: Relationships, support, and influence within coaching practice

This part provides information on the importance of relationships within coaching, how coaches can support their athletes, and the influence over their athletes, which can have a number of different outcomes. In particular, this part contains information on how coaches can build a more effective coach–athlete relationship (Chapter 11), team cohesion (Chapter 12), and provide social support (Chapter 13). There are also chapters on how a coach can maximise motivation (Chapter 14), the motivational climate (Chapter 15), apply self-determination theory (Chapter 16), and promote anti-doping attitudes among athletes through their influence (Chapter 17).

Part VI: Mental skills training for athletes

This part describes different mental skill training techniques and provides practical advice on how a coach can deploy a range of psychological skills such as mental imagery (Chapter 18), develop mental toughness (Chapter 19), maximise confidence (Chapter 20), teach coping effectiveness training (Chapter 21), promote challenge states (Chapter 22), mindfulness training (Chapter 23), and prevent choking under pressure (Chapter 24). These chapters contain scientific evidence that underpins their usefulness and are also supported by sample dialogues to give the coach additional understanding of how to deploy such psychological skills.

Chapter features

Each chapter is set out in same format and includes:

- *Purpose of the chapter*: Every chapter outlines its purpose at the very beginning.
- *Case studies*: All of the chapters, excluding Chapter 1, contain a case study to give the reader a deeper insight and understanding of how coaches can use sport psychology within their coaching. There is also a case study reflection for each case study, which highlights some of the key implications. Thus, this book provides both a theoretical and an applied understanding of the psychological principles of coaching.
- *Summary points*: Each chapter contains a series of bullet points that summarise the key points in the chapter.
- *Practice exam questions*: Each chapter contains five practice exam questions, which will allow the student to practise answering questions, and thus will be very helpful for revision.
- *Critical thinking questions: Applying theory to coaching practice*: Every chapter concludes with five critical thinking questions. These critical thinking questions will assess how the knowledge gained in the chapter can be transferred to real-life coaching scenarios. Some of the new questions within the second edition encourage the reader to reflect on their own coaching practice and identify their strengths and weaknesses based on the new information learned.
- *Case study questions*: A new feature of the second edition is that each chapter contains three questions which are specifically related to the case study presented in the chapter. These questions are designed to encourage you to reflect on the case study and consider alternative approaches, limitations of the psychological approach the coach adopted, and strengths of the coach's approach in the case study.

PART I

Providing sport psychology training as a coach

1

DOS AND DON'TS FOR COACHES WHO PROVIDE SPORT PSYCHOLOGY TO THEIR ATHLETES

Ethics, referrals, and the HCPC

The aim of this chapter is to provide some important information that coaches could consider when they provide psychological support to athletes. More specifically, information is presented on:

- What sport psychology is and what it isn't
- Ethical issues associated with providing sport psychology to athletes: some don'ts and dos
- The regulation of sport psychologists and protected terms
- Referrals
- Practical implications of coaches providing sport psychology.

What sport psychology is and what it isn't

Psychology refers to the scientific analysis of the way human beings behave, think, and feel. As such, sport psychology refers to the way humans behave, think, and feel within sporting contexts, such as training and competition. According to Nicholls and Callard (2012) there are two primary goals of sport psychology: (1) to ensure the psychological well-being of athletes; and (2) to maximise performance. As such, sport psychology and coaching share a common purpose: the performance maximisation of athletes or sports teams.

Ethical issues associated with providing sport psychology to athletes: some don'ts and dos

When a coach provides psychological help to his or her athlete, the coach is entering into what Ebert (1997) termed a dual-role relationship. Brewer (2000) suggested that dual-role relationships are potentially problematic from an ethical perspective. Some scholars even suggested that coaches should not provide psychological help to athletes (e.g. Ellickson and Brown, 1990), because there might be problems establishing a boundary between the coach and the athlete and problems regarding confidentiality, given that coaches often provide public statements to media organisations about their athletes. Additionally, coaches who provide psychological help may not be able to do so without seeing a reduction in their competency as a coach due to time pressures (Buceta, 1993). Perhaps the most important ethical issue relating to coaches providing psychological guidance to athletes relates to whether they are competent to do so without causing harm to the athlete (Koocher and Keith-Spiegel, 1998).

Conversely, others such as Smith (1992) and Brewer (2000) stated that a coach providing psychological help to an athlete is compatible with coaching roles, as long as the coach provides psychology geared towards performance and not clinical concerns. There are several don'ts and do's that coaches could consider when they provide psychological help to athletes:

Don'ts

- Don't provide psychological help for non-performance issues (e.g. depression, drug abuse, alcohol addiction, gambling, eating disorders, or relationships). In instances that these cases are presented to the coach, the athlete should be referred immediately to a clinical psychologist or a general practitioner (Andersen and Van Raalte, 2005).
- Don't put pressure on an athlete to receive psychological help.
- Don't let the psychological help provided to an athlete reduce the quality of coaching provided.

Dos

- Do consult a registered sport and exercise psychologist or clinical psychologist if there are any doubts regarding the aspects of the psychological help you provide or concerns about an athlete.
- Do provide athletes with information on the different psychological skills that can be taught by a coach and the commitment the athlete will need to make before starting any psychology training interventions.

The regulation of sport psychologists and protected terms

Even though a coach may acquire very extensive information on sport psychology and be very effective at creating psychological training programmes, coaches cannot call themselves sport psychologists or advertise for work in this capacity within the United Kingdom, United States, Canada, or Australia if they are not registered within the United Kingdom or are licensed in the United States, Canada, or Australia.

Since 13 May 2009 the Health and Care Professions Council (HCPC) regulates individuals who practise as psychologists under statutory regulation. As such, the terms "registered psychologist", "practitioner psychologist", and "sport and exercise psychologist" are protected terms, and only individuals who are registered with the HCPC can use these titles. There are still examples of the titles being misused in the sport psychology literature such as: "initial contact was made with the first author, a British Association of Sport and Exercise Sciences (BASES) Accredited sport psychologist" (Hays et al., 2010b: 398). Individuals who are accredited by BASES in the sport psychology pathway are breaking the law if they refer to themselves as BASES accredited sport psychologists, given that it is a protected term exclusive to the HCPC and not BASES.

Should a coach wish to become an HCPC registered sport and exercise psychologist, there is a specific pathway, which involves the completion of:

- An undergraduate degree that is accredited by the British Psychological Society (BPS).
- A Masters' degree, which is accredited by the BPS, in Sport and Exercise Psychology.
- Two years of supervision by an HCPC registered sport and exercise psychologist.

Within the United States, Canada, and Australia individuals are required to obtain a licence in order to practise as a psychologist. The formal training involves:

- Achieving an undergraduate degree that is accredited by the relevant country's psychological society (i.e. American Psychological Association, Canadian Psychological Association, or Australian Psychological Society).
- A professional doctorate in psychology.

For clarification, coaches are legally allowed to provide training in the psychological skills outlined in this book, but they cannot call themselves sport and exercise psychologists.

Referrals

A referral is when a coach contacts another professional to help the athlete he or she is working with, because of a lack of competence or expertise to deal with a problem. Referrals might also be made when a coach might not think it is appropriate to work with a specific athlete (Brewer, 2000). A coach should contact a clinical psychologist or ask his or her athlete to contact their general practitioner if the athlete has problems relating to:

- Depression
- Drug abuse

- Alcohol addiction
- Gambling
- Eating disorders
- Relationships.

Under no circumstances should coaches attempt to provide psychological support to athletes for these issues. In circumstances that are performance related and when a coach feels the needs of an athlete are beyond his or her capabilities, the coach should refer the athlete to a registered sport and exercise psychologist.

Referring an athlete to another professional, such as a clinical psychologist or a sport and exercise psychologist, has the potential to be awkward for a coach. The coach should explain to the athlete why a referral has been made, give information about the professional who the referral has been made to, and answer any questions the athlete has.

Practical implications of coaches providing sport psychology

Although many athletes would potentially benefit from receiving training in sport psychology by their coach, some coaches will simply not have the time to learn about different psychological techniques and then implement the techniques with athletes. Before asking an athlete whether he or she would like to engage in some psychological training, the coach should make sure that he or she has enough time to coach the athlete and provide psychological help too.

When coaches have the time and an interest in using sport psychology within their coaching, they can potentially improve the performance, enjoyment, and well-being of the athletes that they coach. As with all new skills, coaching psychological skills will be difficult at times and improvements in athletes' performance may take a long time, but by providing psychological skills training, coaches can provide a more holistic experience for the athlete.

PART II

Identifying the psychological needs of athletes

2

CONDUCTING INTAKE INTERVIEWS

The aim of this chapter is to provide coaches with information regarding how they can establish the psychological needs of an athlete, so that an appropriate intervention can be devised. Information is provided on:

- What is an intake interview?
- The purpose of intake interviews
- The intake interview guide
- Encouraging athletes to open up
- Listening
- Verbal and non-verbal strategies that coaches can employ
- What to expect: impression management strategies that athletes may use.

What is an intake interview?

Intake interviews are often referred to as assessment interviews, initial interviews, or first-contact meetings (Sommers-Flanagan, 2016). In the case of a coach meeting up with an athlete, it will not be the first time the coach has met the athlete, but it may well be the first time that the coach and the athlete have sat down together for a discussion or a chat regarding his or her psychological needs or requirements. An intake interview is when the coach tries to understand some of the issues affecting the athlete, identify the long-term goals of the athlete, discuss potential solutions, and examine barriers that may affect certain solutions (Prevatt and Levrini, 2015). This is achieved by the coach asking the athlete a series of questions and listening to the athlete's responses with the aim of trying to gain more knowledge about the needs of the athlete and the problems that he or she is experiencing (Bernstein and Nietzel, 1980).

The purpose of intake interviews

Coaches may only spend a relatively short time speaking to athletes individually. As such, an intake interview allows the coach to spend a longer period chatting to his or her athlete and is important because it determines how receptive an athlete will be in terms of receiving psychological support (Auld et al., 2005). It is accepted that most athletes will attend a meeting with their coach to discuss psychological approaches if they are experiencing some form of disruption (e.g. changing technique or performance problems that are causing distress; Auld et al., 2005). As such the purpose of an intake interview is for the coach to: (a) identify what is causing the athlete distress; and (b) decide whether the help or advice that he or she can provide will be sufficient to help the athlete (Auld et al., 2005).

In some circumstances, a coach may feel that he or she is not suitably qualified or does not possess the skills to help an athlete. In such circumstances, the coach can make a referral to another professional (see Chapter 1 for making referrals). In other situations, which are within the coach's competencies, he or she can offer a variety of strategies that may help the athlete (Prevatt and Levrini, 2015).

Overcoming nerves

Some coaches with little or no experience of conducting intake interviews may experience anxiety or worry before the intake interview occurs. This can be quite common when a coach interviews somebody for the first time (Auld et al., 2005; Møller, 2014). For intake interviews to be successful, Prevatt and Levrini (2015) recommended that coaches prepare adequately. An excellent way of preparing is to develop an intake interview guide. This provides coaches with a series of questions they can ask.

The interview guide

Taylor and Schneider (1992) developed an interview guide for sport psychologists who want to interview their athletes, but this can also be used by coaches. This is an excellent guide, although some aspects of their guide (i.e. athletes being asked to describe their athletic status, family, and health) might not be necessary, given that most coaches will generally know more about their athlete than a sport psychologist who interviews an athlete for the first time. The interview is based on the coach asking questions about understanding the problem, building a more detailed understanding, influences and consequences, changes prior to the problem starting, and important life events. It is important that coaches realise this is just a guide and that the coach is not required to follow the guide regimentally. That is, the coach might want to change the order of the questions, or he or she might not want to ask all of the questions.

Understanding the issue causing distress

Before a coach can help an athlete it is important that he or she understands the problem from the athlete's perspective (Petitpas, 2000). Taylor and Schneider (1992) suggested that coaches might want to ask questions such as:

- Please describe the problem.
- How frequently does it (the problem) occur?
- When did it first begin?
- How long has it been going on for?
- Where and when is it most likely to occur?
- What do you think causes it?

Building a more detailed understanding

Once the coach has established what the problem is, he or she can start asking some more probing questions that yield much more information on the problem. This provides the athlete with the opportunity to describe his or her experiences in more detail. Based on the guidelines of Taylor and Schneider (1992), the coach might want to ask the following questions:

- Please describe a situation in which the problem occurred. I want you to give me as much detail as possible so I can understand as much as possible.
- Was this the first time that it happened?
- When does it normally occur and is there a consistent pattern?
- What things are going on when the problem is at its worst?
- What things are going on when the problem is at its best?

Influences and consequences

The coach can now ask more probing questions to gather information on the possible influences and consequences (Taylor and Schneider, 1992). As such, the coach might want to ask some of the following questions regarding the athlete's personal influences, social influences, and consequences, which may be related to the problem:

- Who was around you when the situation that you described occurred and what were these people doing? (Social influence question)
- Describe what you were thinking when the incident occurred. (Personal influence question)
- How were you feeling when it happened? (Personal influence question)
- How did you behave? (Personal influence question)
- Please describe what happened after the problem occurred. (Consequence question)
- How did others react? (Consequence question)

Changes prior to the problem starting

Questions relating to factors that changed before the problem started might yield some interesting information. Taylor and Schneider (1992) suggested that questions should be directed towards any physical, mental, technical, and equipment changes. Coaches might want to ask the following questions:

- Please describe the quality and quantity of your training leading up to the problem first occurring. (Physical question)
- Did you experience any illness, injury, or fatigue problems prior to the problem starting? (Physical question)
- How did you feel mentally prior to the problem starting? (Mental question)
- Did you notice feeling more worried or less confident? (Mental question)
- Did you make any technical adjustments prior to the problem starting? (Technical question)
- Did you change any equipment prior to the problem starting? (Equipment question)

Important life events

The questions relating to changes in the athlete's physical or mental state, technical issues, or equipment might not always yield interesting information and the coach could explore whether life events had contributed to the problem. The coach could ask the following questions:

- Please describe some of the most important events in your life.
- Did anything happen in your life away from sport close to the problem occurring?
- Describe any major changes in your life, such as involving your family, friends, or relationships?

Encouraging athletes to open up

For an interview to be of use, it is important that the athlete discloses his or her feelings. Andersen (2000) suggested that athletes are encouraged to talk if the interviewer is engaging, genuine, interested in what the athlete is saying, and does not judge the athlete. This may sound an easy task, but Andersen (2000) stated that it is very difficult. It might be more difficult if the coach is responsible for team selection, because the player might not want to disclose things to the coach that might result in him or her being dropped from a team. This is a difficulty of the coach interviewing an athlete. Even though a coach can reassure the athlete that what he or she says will not influence selection, the athlete might not believe the coach.

Coaches can encourage athletes to open up by the type of questions they ask. Indeed, Auld et al. (2005) stated that coaches would not want athletes to come to an intake interview thinking that all they are required to do is tell their coach about the problem, who will then solve the problem. As such, the coach could avoid asking questions such as "What is the trouble?" or "What brings you here today?" as this does not promote or encourage an open discussion. As such, Auld and colleagues (2005) recommended questions such as "tell me about yourself", "tell me more about the situation in which you first experienced difficulties", or "tell me about how this made you feel" as this encourages the athlete to talk about him or herself in relation to the issues encountered. This would be a good opening question if that has not already been discussed prior to the meeting taking place.

Listening

Even though the questions asked by coaches are very important, it is also imperative that the coach listens to what the athlete has to say in any interview or conversation. According to Giges (2000), words can be clues to an athlete's inner experiences, which may reveal hidden thoughts, feelings, or wants from the athlete. Coaches should listen to every word the athlete says.

Verbal and non-verbal strategies that coaches can employ

In order to make athletes feel more comfortable during the intake and subsequent meetings, Sommers-Flanagan (2016) identified a number of verbal and non-verbal strategies that coaches could use at various stages of the interview. For example, when a coach is listening to an athlete, he or she can engage in a series of non-verbal communication strategies (e.g. head nodding and open body posture), and verbal strategies (e.g. minimal encouragers such as huh, yes, and go on, paraphrasing what an athlete has just said, and reflecting the sentiment of the athlete's feelings). When a coach is listening to the athlete, he or she can use non-verbal strategies such as leaning forward, raising eyebrows, or giving anticipatory gazes, in addition to verbal strategies such as asking open questions or presupposition questions where the coach creates another message (e.g. when you play well against your next opponents, I want you to consider…). In this example, the presupposition is that the athlete will play well against his or her next opponents.

What to expect: impression management strategies that athletes may use

When a person, such as a coach, is providing psychological care to another person and interactions take place, the process of social influence occurs (Heppner and Claiborn, 1989). Social influence includes all techniques and strategies that an individual uses to change someone else's thoughts, feelings, or behaviours (Schneider et al., 2005). It is acknowledged that the individual providing psychological support may use certain behaviours (e.g. verbal or non-verbal communication) to promote positive changes in a person (Strong, 1968), but recent research suggests that the recipient of psychological support may also try to change the thoughts, feelings, and behaviours of the person providing psychological support (Frühauf et al., 2015). Indeed, Frühauf and colleagues found that attempts to influence the psychological provider occurred in 30 per cent of utterances, and included supplication (e.g. attempting to get sympathy and demonstrating they need help), provoking a response (e.g. asking questions), and self-promotion (e.g. portraying the self in a strong light).

As such, athletes may be keen to let their coach know they need help and they may do this by provoking a response and asking direct questions (e.g. "What do you think will be the best mental skill for me?" or "What do you think I should do to cope better?"). Some athletes may also want to show themselves in a good light to the coach (e.g. "I will do everything you suggest, because I want to be the best" or "I try my hardest every training session, so I can improve more"). If coaches consult athletes who engage in supplication and are quite negative about their weaknesses, the coach could also focus on the strengths of the athlete, because focusing on strengths may help alleviate psychological strain (Sachse, 2001). Coaches can be aware of the different ways that athletes present themselves and remember to ensure that questions are positively worded if athletes focus too much on negative aspects.

CASE STUDY 2.1 INTERVIEWING AN ATHLETE

The following case study represents an excerpt of the dialogue between a coach (Darren, a 45-year-old cricket coach) and Matthew (a 21-year-old minor county league player). Darren has seen a deterioration in Matthew's demeanour and performance. This part of the intake interview focuses on the start of the interview in which Darren asks Matthew to describe his situation or circumstances.

Darren: Thanks for coming to see me Matthew.

Matthew: I have been wanting to speak to you for a while now, as I have been really struggling this season, and it is not getting any better.

Darren: I would like you to describe all aspects of what is going on. In this chat today, I would like to ask you about what is currently happening, the possible influences, any changes that might have occurred, and even parts of your family life. From what the other lads have said and what you have told me, I know you have been having a few problems there. The purpose of this chat is to help me understand how best I can help you. I want to assure you that what you say in our chat will not influence team selection. I would like you to describe the problem.

Matthew: I can't concentrate when I play. I am playing matches thinking about my dad and wondering how long he has left.

Darren: Does this happen in every match?

Matthew: Yeah, it seems to. Although when we play other teams at the top of the league I seem to be able to concentrate better.

Darren: In the matches when you have struggled to concentrate, do you struggle for the whole match?

Matthew: No.

Darren: Could you tell me more about when you concentrate and when your concentration goes?

Matthew: My concentration usually goes when I'm fielding. When I'm bowling I can usually concentrate, although sometimes I do struggle a bit. When the match is close I don't have any problems.

Darren: When did you notice this starting?

Matthew: It was a month ago, just after my dad first got his diagnosis.

Case study reflection

Some coaches may find interviewing their athletes quite difficult, because it is not an easy process. It may result in athletes disclosing information that coaches are not comfortable hearing. Coaches may also feel that their skills are not competent to help the athlete. In these instances the coach should refer the athlete to a more suitably qualified individual such as a clinical psychologist or a counsellor.

Summary points

- Interviews can help coaches gain an understanding of problems that may affect their athletes, which then might determine how the coach helps the athlete.
- Coaches can adapt the interview guide proposed in this chapter.

Practice exam questions

1   What is the purpose of interviewing an athlete?
2   Identify and elaborate on the factors that may influence the extent to which a coach understands an athlete's problem based on an interview.
3   Discuss the importance of asking questions relating to an athlete's life.
4   Discuss the importance of listening to an athlete's response.
5   Describe the importance of identifying problems before providing psychological skills training.

Critical thinking questions: Applying theory to practice

1 What can a coach do to encourage an athlete to open up about his or her feelings?
2 Design your own interview schedule and justify each section.
3 What can coaches do if they suspect an athlete is hiding information?
4 What can coaches do if they hear information that goes beyond their own competencies?
5 Discuss the factors that influence how affective an interview will be in providing information to guide any interventions.

Case study questions

1 What influence strategies does Matthew use?
2 What questions could Darren ask to find out if a referral is necessary?
3 How would Darren make a referral?

3

USING QUESTIONNAIRES TO ASSESS THE NEEDS OF ATHLETES

The purpose of this chapter is to provide information on how coaches can use questionnaires to gather information about their athletes. Information is provided on:

- Advantages of questionnaires
- Disadvantages of questionnaires
- Uses of questionnaires
- Questionnaires that coaches can use.

Advantages of questionnaires

A questionnaire is a series of written questions, which provides the athlete with set choices regarding how he or she will answer each question (i.e. by circling 1, 2, 3, 4, 5). An advantage of questionnaires is that they are generally quick to complete (Nicholls et al., 2007), which is important for coaches who have little time. Questionnaires can be used to generate objective scores regarding a psychological quality that an athlete might experience (e.g. anxiety or stress). Coaches can use these objective scores to compare scores with other athletes or data from published research. These comparisons may be useful in providing the coach with objective information.

Disadvantages of questionnaires

A limitation of questionnaires is that they do not allow athletes to explain their answers or document their experiences. Athletes might find the process of completing questionnaires tiresome and pointless. It is important that coaches explain why questionnaires are being completed. Another possible limitation of questionnaires is that they might be subject to athletes over-emphasising their abilities, because it might be more socially desirable to do so.

CASE STUDY 3.1 MONITORING CHANGE USING QUESTIONNAIRES

Paul, a 64-year-old tennis coach, decided to assess Victoria's mental toughness, using the Mental Toughness Questionnaire-48 (MTQ48; Clough et al., 2002), after she complained of not being able to play in pressurised situations, lacking commitment, confidence, and failing to control her emotions during matches. Paul could have used a variety of questionnaires, but decided to use the MTQ48 as he knew this questionnaire would provide him with some useful data and could identify areas that Victoria could work on. The results are shown in the figure below.

Mental Toughness Scores – September	
Total Mental Toughness	112
Challenge	24
Commitment	12
Emotional Control	12
Life Control	32
Interpersonal Confidence	22
Ability Confidence	10

As Victoria could improve upon her mental toughness score, Paul developed a mental toughness training programme for Victoria. This lasted an entire season and involved optimism training, coping effectiveness training, goal setting, and sport intelligence training. Paul also created a variety of different drills that simulated pressurised situations in matches, which had consequences. For example, if Victoria did not perform to a particular standard on a forehand drill, she knew she would have to do a shuttle run. This gave Victoria an incentive to perform well. She agreed that this drill and the consequence of not performing well increased her pressure levels, but she believed that she was more equipped to deal with the pressure through the coping effectiveness training she received. Paul also reflected on his own coaching behaviours to ensure that he was fulfilling Victoria's basic psychological needs. He monitored her mental toughness scores every three months (see the figures below).

Mental Toughness Scores – December	
Total Mental Toughness	124
Challenge	22
Commitment	14
Emotional Control	14
Life Control	32
Interpersonal Confidence	26
Ability Confidence	16

Mental Toughness Scores – March	
Total Mental Toughness	138
Challenge	24
Commitment	24
Emotional Control	16
Life Control	32
Interpersonal Confidence	26
Ability Confidence	16

Mental Toughness Scores – June	
Total Mental Toughness	144
Challenge	24
Commitment	24
Emotional Control	16
Life Control	32
Interpersonal Confidence	26
Ability Confidence	20

As Victoria continued to improve her performance in the pressure drills that took place in training, Paul increased the performance standards required to avoid a shuttle run, so that the pressure she experienced was also gradually increased.

Victoria's mental toughness increased throughout the season, which Paul felt was a result of the mental toughness training she received. In particular, he thought the pressure drills were useful and that Victoria had the psychological tools to cope with them, which she could take into matches and other stressful encounters in her life.

Case study reflection

Questionnaires are useful to provide objective measures of the effects of interventions. Sceptics might argue that coaches could just ask an athlete whether he or she feels more mentally tough or not, but questionnaires provide an objective measure and enable subtle changes to be assessed over time.

Uses of questionnaires

Coaches can use questionnaires to assess the extent to which an athlete might be afflicted by a condition (e.g. anxiety) and the strategies athletes may use (e.g. coping). Questionnaires can also be used to monitor any changes that occur within an athlete by being completed on a regular basis.

Questionnaires that coaches can use

There is an array of questionnaires, published in peer reviewed articles and books, which measure a variety of different psychological constructs in the sport literature. Also a number of questionnaires are available on the internet. Coaches should consider the quality of the questionnaire they use and where possible, they should avoid disseminating questionnaires that are not supported by published research. The list of questionnaires in Table 3.1 documents some of the questionnaires that coaches can use. This list is by no means comprehensive, but represents questionnaires that are related to the psychological constructs mentioned in this book.

TABLE 3.1 Questionnaires widely used within the sport literature

Name of questionnaire	Authors	Construct measured by questionnaire	Brief description
Revised Sport Motivation Scale (SMS-II)	Pelletier et al. (2013)	Motivation	30-item questionnaire measures intrinsic regulation, integrated regulation, identified regulation, introjected regulation, external regulation, and amotivated regulation.
The Cognitive and Affective Mindfulness Scale—Revised (CAMS—R)	Feldman et al. (2007)	Mindfulness	12-item questionnaire assesses an athlete's mindful approach to thoughts and feelings.
Performance Enhancement Attitudes Scale	Petróczi and Aidman (2009)	Attitudes towards doping	19-item unidimensional questionnaire assesses attitudes towards doping.
Stress Appraisal Measure	Peacock and Wong (1990)	Stress appraisals	28-item questionnaire measures primary and secondary appraisals.
Athletes Received Support Questionnaire	Freeman et al. (2014)	Social support	22-item questionnaire assesses emotional, esteem, informational, and tangible support received by an athlete.
Behavioural Regulation in Sport Questionnaire (BRSQ)	Lonsdale et al. (2008)	Self-determined motivation	24-item questionnaire measures the extent to which an athlete's motivation is self-determined.
Health Care Climate Questionnaire	Adapted version used by Healy et al. (2014)	Coach behaviour	This questionnaire measures the extent to which the coach displays autonomy supportive coaching behaviours.
Controlling Coach Behaviours Scale	Bartholomew et al. (2010)	Coach behaviour	This questionnaire measures the extent to which the coach displays controlling behaviours.

Name of questionnaire	Authors	Construct measured by questionnaire	Brief description
Coach–Athlete Relationship Questionnaire (CART-Q)	Jowett and Ntoumanis (2004)	Coach–athlete relationship	11-item questionnaire assesses the athlete's perceptions of closeness, commitment, and complementarity with their coach.
Empowering and Disempowering Motivational Climate Questionnaire-Coach (EDMCQ-C)	Appleton et al. (2016)	Motivational climate	37-item questionnaire assesses the extent to which the climate is empowering or disempowering.
Sport Emotion Questionnaire (SEQ)	Jones et al. (2005)	Emotions	20-item questionnaire measures three unpleasant emotions (i.e. anger, anxiety, and dejection) and two pleasant emotions (i.e. excitement and happiness).
Achievement Goals Questionnaire	Conroy et al. (2003)	Achievement goals	12-item questionnaire containing four subscales: (1) Mastery Approach; (2) Mastery Avoidance; (3) Performance Approach; and (4) Performance Avoidance goals.
Test of Ability in Movement Imagery (TAMI)	Madan and Singhal (2013)	Imagery ability	10-item questionnaire instructs athletes to perform 10 different movements. Each question requires the participant to perform a sequence of 5 movements. It is also associated with 5 images of different body positions, with one correct answer for each question.
Trait Sport Confidence Inventory (TSCI)	Vealey (1986)	Trait sport confidence	13-item questionnaire in which athletes rate how confident they normally are when playing sport.
Sources of Sport Confidence Questionnaire (SSCQ)	Vealey et al. (1998)	Sources of sport confidence	9-dimension questionnaire relating to how athletes derive their confidence.
Mental Toughness Questionnaire-48 (MTQ48)	Clough et al. (2002)	Mental toughness	48-item questionnaire containing six subscales: challenge; commitment; personal control; emotional control; ability confidence; and personal confidence.

continued…

Table 3.1 continued...

Name of questionnaire	Authors	Construct measured by questionnaire	Brief description
Mental Toughness Index	Gucciardi et al. (2015)	Mental toughness	8-item unidimensional measure of self-reported mental toughness.
Mental Toughness Inventory	Hardy et al. (2014)	Mental toughness	8-item questionnaire that is completed by the coach regarding a specific athlete. The coach answers questions about the athlete's ability to perform well in pressurised situations.
Coping Inventory for Competitive Sports	Gaudreau and Blondin (2002)	State coping	39-item questionnaire measures what an athlete does to cope and includes three dimensions: task-oriented coping; distraction-oriented coping; and disengagement-oriented coping.
Dispositional Coping Inventory for Competitive Sports	Hurst et al. (2011)	Dispositional coping	37-item questionnaire measures what an athlete would usually do to cope and includes three dimensions: task-oriented coping; distraction-oriented coping; and disengagement-oriented coping.

Practice exam questions

1 Discuss the advantages of using questionnaires.
2 Describe the disadvantages of using questionnaires.
3 What are the implications of using questionnaires that do not have research to support them?
4 Compare and contrast the State Sport Confidence Inventory and the Trait Sport Confidence Inventory.
5 To what extent do questionnaires provide reliable information? Discuss.

Critical thinking questions: applying theory to practice

1 Describe why a coach would use a questionnaire to measure traits.
2 Discuss why coaches might use stated versions of a questionnaire.
3 Questionnaires are a useful way of measuring psychological constructs. Discuss.
4 Describe how a coach could use interview data along with questionnaire data.

5   Should coaches compare questionnaire results among their athletes? Discuss.

Case study questionnaires

1   Discuss the appropriateness of using the MTQ48 in this instance.
2   Identify other questionnaires that Paul could have used.
3   Discuss how else Paul could increase his understanding of how Victoria's mental toughness changed over time.

PART III

Facilitating awareness among athletes

4

GOAL SETTING

The purpose of this chapter is to provide information on how coaches can set both individual and team goals for their athletes. In particular, information is provided on:

- Defining goals
- The benefits of goal setting
- Types of goals
- Goal-setting styles
- Short-term, medium-term, and long-term goals
- Helping athletes set SMARTS goals
- Setting individual goals
- Setting team goals
- Problems that may prevent effective goal setting.

Defining goals

A goal refers to an objective that an athlete may have, a target of an athlete in relation to sport, or even a desired standard that an athlete wants to achieve in relation to a specific task or sport, and within a specific time limit (Locke and Latham, 2002).

The benefits of goal setting

Locke and Latham (1990, 2002) conducted a review that included 35 years' worth of research regarding the effects of goal setting. They found that:

- Specific goals were consistently associated with enhanced performance on more than 100 different tasks, which involved over 40,000 participants from more than eight countries. Goals enhanced performance by directing the attention and effort of athletes towards goal-relevant activities. As such, a coach who asks his or her athletes to do their best will not get the best performance from his or her athletes. Locke and Latham argued that asking people to do their best allows for a wide range of acceptable performance levels. This is not the case when a goal level, such as performance standard (e.g. percentage of successful fairways hit in golf) is specified. These findings were echoed by Staufenbiel et al. (2015) who reported that goal setting contributed to enhanced performance in soccer.

- Goals give an energising influence, and may result in athletes exerting more effort compared with those with no goals.
- Goals encourage people to plan strategies to enable them to achieve their goals.
- Goals ensure that athletes remain persistent during times of adversity (e.g. being dropped from a team or losing two matches in a row), because the athlete has something he or she wants to achieve.

Other researchers such as Martin et al. (2009) and Kingston and Hardy (1997) also found that:

- Goal setting has a positive impact on teams. Indeed, goal-setting interventions positively impacts on both team performance and how cohesive a team is.
- Goal-setting programmes also positively impact different psychological constructs. For example, Kingston and Hardy (1997) found that self-efficacy, cognitive anxiety, and confidence levels were all improved among a sample of golfers.

More recently, researchers such as Wilkman et al. (2014) conducted a 12-week goal-setting intervention and monitored the athletes' fear of failure before the study started, after the completion of the 12-week goal-setting intervention, and then 12 weeks after the intervention finished. Interestingly, the athletes' fear of failure decreased following the goal-setting intervention, but returned 12 weeks following the intervention. As such, this finding could imply that coaches need to regularly encourage athletes to set goals in order for them to experience the benefits.

Types of goals

Burton et al. (2001) suggested that there are three different types of goals, which are related to the outcome of competitions, the standard of performance, and the actions athletes must engage in to perform well. These goals are referred to as outcome goals, performance goals, and process goals.

- *Outcome goals* are related to the result or outcome of a particular match or competition, and may include the position the athlete finishes in a competition, whether he or she wins, or even whether an athlete earns a professional contract. Although it is important that coaches set outcome goals, because sporting success is often determined by winning or losing, it is also crucial that coaches understand some of the possible disadvantages of outcome goals. For instance, outcome goals are only partially controllable by an athlete or a team, because the outcome of a match is determined by factors that an athlete or team cannot control, such as the performance of the opponents or the decision making of an official. As such, a cross-country runner may finish seventh in a race, and thus performed to his or her potential in that race, but was not fast enough to win at his current fitness level, so an outcome goal of winning would result in the athlete feeling disappointed. As such, coaches should not rely too heavily on outcome goals, because they can negatively affect motivation. Indeed, coaches are encouraged to use outcome goals in combination with performance and process goals.

- *Performance goals* are related to athletes achieving specific standards of performance, usually in relation to an athlete's previous levels of performance such as their personal best. Performance goals are not concerned with outcomes or results, only standards of performance. For example, a golfer might want to improve the number of fairways he or she hits by 10 per cent in a season, from 35 per cent to 45 per cent.

- *Process goals* focus on the actions an athlete needs to perform to be successful. For example, a soccer player who takes free kicks for his or her team could want to improve his or her follow through when striking the ball. As such, process goals enable athletes to improve their performance by focusing on improving techniques that are associated with enhanced performance.

Goal-setting styles

Burton and Naylor (2002) found that athletes have goal-setting styles. That is, athletes will set particular types of goals depending on their personality without any help from their coach. Therefore, athletes have a pre-disposition to set certain types of goals. According to Burton and Naylor there are two types of goal-setting styles:

- *Performance-oriented*: Athletes who have a tendency to set goals that are related to their own self-improvement, rather than to demonstrating their ability in comparison with other athletes, are said to have a performance-oriented goal-setting style. Athletes with this goal-setting style tend to focus on improving their performance and are less concerned with results. Athletes with performance-oriented goal-setting styles are likely to set goals that are difficult and challenging, and are not concerned about making mistakes or failing. This is because their main motivation is to improve as an athlete. As such, athletes with a performance-oriented goal-setting style are comfortable about playing opponents who have more skill, because they judge success on their own performance and any improvements they have made, as opposed to the outcome of a match or competition.

- *Success-oriented*: Athletes who have a tendency to set goals that involve social comparisons with their competitors or team mates (e.g. beat a specific opponent) are classified as having a success-oriented approach to goal setting. Coaches should be aware that athletes who have a tendency to set success-oriented goals may avoid setting themselves challenging goals, because they are worried about the humiliation they might experience when failing to achieve their goals and what other people will think about them if they fail to achieve their goals. Therefore, athletes with this goal-setting style will only set goals they know they can achieve.

Short-term, medium-term, and long-term goals

Coaches should be aware that goals can be short-term, medium-term, or long-term:

- Short-term goals refer to desired achievements that may happen shortly after a goal is set, usually within a week, such as an athlete winning his or her match the following day or the following week.
- Medium-term goals refer to desired achievements that may happen from a week to several months ahead, such as an athlete wanting to make a set number of appearances during a season or to win a specific number of races within a season.
- Long-term goals relate to desired achievements that may happen from a few months to many years after a goal is set. For instance, a long-term goal of a 15-year-old golf player might be to win a major before his or her 40th birthday.

It is very important that coaches help their athletes to set a variety of short-term, medium-term, and long-term goals. Long-term goals are crucial for helping athletes develop a sense of purpose regarding what they do. This should also make sacrifices they have to make more bearable, because they know the sacrifices are being made for the good of their goal. Additionally, medium-term and short-term goals can make longer-term goals seem more achievable to athletes. The coach can tell his or her athletes that they will eventually succeed in achieving their long-term goals, if they regularly achieve their short- and medium-term goals.

Helping athletes set SMARTS goals

Smith (1994) developed a guide for helping coaches to set effective goals, by using the acronym SMARTS, which refers to specific, measurable, action-orientated, realistic, timely, and self-determined goals:

- *Specific*: Coaches should help their athletes set goals that are clear. That is, the athlete states exactly what he or she wants to happen (e.g. improve pass success by 10 per cent, from 65 per cent to 75 per cent, by the end of the season). Locke and Latham (2002) found that specific goals result in enhanced performance.
- *Measureable*: Goals should be measurable, so athletes will know whether they have been successful in achieving their goal. When athletes can see that they have improved, their motivation levels may also increase. This can, in turn, result in athletes making even more improvements.
- *Action-oriented*: In addition to helping athletes set goals, coaches should facilitate a discussion regarding how an athlete can achieve his or her goals and what he or she will have to do to achieve these goals.
- *Realistic*: When helping athletes set goals, coaches must ensure that the goals athletes set are realistic and encourage them to modify their goals if they are not realistic. If a goal is not realistic and an athlete has little or no chance of achieving his or her goal the athlete may become very frustrated and de-motivated. Conversely, if athletes set goals that are too easy they may become very bored. As such, goals should be achievable, but should push the athlete to work hard to achieve the goal.
- *Timely*: All goals should involve a specified time period in which the athlete wants to achieve the particular goal. This may involve a goal being set for the next match or a goal that might not be achieved for many years, but there is still a time limit set.
- *Self-determined*: Goals should be set by the athlete or by the team, rather than by a coach. Coaches can have an input in the goals, but Locke and Latham (2002) found that goals are more effective when the individual is committed to his or her goal.

Setting individual goals

Coaches can work with athletes to set individual goals or to help teams set goals. Coaches working with athletes from individual sports may find setting goals more straightforward because there is only one athlete to work with and it is more likely that the athlete will be committed to the goals he or she sets. Conversely, it might be more difficult to ensure an entire team agree with and are committed to the team goals. However, regardless of whether an athlete plays an individual sport (e.g. tennis) or a team sport (e.g. soccer) he or she should have individual goals.

Coaches can help and encourage their athletes set their own goals by adopting the SMARTS goal-setting principle, as proposed by Smith (1994). Coaches should also encourage athletes to set a variety of short-, medium-, and long-term goals. It is important that coaches do not set their athletes' goals, because they will not be committed to achieving these goals. Research by Shilts et al. (2004) found that if people are provided with information to set their own goals they are more committed. Furthermore, coaches should also support their athletes regarding the goals they set. This should involve coaches being supportive and encouraging about their athletes achieving their goals.

Setting team goals

As mentioned in the section on the benefits of goal setting, the meta-analysis by Martin et al. (2009) indicated that team goal-setting programmes have a positive impact on team cohesion and team performance. It is therefore important that coaches have an understanding of team goal setting and encourage their teams to set team goals. A team's goal can be defined as "the future state of affairs desired by enough members of a group to work towards its achievement" (Johnson and Johnson, 1987: 132).

Widmeyer and Ducharme (1997) provided information on how coaches can set team goals more effectively. In particular, they outlined six key principles for effective team goal setting and a rationale for each principle:

1   *Establish long-term goals first:* Although short-term goals are those that are achieved first and are likely to be more realistic, athletes are more likely to agree with the long-term goals that they want to achieve whilst playing for a team. Coaches should still apply the SMARTS principle to setting long-term goals, and all goals for that matter, with these long-term goals being specific and realistic.

2   *Establish clear paths to long-term goals:* Coaches should help athletes establish clear paths regarding how their teams can reach their long-term goals. This can be achieved by encouraging athletes to set short-term team outcome, performance, and process goals. For example, a team's long-term goal could be to finish at least second in the league, so the coach could encourage the players to split the league into 10 segments containing three games each. The short-term outcome goal could be to win at least two games per segment, which if achieved would allow the team to achieve their long-term goal. In order for the team to achieve their outcome goals, they could be encouraged to set performance goals that will make the outcome goal realistic, such as not conceding more than five goals in any three segments and taking at least 40 shots per segment. Short-term team process goals would focus on the processes that determine successful performances, which will vary from sport to sport. This might include reducing the number of two-on-ones when defending in rugby to zero per match, but increasing the number of two-on-ones when attacking by 10 per cent.

3   *Involve all team members when developing team goals:* It is important that all team members have an input in developing their team goals. This could potentially be quite challenging for a coach who coaches a team with many athletes such as rugby union or American football. Asking athletes to publically provide input into a team's goal might not be a wise decision by a coach, because athletes will be concerned about what other team

mates think when they set team goals. Coaches could ask their players to anonymously write down their goals for the team on a piece of paper and collect these ideal goals for the team. The coach could then collate and present these to the team to discuss which goals are realistic, with the view of developing team goals that all athletes are committed to achieving.

4   *Monitor the progress of team goals:* Coaches should monitor and record the progress of their teams in achieving their short-, medium-, and long-term goals. This information should be presented to the players, which might facilitate discussion if teams are not performing as well as they like, regarding what they could do differently to get back on track. Monitoring goals provides motivation to athletes and encourages them to focus on their team goals (Hampson and Harwood, 2016).

5   *Reward team progress in achieving team goals:* It is important that coaches reward players when they make progress in achieving their team goals. This could be in the form of praise or having a social activity that the players will enjoy, which may foster even more team spirit.

6   *Foster collective efficacy regarding team goals:* Teams with athletes who are more confident in achieving their goals will perform better. Coaches can enhance their team's belief in their ability to be successful by employing techniques that maximise the chances of team success, such as ensuring optimal preparation. Other techniques could include the coach providing information regarding how goals can be achieved and practising relevant drills in training sessions. For example, if a team has a process goal of limiting the opposition to zero two-on-ones when defending per rugby match, the coach could have players practise defensive drills that make this more likely, and thus enhance players' confidence regarding achieving their team goal.

Problems that may prevent effective goal setting

Although goal setting seems a relatively straightforward process, some common problems may arise:

- Some athletes may not want to set themselves goals, because they feel that goal setting takes up too much time. Other athletes might not want their goals to become public knowledge (Murphy, 1996). Coaches can inform athletes that goal setting is an important process that will remain confidential.
- Athletes might fail to adjust their goals if they struggle to accomplish their targets (Burton, 1989). If an athlete is half-way through his or her season and will not achieve the seasonal goal of finishing in the top five of the rankings, he or she may experience a decline in motivation. Coaches can help monitor an athlete's progress in achieving his or her goal and then encourage them to adjust their goals if they are not going to achieve them.
- Athletes might not be motivated by their goals. As such, coaches should work with athletes and monitor the effects of goals on motivation levels by

chatting to athletes or administering motivation questionnaires. Coaches should regularly monitor the impact that goals have on athletes.

- Coaches should encourage athletes not to set too many goals. If athletes set too many goals their attention will not be focused on achieving specific goals because they have too many things to think about. As Locke and Latham (2002) pointed out, goals work because they focus the mind. Although athletes may set a few goals, coaches could encourage athletes to focus on two or three goals at a time. Once the athlete has achieved these goals they could work towards achieving their other goals or setting new goals.
- One factor that may prevent athletes from achieving their goals is barriers. Helping athletes remove these barriers may be pivotal in helping them succeed and experience higher levels of motivation. As such, the coach should work with the athlete to identify the barriers that may prevent the athlete from achieving their goals, by discussing barriers and their impact. These barriers might include other commitments that prevent athletes from doing the necessary practice needed to reach his or her goals (e.g. education, work, or family). If the barriers cannot be overcome, coaches should encourage athletes to adjust their goals accordingly.
- Some athletes might focus too much on outcome goals (Hampson and Harwood, 2016), so it is important that coaches encourage athletes to focus on process goals.

CASE STUDY 4.1   WORKING WITH AN ADOLESCENT BASKETBALL PLAYER TO DEVELOP GOALS

Dave is a 59-year-old coach, who has been coaching basketball at national level for over 25 years. One of his players, Michael, is a 14-year-old who is already playing under-18 national basketball. Although Michael is highly motivated, Dave feels Michael should set some goals. After an individual training session, Dave asked Michael to arrive 30 minutes early for the next session, so they can set some goals.

Dave started the goal-setting session by explaining what goals are and the potential benefits of setting goals. He then asked Michael whether he set goals for himself and what those goals were, to see if Michael was likely to set performance-oriented or success-oriented goals. It turned out that Michael did not really set any goals for himself, other than to play for his country at the Olympics. Dave told Michael that this goal was a good starting point. He also explained the concept of setting short-term and medium-term goals that were related to outcomes, performance, and processes to help Michael achieve his ultimate aim of playing for his country at the Olympics.

Dave was conscious of the fact that he wanted Michael's goals to be his own goals and did not want to force his own goals on Michael. After explaining the different types of goals, he asked Michael to pick several outcome, performance, and process goals. Although Dave wanted Michael to choose his own goals, he provided guidance for Michael using the SMARTS principles of goal setting. For instance, Dave suggested that Michael's goals should be specific because these would focus his attention, measureable so they could monitor his progress, realistic, and set within specific time frames. Michael set several goals, such as playing for his national under-16 team at the world championships and starting all of the matches. He also wanted to improve his shooting accuracy, and in particular his follow through when shooting. Dave encouraged him to focus on three specific goals, and asked Michael what he thought he had to do to achieve his goals. They then developed a two-month training programme to work on Michael's acceleration, shooting, and passing. They planned to review Michael's progress after two months and adapt the programme if necessary, but Dave wanted Michael to always have goals to work towards so intended to regularly meet with Michael to monitor his progress.

Case study reflection

Goal setting is a power tool that coaches can use to maximise the performance of their athletes in addition to the well-being of athletes (i.e. reduced cognitive anxiety and enhanced confidence). It is important that coaches regularly monitor the progress of their athletes and support them in achieving their goals. If a coach feels his athlete is struggling to achieve his or her goals, the coach should encourage the player to adjust his or her goals.

Summary points

- A goal refers to an objective, target, or a desired standard that an athlete wants to achieve in relation to a specific task or sport.
- Goal setting is associated with numerous benefits such as enhanced performance, team cohesion, and they also have a motivating effect on athletes.
- There are three types of goals: (1) outcome goals; (2) performance goals; and (3) process goals.
- Coaches should help athletes set effective goals by adhering to the SMARTS principle of goal setting.
- Athletes should be encouraged by their coach to monitor their progress in attaining their goals, and adjustments should be made if necessary.
- It is important that athletes do not set too many goals.

Practice exam questions

1   Compare and contrast the advantages and disadvantages of goal setting.
2   Discuss the implications of setting too many outcome goals.
3   Athletes are pre-disposed to set certain types of goals. Discuss.
4   Critically examine the relationship between goal setting and performance.
5   Discuss the implications of coaches setting team goals without consulting their athletes.

Critical thinking questions: applying theory to practice

1   Reflect on your own coaching experience and describe how you have used goal setting in your own coaching practice.
2   Design a goal-setting intervention, adhering to the SMARTS principles.
3   Discuss the implications of players focusing too much on long-term goals.
4   Coaches can alter an athlete's predisposition to set goals. Discuss.
5   How can coaches prevent problems occurring when their athletes engage in goal-setting interventions?

Case study questions

1   How could setting goals benefit Michael in the short-, medium-, and long-term? Discuss.
2   Why is it important that Dave encouraged Michael to set his own goals?
3   Discuss why Dave wanted Michael to continue working towards goals.

5

PERFORMANCE PROFILING

The purpose of this chapter is to provide information on how coaches can use performance profiling with individual athletes and in team settings. As such, information is provided on:

- A definition of the performance profile
- Benefits of performance profiling
- How does the performance profile work?
- Monitoring progress
- Team performance profiling
- Coach performance profiling.

A definition of the performance profile

The performance profile was developed to enhance an athlete's self-awareness regarding the characteristics that facilitate successful performance and to enhance the coach's understanding of the athlete's viewpoint (Butler, 1989; Butler et al., 1993). As such, performance profiling is a method of allowing coaches to understand how athletes rate themselves in the qualities that are needed to be successful in their sport. Coaches can use this information to help develop training schedules in the areas where athletes feel they could improve (Butler, 1996a).

Performance profiling is embedded in Kelly's (1991) Personal Construct Theory (PCT). The major tenet of the PCT is that individuals continually strive to make sense of the world that they are in, and themselves, by constructing personal theories. This leads to individuals anticipating what will happen in given situations (e.g. playing a highly ranked player at tennis) and these theories are either validated when the match is played or are revised (Butler and Hardy, 1992). As such, PCT is concerned with the athlete's view or perception. The PCT has two fundamental principles according to Butler (Butler, 1996a; Butler et al., 1993):

1   Each athlete has a unique way of making sense of his or her experiences in sport, which might otherwise remain at a low level of consciousness if he or she does not engage in performance profiling.
2   In order to understand an athlete's point of view, it is essential that the coach sees things from the athlete's perspective. Coaches and athletes may have a tendency to see things from their own perspective, because they both have a unique set of experiences (e.g. playing vs. coaching).

Benefits of performance profiling

Sport psychology scholars (e.g. Dale and Wrisberg, 1996; D'Urso et al., 2002; Jones, 1993; Weston et al., 2011a, 2011b) reported a number of benefits of the performance profile:

1   Helping athletes identify the qualities that are associated with successful performances in their chosen sport.
2   Helping athletes identify their own strengths and weaknesses.
3   Fostering an athlete's understanding of his or her abilities and what is required to be successful in his or her chosen sport.
4   Enhancing an athlete's motivation if a performance profile is completed at least three times in a six-week period.
5   Allowing athletes to monitor their own progress.
6   Facilitating a discussion between the coach and the athlete.
7   Enhancing communication between athletes in team settings.
8   Taking responsibility for one's own development.
9   Setting new and challenging goals.

How does the performance profile work?

Traditional methods of providing psychological support would involve a coach deciding what an athlete needs and then delivering an intervention to help the athlete's psychological needs (Jones, 1993). However, in this process the athlete is relatively passive and has little say regarding what psychological skills he or she receives. This may reduce an athlete's motivation to engage in and adhere to any psychological intervention (Butler and Hardy, 1992). The performance profile eradicates athletes being passive, because they are instrumental in the performance profile procedure.

The performance profiling procedure involves three main stages as follows:

Stage 1

The coach asks the athlete to list the qualities that the athlete feels are the most important for success in their sport. As such, the athlete would list a variety of qualities that the best players in his or her sport possess, which will include:

- Physical (e.g. stamina, acceleration, agility, etc.)
- Technical (e.g. serving in tennis, shooting in soccer, or passing in rugby, etc.)
- Tactical (e.g. understanding of sport-specific tactics, etc.)
- Psychological (e.g. ability to cope with stress, confidence, or mental toughness).

Players would write this information down in a table. An example of a completed table is presented in Table 5.1. This table represents a soccer player's performance profile. It is important that coaches encourage their athletes to complete the table honestly and it should reflect their own opinions.

Stage 2

Stage 2 involves two distinct processes. Firstly, the coach asks the athlete to rank the 12 most important qualities that he or she has identified in Stage 1. Quality 1 is the most important, whereas Quality 12 is the least important quality that the athlete has listed. Sometimes athletes may struggle to think of 12 qualities, but they should still rank the qualities in order of importance, whether they have identified 10 qualities or only five qualities. The second process involves the athlete writing down what each quality means. Some athletes might find this difficult, but it is important that they write down the meaning of the quality so that there is no confusion about it at a later date. Athletes would list this information in a table. Table 5.2 is an example of a completed table by the same soccer player who completed Table 5.1.

Stage 3

Stage 3 also contains two processes. First, the coach asks the athlete to write down the qualities the athlete has listed in the performance profile and then rate his or her current ability out of 10. A score of 10 indicates that the athlete cannot

TABLE 5.1 Physical, technical, tactical, and psychological characteristics

Physical	Technical	Tactical	Psychological
Acceleration	1st touch	Positional play	Manage stress
Speed	Passing	Set play defensive formations	Mental toughness
Stamina	Shooting		Motivation
Agility	Heading		Concentration
Explosive strength			Managing anger
Flexibility			
Core strength			

TABLE 5.2 Example of completed table of important qualities

Rank order	Quality	Meaning
1	1st touch	Being able to control the ball well when I first get it, which gives me time
2	Acceleration	Being quick over the first 5 metres
3	Stamina	Being able to run for the whole 90 minutes
4	Positional play	Knowing where to be at the right time
5	Managing stress	Not letting my nerves get the better of me
6	Shooting	Accurate and powerful shots at goal
7	Passing	Making sure passes are hit with the right pace and in the right direction
8	Agility	Being able to change direction quickly
9	Concentration	Not letting unrelated thoughts affect me
10	Speed	Running as fast as you can
11	Flexibility	Range of movement in my joints to prevent injury
12	Managing anger	Not letting anger get the better of me

improve in a particular area, whereas a score of 1 suggests that the athlete has much room for improvement. Second, the coach asks the athlete to write down action points which represents what the athlete feels he or she needs to do. See Figure 5.1 for an example of a completed performance profile.

Assessing athlete and coach discrepancies

Once the athlete completes his or her performance profile, Butler (1996a) suggested that the coach should rate the athlete in each characteristic to assess the discrepancy between the coach and the athlete. Ideally, the coach would rate the athlete on the qualities without knowing how the athlete rated him or herself. Large discrepancies between the coach and the athlete require discussion between the coach and the athlete in which the two parties discuss their reasons for awarding their score. Butler (1996a) argued that it is often the areas of mismatch between the coach and the athlete that contribute to tension between the two people and even to a lack of progress. If the coach and the athlete still disagree after a discussion, they could ask the opinion of another coach or use video feedback, so that the athlete can see the coach's perspective.

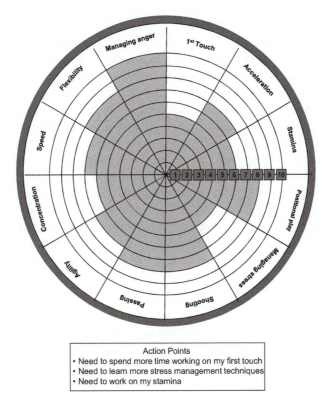

Action Points
- Need to spend more time working on my first touch
- Need to learn more stress management techniques
- Need to work on my stamina

FIGURE 5.1   Completed performance profile

Monitoring progress

Coaches can monitor their athlete's level of improvement by asking the athlete to complete a performance profile on a regular basis, such as once a month. Improvements in qualities that athletes are working towards can instil confidence and also illustrate to the coach that their training programme is effective or whether it needs altering (Butler, 1996b).

Team performance profiling

Research by Dale and Wrisberg (1996) indicated that performance profiling can be very useful in team settings. Team performance profiling involves a team identifying the characteristics associated with successful teams and then rating themselves in each characteristic. Dale and Wrisberg (1996) developed a three-step procedure which coaches can use for team performance profiling:

- *Initial team meeting*: The coach should call a team meeting, ideally at the start of the season, to integrate any new members of the team, and then explain what the performance profile is. Additionally, the coach should also explain the benefits of team performance profiling, such as allowing the coach and team members to gain an insight into each other's opinions.

• *Individual performance profiling*: The coach asks each athlete to go through the three stages outlined in this chapter, in order for them to complete their own individualised performance profile. Once the athlete has completed his or her own performance profile, the coach then rates the athletes on the characteristics that they have selected. This process may facilitate discussions between the team members and coaches, especially when there are any discrepancies.

• *Team performance profiling*: Athletes then go through the same three stages of the performance profile, but this time it is related to the team. So instead of athletes describing the characteristics of successful performers in their sport, they identify the characteristics of successful teams (Stage 1), rank the 12 most important characteristics and provide a meaning for each (Stage 2), and then individually rate their current scores out of 10. Each athlete's score contributes to the overall team average, which is plotted on the performance profile (Stage 3).

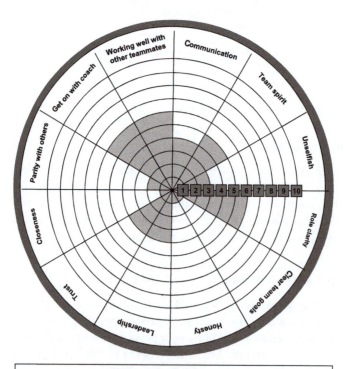

Action Points
• Develop team spirit and get to know each other more on pre-season tour of Scotland
• Organise social events so players, especially the new players, can get to know each other better
• Ensure that individual roles and positions with the team are clarified

FIGURE 5.2 Team performance profile

Coach performance profiling

Dale and Wrisberg (1996) also suggested that coaches could ask their teams to profile their ideal coach behaviour, with the view of allowing coaches to maximise their behaviour. The coach would ask his or her team to collectively identify ideal coach behaviours (Stage 1), rank the 12 most important characteristics and define their meaning (Stage 2), and individually rate their coach on each characteristic which contributes to a mean score that is plotted on the performance profile (Stage 3).

CASE STUDY 5.1   A SEASON-LONG PERFORMANCE PROFILING INTERVENTION IN PROFESSIONAL RUGBY UNION

Ian is a 45-year-old professional soccer coach, who has previously used the performance profile to good effect with injured players during their rehabilitation, but not in a team setting. In the close season a number of players have left his club and the team recruited 12 new players. As such, Ian thought it could be useful to conduct a performance profiling session to help integrate his new players. Ian also planned to have a performance profiling session once every two months to allow his players to monitor their progress. In the initial meeting, Ian explained what performance profiling was and how it could benefit his players. In particular he emphasised that if all his players could make small improvements in many areas then their overall performance would improve. Once the players completed their own performance profile, Ian asked them to consider the characteristics of successful teams in a brainstorming session. The players identified 27 different characteristics, and they decided that some characteristics were quite similar. By consensus, the players picked the 12 most important characteristics and spent 20 minutes or so describing each characteristic, before rating themselves. The performance profile presented in Figure 5.2 is the outcome of this meeting.

Ian held meetings every two months with his players in which they completed a team performance profile. The team performance profile from April is presented in Figure 5.3. The team improved in a number of areas by putting in lots of hard work on different elements throughout the season. The team also established action points for the following season.

Case study reflection

The performance profile can be an excellent tool in both individual and team sport settings if used correctly. It is essential that coaches are not prescriptive when conducting performance profile sessions, and allow athletes to complete their own performance profile. The benefits of the performance profile will be much greater if it is completed on multiple occasions.

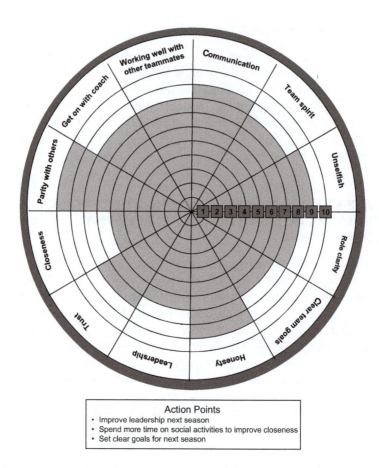

FIGURE 5.3   April performance profile

Summary points

- Performance profiling is based on Kelly's (1991) Personal Construct Theory.
- Performance profiling is a method of allowing coaches to understand how athletes rate themselves in the qualities that are needed to be successful in their sport.
- Performance profiling can be beneficial to athletes and is associated with enhancing athletes' motivation.
- Performance profiling can be conducted with individual athletes or with teams.

Practice exam questions

1   Discuss the origins of the performance profile.
2   Performance profiling can enhance motivation. Discuss.

3   Describe the benefits of performance profiling.
4   What are the benefits and possible negative effects of performance profiling?
5   Critically evaluate the advantages of team performance profiling.

Critical thinking questions: applying theory to practice

1   Describe how performance profiling may cause conflict between the coach and the athlete.
2   Describe how a coach would plan a performance profiling intervention over a season for an elite athlete.
3   Discuss why some coaches may be reluctant to conduct coach performance profiling with their team.
4   What are the implications of coaches who are too vocal when athletes create their own performance profile?
5   What difficulties may coaches encounter when conducting team performance profiling sessions? Discuss.

Case study questions

1   If you were Ian, how would you explain the performance profile and the processes involved to a team?
2   Discuss the importance of the players selecting the 12 characteristics.
3   How could Ian resolve any conflict if the players disagreed about the 12 characteristics they wanted to select?

PART IV

Coaching different populations

How to support the needs of different athletes

part II

6

COACHING CHILDREN

The purpose of this chapter is to provide information on the factors that coaches could consider when coaching children. Children are classified as athletes aged between 4 and 11 years of age. Specifically, in this chapter information is provided in relation to children and:

- Enhancing learning
- Self-awareness of coaching behaviour
- Enhancing positive experiences: fun and enjoyment.

Enhancing learning

Coaches who regularly coach children will probably have coached a child's first experience in a particular sport. This is because children try many sports, often prompted by their parents, to see if the child enjoys or has any talent for the sport (Côté, 1999). Coaching a child who is new to a particular sport might be difficult if the child struggles to learn different skills or techniques.

Learning amongst children can be enhanced by the coach giving the child the choice about when he or she receives performance feedback, also referred to as knowledge of results (Chiviacowsky et al., 2008b). However, before information is provided on how to enhance learning among children, coaches should be aware of the differences between children and adults in their capacity to deal with information (Badan et al., 2000).

As a child progresses through childhood, his or her motor behaviour (e.g. ability to perform different movements skilfully) will develop, due to (1) hardware and (2) software changes (Connolly, 1970). Hardware refers to changes that occur due to growth such as increases in height and weight. Software changes refer to an individual's ability to use different structures. Essentially, the individual becomes more efficient at processing information. For example, Lambert and Bard (2005) found that reaction time decreased from early childhood to adolescence.

At the present time much less is known about a child's information processing abilities than about adults' abilities (Chiviacowsky et al., 2008b), but asking children to tell the coach when they want to receive feedback may accelerate the learning process when children are learning new tasks. For example, Chiviacowsky and colleagues found that children's performance in a bean bag throwing exercise could be improved when the children decided when to receive feedback as opposed to when the children had no choice on when they received feedback. The children also required knowledge of results less often as they continued in the throwing task. This trend of the children requiring less feedback about their results indicates that the children learned more effectively (Wulf and Shea, 2004). Therefore coaches who ask their child athletes to tell them when they want information on the knowledge of results should expect fewer requests as a child progresses in an activity.

Furthermore, the findings from Chiviacowsky et al. (2008b) also indicated that children preferred feedback after successful attempts. Indeed Chiviacowsky et al. stated there may be a temptation for coaches to provide feedback after unsuccessful attempts only. This is because the coach may assume that this is when the child needs the most help in order to guide the child and correct any erroneous movement patterns in a skill. However, the children in the Chiviacowsky et al. (2008b) study only asked for successful feedback. Therefore, coaches should ask children to tell them when they want feedback or knowledge of results and refrain from providing the child with feedback when they have been unsuccessful at performing a specific task, because it is not conducive to effective learning.

Learning may also be enhanced by coaches encouraging children to ask for feedback more often when a new skill is being learned. This is because children often have a tendency to ask for feedback at less than the optimal rate according to research (Chiviacowsky et al., 2008a). The onus is on the coach to act in a supportive and encouraging manner so that children feel comfortable in regularly asking for feedback. Although this may be advantageous to learning among children, providing regular feedback to child athletes may only be possible when a coach is coaching an individual or a small group as opposed to a group of 20–30 children.

Another strategy that coaches could employ to facilitate learning in timing-based skills among children, especially when timing of movements is a crucial factor such as swimming, cycling, or evening running, is to teach children a counting strategy. This has been found to enhance learning on cycling tasks among younger children, between five and seven years of age, and older children aged between eight and ten years (Liu and Jensen, 2011). For example, a coach could administer the instructions "You are at 50 right now, try and keep the same pace" to a swimmer. It is especially important that coaches encourage younger children to use strategies, because they do not automatically use strategies. Ellis (1992) stated that timing is especially important for sports, so improving a child's timing has the potential to benefit performance.

Another method that coaches can use to enhance learning among children is to provide instructions that promote an external focus. For example, Flores et al. (2015) conducted a study in which children were assigned to an external focus group (i.e. instructions directed the attention of the children to the effects of their movement on a balance task), an internal focus group (i.e. focused attention on bodily movement), or a control group (i.e. did not receive instructions about the body during a balance task). Those in the external focus group learned quicker than the internal or control groups. These results were replicated in a throwing task, as Perreault and French (2015) found that children who were assigned to the external feedback group experienced a distinct advantage over the children in the internal focus group.

Another technique that coaches can employ to enhance learning among children is to limit the number of errors children make during training, as Capio et al. (2013) found that this enhanced the learning of a throwing task. This was achieved by devising a throwing task that gradually increased in difficulty in comparison with another group whose throwing task got easier. By gradually increasing the difficulty of the task, the children made fewer errors because their proficiency increased, and their performance at throwing was better than the group who completed the throwing task that got easier. As such, coaches can promote learning by devising tasks that get harder as a child's skill improves and thus reduce errors in practice.

Self-awareness of coaching behaviour

It is essential that coaches consider their behaviour whether they coach children, adolescents, or adult athletes. Quite often, coaches are not aware of their behaviour, with many coaches often being "blissfully unaware of how they behaved" (Smith and Smoll, 1997: 18). Millar et al. (2011) reported that the discrepancy between a coach's actual and reported behaviour may be as high as 40 per cent. Sport has the potential to benefit children in a number of ways, but if the coach behaves poorly, it has a detrimental impact on the well-being of children and reduces enjoyment (Smith and Smoll, 1997).

Researchers found that male coaches behaved differently to female coaches, with male coaches generally offering less encouragement than female coaches (Dubois, 1990; Walters et al., 2012; Wandzilak et al., 1988). Indeed, in the study by Walters and colleagues, male coaches made 29 per cent more negative comments than female coaches. Negative comments by the coaches included "Great shot" when indeed the athlete had hit a poor shot, "You need to shoot earlier", or "You committed yourself too early". It is essential that coaches refrain from expressing negative comments, especially to children, because Smoll and Smith (2006) suggested that negative behaviours or comments made by coaches are likely to induce feelings of resentment among children and may even result in some children ceasing sports participation. Coaches may make negative comments if they are frustrated due to their team or athlete not performing at the level they would desire. Coaches who overemphasise the importance of winning negatively influence dropout rates, self-esteem, and stress (Siegenthaler and Gonzalez, 1997). Furthermore, if a coach emphasises performance outcomes then a performance-motivational climate will develop, which is not conducive to athlete well-being, enjoyment, or motivation.

Another concerning finding from the Walters et al. (2012) study was that coaches were more critical of male athletes than female athletes, because coaches perceived females to be less talented (Horn et al., 2006). Additionally, coaches from sports of more national significance were also more critical of child athletes. It is essential that coaches are: (a) aware of how negative behaviour may impact upon child athletes; and (b) are aware of their own behaviour when coaching.

Enhancing positive experiences: fun and enjoyment

The main reasons why children participate and continue participating in sport are because it is fun and enjoyable (Crocker et al., 2004; Atkins et al., 2015). One of the main reasons why children cease participating in a sport is because it makes them unhappy (Cary, 2004). Indeed, Cary found that 44 per cent of parents said their child had dropped out of playing sport because it made them unhappy. For these reasons, it is essential that coaches make participating in sport a fun and enjoyable experience for all children.

Scanlan and Lewthwaite (1986) developed a model to explain the sources of fun and enjoyment among children. The model contains four elements, described below. Coaches should understand this model and implement the model within their coaching. Maximising the outcomes in each of the four categories will make sport more fun and enjoyable for children (MacPhail et al., 2008).

1   *Intrinsic achievement* refers to a child's perception of his or her competence. It is related to the amount of improvement made, whether a skill has been successfully mastered or not, and perceptions of ability.
2   *Extrinsic achievement* relates to perceptions of competence achieved through feedback from a coach or achieving recognition from a coach.
3   *Intrinsic non-achievement* includes both competition and movement factors. For example, participating in competitions can be very exciting, and the movement sensations that a person experiences when playing sport can be very satisfying.
4   *Extrinsic non-achievement* involves non-performance sources of fun, such as a child making friends through playing sport, spending time with their friends through playing sport, or even the feeling of being affiliated with a particular team.

A coach can maximise the enjoyment of a child by creating tasks that promote feelings of competence, provide feedback that denotes competence, and provide children with an element of competition. Finally, the coach can tell the children that they are all important members of the team or club and that their affiliation is highly appreciated and respected.

CASE STUDY 6.1 ENHANCING LEARNING AMONG CHILDREN

Abby is a 24-year-old full-time tennis coach, who coaches a variety of different levels and ages. She was recently asked to attend an inner city school to provide a coaching session to 7- and 8-year-olds who had never played tennis before. The session was conducted in a gymnasium, so there was limited space available. Further, Abby only had five one-hour sessions with the children, so she was conscious that she wanted to maximise the time spent with the children by ensuring that learning was accelerated as much as it could be.

In order to maximise learning, Abby adopted a number of approaches. First she developed a number of drills that were assigned a station number. Once the class arrived Abby explained the drill for each specific station, asked the children to decide which station they would attend first, and explained that they would be spending around 5 to 10 minutes per station. As it was the children's first experience of playing tennis, the drills were designed to minimise errors. For example, at Station 4, the children were asked to throw and catch a tennis ball with their partner. To limit the times the ball was dropped, the children stood 1 metre apart. Abby was going to increase this distance over the coming weeks as the children's throwing and catching ability improved.

Another strategy that Abby employed was to promote an external focus among the children. She did this by providing instructions that encouraged them to deploy an external focus when completing the different stations (e.g. when you throw the ball to your partner, try and make it spin backwards as you let go, balance the ball on your racquet like a waiter balances plates on his hand, and focus on the centre of racquet as you hit the ball). She also said that she would provide help and guidance only when the children wanted it, and that they could receive help or advice by asking Abby a question.

In addition to maximising learning among the children, Abby also wanted the sessions to be fun. By making the tasks more difficult as the skills of the children progressed Abby thought that she would be enhancing the children's perceptions of competence. She was also very aware of her body language and tone of voice.

Case study summary

Coaching children's first experience of a sport could be very challenging for coaches, as some children might get incredibly frustrated if they are unable to learn the key skills that are required. Coaches can increase the speed at which children learn, and thus hopefully minimise frustration, by adopting strategies such as providing choice regarding the activities that are carried out, encouraging children to ask for feedback, promoting external focus via instructions and feedback, and limiting the number of errors in practice by devising drills that become progressively more difficult as children improve.

Summary points

- Coaches can enhance learning among children by providing feedback when they want it.
- Learning can be maximised by devising drills that become progressively more difficult, so that errors are reduced.
- Coaches should encourage athletes to have an external focus through their feedback and instructions.
- Coaches should be aware of their behaviour and the consequences of negative comments.
- Sport should be fun and enjoyable to maintain participation rates among child athletes.

Practice exam questions

1 Discuss the role of feedback in influencing learning among children.
2 Discuss the influence attentional coaching styles on learning among athletes.
3 Discuss how providing choice to children influences learning.
4 Discuss how coach behaviour affects children.
5 Discuss the influence of the coach on how a child enjoys sport.

Critical thinking questions: applying theory to practice

1 Discuss ways in which coaches can become more aware of their behaviour.
2 What can a coach do to enhance learning among children?
3 Reflect on your own behaviour when you have coached a child or children. Identify the positive and negative comments that you made.
4 How can coaches make training sessions more enjoyable for children?
5 Design a training session that limits the number of errors a child makes.

Case study questions

1 Design four drills that Abby could have used with the children and comment on how they could be made progressively more difficult.
2 Develop some instructions for your own sport that promote an external focus among athletes.
3 Abby decided to only provide feedback when the children wanted it. Discuss the advantages and limitations of this approach.

7

COACHING ADOLESCENTS

This chapter provides information on the factors that coaches could consider when they coach adolescent athletes. In this chapter, information is provided in relation to coaching adolescent athletes and:

- Adolescence
- Coach behaviour
- Practice activities and instruction
- Understanding and reducing dropout
- Enhancing self-esteem, well-being, and enjoyment.

Adolescence

Athletes who are between 12 and 18 years of age are classified as being adolescents in this chapter. Adolescence has the potential to be a stressful period, due to the development changes that occur in this stage of a person's life (Compas et al., 2001). Athletes may experience physical, physiological, emotional, social, and cognitive changes during this period (Boekaerts, 1996).

Coach behaviour

Effects of and desired coach behaviour

It is essential that coaches are aware of their behaviour when coaching adolescent athletes, because coach behaviour has a number of implications. In addition to influencing intrinsic motivation, it is also related to aggression (Chow et al., 2009). Indeed, Chow et al. (2009) found that coaches who perceived they had stronger beliefs in their abilities to coach sport and lead their team to success resulted in players who were more likely to commit violent acts of aggression than players who were coached by coaches with weaker beliefs in their ability to be successful. Chow et al. suggested that coaches who possessed strong judgements about their ability to coach may view aggressive behaviour as legitimate, given that it might result in a team winning and thus achieving the coach's goal. Additional research by Rieke et al. (2008) found that coaches who demonstrated a caring behaviour, involved athletes in making decisions, and wanted others to grow personally were associated with athletes who were more satisfied, mentally tough, task-oriented, and intrinsically motivated. These studies reveal the importance of coach behaviour, but did not explore how coaches behaved during competitions. More recent research has assessed how coaches behave during competitions.

In-game behaviours of coaches

Smith and Cushion (2006) examined how professional soccer coaches behaved during matches. They categorised behaviour into three types: (1) developing performance (e.g. use of silence, use of instruction, mistake correction, decision making, and purpose of games); (2) support and encouragement (e.g. use of praise, scolding, use of names, and verbal statements to intensify the efforts of players); and (3) coaches' role and influences (e.g. the coach's job and coach's knowledge and experience). The most frequently reported in-game behaviour was the use of silence. Coaches need to be careful when adopting the strategy of silence, because some athletes might perceive that a coach is conducting ineffective coaching (Jones et al., 1995). However, Smith and Cushion (2006) contended that the use of silence was an appropriate behaviour because it allowed the coaches to monitor their team and performance, before reflecting on deploying an intervention. Other research concurred with the findings of Smith and Cushion, an instruction appears to be the most frequent coach behaviour with samples of adolescent soccer players in the United Kingdom (Ford et al., 2010).

Interestingly, Ford and colleagues (Ford et al., 2010) examined skill and age-related differences and found that elite adolescent soccer players received more coaching behavioural responses in training activities that replicated match conditions than non-elite athletes. Furthermore, older soccer players in the under-16 category received more coaching behavioural responses than those in the under-9 and under-13 years of age category. These findings have a number of implications for players and it appear that the behaviours may result in a number of undesirable consequences. Indeed, Smith and Cushion (2006) acknowledged that the in-game behaviours of coaches were focused on developing the performance of the players to the detriment of creating a supportive and encouraging environment. Indeed, the instructional approach adopted by coaches as opposed to more supportive and encouraging behaviour may result in decreased intrinsic motivation (Bengoechea and Strean, 2007), decreased satisfaction among athletes (Rieke et al., 2008), and even lower mental toughness scores (Gucciardi et al., 2008). However, other research implied that adolescents require coaches to demonstrate instructional approaches in training (Martin et al., 2003), so athletes may also require this in matches. However, research is required to assess the effects of in-game coach behaviour among athletes to assess the impact of coaches mainly providing athletes with instructional behaviours as opposed to supportive and encouraging instructions.

Another issue with coaches providing so many instructional behaviours relates to the development of the athlete. There is evidence to suggest that coaches who provide frequent verbal instruction, feedback, or demonstrations may indeed provide too much information to athletes, which can prevent them from engaging in their own problem-solving process (Williams and Hodges, 2005). There have been calls for coaches to provide less instruction to athletes, which is representative of the instruction they would receive in a match. Ford et al. (2010: 493) stated that learners will eventually have to perform in competitions on their own and without direct guidance or instruction from a coach. Therefore, Ford et al. (2010) stated that the challenge for coaches is "to provide the least amount of instruction possible so as to enable athletes to solve problems independently".

Practice activities and instruction

There appears to a be a discrepancy between what coaches actually do and research regarding skill acquisition, motor learning, and expert performance among adolescent athletes (Ford et al., 2010). Indeed, it has been argued that practice should reflect competition for athletes to make improvements from their training (Singer and Janelle, 1999). For example, elite wrestlers reported that mat work was the most important part of their training, whereas gymnasts have adapted their training to spend more time engaged in activities that were similar to competition (Law et al., 2007). However, the results by Ford et al. indicate that adolescent soccer players spend 65 per cent of their training time in activities that are not closely related to actual competition, whereas only 35 per cent of practice time involved activities that were similar to playing soccer.

Ford and colleagues (2010) stated that this finding is very worrying, given that adolescence might be a key period in which the skills associated with playing soccer are developed (Proteau et al., 1992). Others advocated that only activities relevant to competition should be practised (Williams and Hodges, 2005). Indeed, sport-specific practice was associated with adolescent athletes being more likely to be selected for their national team (Forsman et al., 2016). It is apparent that adolescent athletes should spend more time in activities that are relevant to competition. In addition to enhancing the likelihood of an athlete being selected for a national team, sport-specific practice was also associated with superior technical, tactical, and psychological skills (Forsman et al., 2016). One of the reasons why sport-specific practice may have enhanced psychological skills is because such practice, in which athletes are required to perform under pressure, may foster the development of new coping skills via athletes learning through experience to cope (see Tamminen and Holt, 2012) and/or facilitate the development of mental toughness (see Bell et al., 2013). In addition to competition-relevant activities developing perceptual, cognitive, motor, and technical skills, tactical understanding, and psychological skills, they may also enhance intrinsic motivation. This is because athletes are more motivated when they perceive tasks to be relevant (Nicholls, 1989). Future research could explore the effects of playing form activities on intrinsic motivation among adolescent athletes.

Understanding and reducing dropout

A recent systematic review, with meta-analysis, of 10 studies revealed that 23.9 per cent of adolescent soccer players drop out on an annual basis (Møllerløkken et al., 2015). The authors of the systematic review reported that this number is relatively stable during adolescence, but that the dropout rates are higher for female (26.8 per cent) than male (21.4 per cent) adolescent soccer players. These dropout rates were similar to another study by Baron-Thiene and Alfermann (2015), who reported a dropout rate of 29.6 per cent among elite German athletes. Interestingly, dropout rates were also higher for female and individual sport athletes.

It is therefore important that coaches understand the reasons why adolescent athletes drop out so they can eliminate some of the risk factors associated with dropout. A review by Weiss and Williams (2004) identified conflict of interests, lack of fun, arguments with coaches, and a lack of playing time as the main reasons for dropping out of sport. Other factors that influence dropout rate are:

- Achievement goals (Gardner et al., 2016a, 2016b, 2017)
- Burnout (Isoard-Gautheur et al., 2016a)
- Relative age effects (Lemez et al., 2014)
- Motivation (Baron-Thiene and Alfermann, 2015; Francisco Guzmán and Kingston, 2012)
- Physical and psychosocial reasons (Fraser-Thomas et al., 2008).

Achievement goals

Gardner et al. (2016b) proposed that mastery-approach goals (i.e. an athlete wanting to improve a previous standard of their own performance) were thought to be associated with athletes being less likely to drop out. Conversely, Gardner and colleagues predicted that performance-avoidance goals (i.e. an athlete not wanting to be the worst on his or her team) would be linked to higher levels of dropout, because these types of goals are associated with athletes not enjoying themselves.

Burnout

Burnout is a multi-dimensional construct that consists of (1) emotional and/ or physical exhaustion, (2) evaluating one's performance negatively, and (3) showing a lack of concern for one's sport (Raedeke and Smith, 2009). Isoard-Gautheur et al. (2016a) examined the relationship between burnout and participation rates after six years, among elite handball players, aged between 14 and 18 years old. Those who reported higher levels of burnout were much less likely to be playing handball six years later.

Relative age effects

The relative age effect states that athletes who are born in the first two quartiles of a selection year are more likely to be selected for teams and have a greater chance of success, because these adolescents are generally heavier, taller, and stronger (Helsen et al., 1998). Lemez et al. (2014) reported that dropout rates were highest among those born in the third and fourth quartiles.

Motivation

Another factor that influences dropout rates is motivation. Francisco Guzmán and Kingston (2012) found that athletes who persisted in their sport were more likely to have self-determined motivation and have their basic psychological needs (e.g. autonomy, competence, and relatedness) met.

Physical and psychosocial reasons

Fraser-Thomas et al. (2008) conducted a study that assessed the physical and psychosocial reasons for dropout among a sample of 25 swimmers who had dropped out and 25 swimmers who were currently engaged in swimming and were aged between 13 and 18 years of age. The results revealed that physical factors and psychosocial factors were related to dropout among these swimmers. With regard to physical factors, it was found that those who dropped out took part in few activities outside of school and spent less time participating in swimming. Additionally, those who had dropped out were more likely to have had the status of being a top swimmer in their childhood, started supplementary dryland training earlier, and went to a swimming camp earlier than those engaged in swimming. Fraser-Thomas and colleagues suggested that the swimmers who dropped out might not have been psychologically capable of handling the pressure of being a top swimmer, which indicates the need for coaches to provide athletes with the psychological skills training to ensure they are capable of coping with stress or pressure, or even the disappointment of being a child star, but mediocre in adolescence (Hill, 1988). Fraser-Thomas et al. (2008) identified psychosocial factors as a reason for the swimmers dropping out, such as receiving less one-on-one coaching throughout development. Another factor that was related to dropout was parents. Many of the swimmers who dropped out had parents who competed at a high level. Also, those who dropped out were less likely to have best friends who were involved in swimming and the dropouts were also the youngest in their training group.

It appears that adolescents do not make a "snap" decision to drop out. Dropping out of sport is a process. In this process the adolescent athletes make an ongoing cost-benefit evaluation of participating in their sport, which could involve weighing up a lack of playing time (cost) with the amount of improvement that has been made (benefit) (Fraser-Thomas et al., 2008).

From a coaching perspective, these findings indicate that coaches need to think carefully about how they formulate and structure training. It is clear, however, that coaches need to make sports training and competition more fun and enjoyable for adolescent athletes, which could mean delaying when athletes attend residential training camps (Fraser-Thomas et al., 2008). Additionally, coaches could also consider what athletes do at the training camps and reduce the amount of training at these camps. This would leave more time for additional activities that athletes perceive as fun and enjoyable. Coaches can also reduce dropout by promoting mastery goals, meeting the psychological needs of their athletes, and designing training drills that do not give an advantage to older athletes and thus reduce the impact of relative age effects.

Enhancing self-esteem, well-being, and enjoyment

Self-esteem refers to an athlete's overall evaluation of his or her sense of worthiness and indicates a person's feelings regarding skills, abilities, and social relationships (Rosenberg, 1979). Additionally, self-esteem is a useful indicator of a person's well-being (Coatsworth and Conroy, 2006). Promoting and enhancing self-esteem is desirable, because individuals who are high in self-esteem are thought to be more psychologically healthy (Taylor and Brown, 1988). Conversely, individuals who have low self-esteem may be more likely to experience stress (Tennen and Affleck, 1993). In general, it is accepted that self-esteem influences current and future behaviour (Harter, 1999). There is a widely held notion that adolescents who participate in sport benefit from increased levels of self-esteem (Marsh and Kleitman, 2003).

Although participating in sport has the potential to boost self-esteem, this is very much dependent on the coach. Research indicates that coaching behaviours account for variances in self-esteem (Smith et al., 1983) and that athletes with lower self-esteem are more sensitive and responsive to instructive and supportive behaviours from a coach (Smith and Smoll, 1997). With this in mind, a number of programmes attempted to improve coach behaviours with the aim of enhancing self-esteem among athletes. One of the most recent interventions was created by Coatsworth and Conroy (2006), who developed a two-hour coach training programme adapted from Coach Effectiveness Training (Smith and Smoll, 1997). Smith and Smoll emphasised the consequences of coaching behaviour, how coaches should evaluate success and failure, benefits of and techniques for team building, creating a mastery achievement goal climate, supporting coach behaviours and eliminating punitive coaching behaviours. Overall, the intervention was successful in enhancing self-esteem, especially among younger adolescents and females with lower self-esteem at the start of the study.

Coaches can also enhance the well-being of adolescent athletes by supporting them in the choices they make and soliciting input. For example, Adie et al. (2012) found that environments created by coaches that solicit athletes' responses and opinions convey that the coach trusts the athlete. Allowing athletes to make their own choices or decisions increases well-being. Furthermore, this type of coaching environment may even reduce symptoms of overtraining among athletes (Adie et al., 2012).

In terms of making sport a more enjoyable experience for adolescent athletes, Fry and Gano-Overway (2010) found that athletes who perceived a caring sporting environment were more likely to report higher enjoyment scores. A caring environment was characterised by warmth, safety, acceptance, and willingness to help each other. There was also a number of other interesting results with regard to athletes being in a caring environment. Athletes in a caring environment were more likely to report positive attitudes towards their team mates, greater commitment to their sport, and engage in more caring behaviours towards their team mates.

CASE STUDY 7.1   REFLECTIONS ON A TRAINING SESSION

The following case study represents Kim's reflection on a practice session in the diary she keeps. Kim is an ex-international hockey player and is the coach of a regional under-18 squad that contains 18 players.

> The players were a bit low after Saturday's defeat and I felt it was really important to speak to them all at the start of session, and I am really glad that I did. I tried to be very empathetic towards the players and supportive and wanted them to voice some of the reasons behind the defeat and poor performance. This worked really well as the players identified a number of factors that I had also noticed but they all seemed to take ownership of the situation and devised their own strategies regarding what we could work on. I also provided some feedback in areas that I felt we could improve on and asked for opinions from the athletes. After some positive discussion the players seemed to be uplifted, because they felt if we made improvements in the areas we had identified team performance would improve. One of the key areas the players identified was playing under pressure. As such I created some training matches that gave the players less time on the ball so they would become more used to playing with less space and time. I did this by reducing the size of the pitch by initially playing 9 versus 9 on a half pitch for 15 minutes. I then

reduced the pitch even further to give the players even less space. I also provided some coping training to the players so that they could cope with the increased pressure that they experienced in training.

This was a challenge for the players and I tried to be encouraging which I think really helped as more mistakes were being made, but deep down the players knew they needed to improve in this area of the game and I think most of them saw the benefits of this and quite a few asked if we could do this in future. I know that it is not going to be a quick fix, but I feel confident that the players believe that they will improve as the season progresses and that today's session helped lift their spirits. I am looking forward to the next session with the players.

Case study summary

In this case study Kim described how she attempted to provide the players with input and decision making in a manner that was caring and supporting. She also tried to place an emphasis on the players improving and set up a training activity that was relevant to matches with the aim of helping the players become accustomed to playing under pressure with less time on the ball.

Summary points

- Coach behaviour can influence aggression, decision making, and mental toughness among adolescent athletes.
- The majority of in-game behaviour by coaches appears to be of an instructional nature.
- Practice activities in training should replicate match conditions to help develop adolescent athletes, but it appears that players might only spend a third of their practice time in match-like conditions.
- Around 25 per cent of adolescents may drop out each year.
- Female and individual sport athletes are more likely to drop out than males or team sport athletes.
- There is a relationship between the age at which adolescents increase the amount of training (e.g. attend training camps) and drop out.
- Dropout rates could be reduced by coaches delaying specialised training camps and providing psychological support to adolescent athletes to help them combat stress.
- Decreasing the impact of relative age effects in training drills, reducing burnout, and promoting mastery goals may also reduce dropout.
- Ensuring that an athlete's psychological needs are met (e.g. autonomy, competence, and relatedness) may also reduce dropout.

- Coaches can enhance the self-esteem of adolescent athletes by placing less emphasis on outcome and more emphasis on rewarding improvement, and viewing that as success, acting in a supportive manner, and refraining from administering punitive coaching behaviours.
- Coaches can also enhance the well-being of the adolescent athletes they coach by supporting them in the choices they make and soliciting input and decision making.

Practice exam questions

1   Describe the discrepancies between adolescent athletes' preferred behaviour and the in-game behaviour of coaches.
2   Discuss how the relative age effects influence dropout.
3   Discuss the role of the coach in promoting self-esteem among adolescent athletes.
4   Coaches are responsible for the aggressive behaviour of their athletes. Discuss.
5   Describe the process in which an athlete drops out.

Critical thinking questions: applying theory to practice

1   How can coaches make training sessions more realistic of matches and what are the implications for performance?
2   Identify and discuss how coaches can devise training programmes with the goal of reducing dropout among adolescent athletes.
3   What can a coach do to develop a caring environment?
4   Design some training drills that do not provide an advantage to stronger, taller, and heavier athletes and which thus counter the relative age effects.
5   Describe how coaches can facilitate the development of adaptive achievement goals (i.e. approach achievement goals) and reduce the likelihood of athletes having avoidance type achievement goals.

Case study questions

1   What else could Kim have done to demonstrate empathy?
2   Discuss why Kim provided coping training in addition to pressurised training matches in training.
3   Discuss the importance of reflection for coaching practice.

8

COACHING ADULTS

The aim of this chapter is to provide information on the factors that coaches should consider when they coach adult athletes, who are classified as being 18 years of age and older. In this chapter, information is provided in relation to adults and:

- Andragogy: learning among adults
- Effects of coach behaviour
- Antecedents of coaching behaviour.

Andragogy: learning among adults

Although coaches might expect to be coaching athletes with years of experience when they coach an adult athlete, this might not always be true. Adults are likely to take up new sports for a number of reasons. For example, athletes who participate in contact sports such as rugby union might take up new sports that put less strain on their bodies such as swimming or tennis. Older athletes who are not capable of performing how they want in tennis, due to their reduced speed, might take up sports such as golf or bowls. It is therefore essential that coaches understand how adult athletes learn in order to maximise their coaching efficiency.

In comparison with children, less is known about how adults learn. The term pedagogy is a familiar term in sport science journals and originates from the Greek words *paid* which means child and *agogus* which means leader of. Pedagogy literally means teaching children (Knowles et al., 2011). The term that refers to the understanding and supporting of learning among adults is andragogy. It is important to note that the word andragogy is not a new term, as the use of this word dates back to Alexander Kapp who used it way back in 1883 (Reischmann and Jost, 2004).

Lindeman (1926) identified key principles among adult learners, which were subsequently supported by research (Knowles et al., 2011), Merriam and

Brockett (1997) stated that little has changed with regard to why adults want to learn and the best ways of helping adults learn. As such, Lindeman stated that:

1   Adults become motivated to learn skills when they experience needs and interests, which they feel that learning will satisfy.
2   Adults are oriented to learning that is life-centred and thus adults will want to learn when they feel that learning will benefit their wider life.
3   Adults often rely on their previous life experience when learning, so coaches should use experience as a core component of coaching adults. Within a sport setting, coaches could relate back to athletes' previous experiences of playing other sports if they are similar.
4   Adults also have a very deep need to be self-directing. The role of the coach is not to transmit his or her knowledge to the athlete; rather, the coach's role is to engage in a mutual process of enquiry with the athlete.

Based on these four points, Knowles (1995) developed eight principles that form a process to help adults learn more effectively that can be applied by coaches:

1   *Preparing learners:* It is crucial that adults are given information regarding the tasks they will be engaged in at the start of each session and why they are relevant. For example, a coach who is teaching an adult to swim could say that he or she would like the swimmer to work on his leg kicks in a session, to increase swimming speed.
2   *Developing the climate:* Coaches should teach athletes in a relaxed fashion that is supportive, collaborative, and respectful. Furthermore, coaches should also be open to the athletes' ideas. Many adult athletes will have their own ways of learning based on their previous experiences in sport and non-sport settings.
3   *Planning:* Coaches should involve the athlete in regard to the activities that the athlete will be engaged in.
4   *Diagnosis of needs*: The coach and the athlete should mutually assess the current state of the athlete's abilities and what they feel the athlete needs to work on to improve.
5   *Setting objectives:* The coach and the athlete should work together to set realistic objectives regarding improvement and standards of attainment. For example, an adult golfer may have the objective of attaining a handicap of 5 within 12 months of starting golf, which might be unrealistic. In this instance the coach could question whether the golfer thinks that would be realistic and could give his opinion on the amount of time the golfer would have to spend practising in order to get his handicap down to 5 in such a short space of time.
6   *Designing learning plans:* Adult athletes like to understand why they could benefit from learning new skills. The coach could identify what Knowles (1995) termed "problem units" that would then help determine a learning plan. Within a sporting context, a problem unit would refer to aspects of a person's ability that might prevent him or her from reaching a desired level

of ability. For example, a tennis player might not be serving as he would like to because he (1) has a poor ball toss, (2) does not have adequate power to hit the ball as hard as he wants to, (3) lacks explosive power, (4) has poor racquet position when he draws his racquet back in preparation for hitting the ball. As such, each point would be considered a problem unit. The coach could design activities that the athlete could engage in to learn new skills to eradicate each problem unit and thus serve better.

7   *Learning activities:* Adult learners will learn more effectively when the coach relates learning to an athlete's previous experience. For example, a retired tennis player may take up golf and the coach could relate aspects of golf to tennis when coaching. For example, the tennis player would be familiar with slicing the ball and hitting topspin shots, which is similar to golf when golfers hit a drawn shot or a fade. By explaining the concept of a fade as a slice and a draw as a topspin shot, the player can use his or her previous experiences and relate them to golf.

8   *Evaluation:* Coaches should regularly evaluate the progress made by an adult learner and involve the learner in the process. That is, the coach could ask the learner for his or her opinions on progress made. The athlete and the coach could share their own ideas, which then might shape future training sessions.

Enhancing learning through control

Although the eight principles developed by Knowles (1995) were not specifically designed for sports coaches who coach adult athletes, many of the principles have been supported in the sport science literature. In summary, these eight principles indicate that the adult athlete should be given a choice when learning. Within motor learning research, experimenters attempted to explore how giving adults choices influences learning when practising. Giving an athlete choice is often referred to as self-control (Wu and Magill, 2011).

One of the first studies that explored self-control and learning among adults was by Janelle et al. (1995). They allowed the adults to control when they received feedback during practice for learning a ball-throwing task. Janelle and colleagues found that giving the adult learners this choice improved learning. Interestingly, Janelle and colleagues found that those in the self-controlled group asked for feedback after 20.8 per cent of trials in the first trial block, but after only 6.7 per cent in the second trial block. From a coaching perspective, this would indicate that coaches should give athletes less feedback as they continue their learning.

Giving adults the choice regarding observations (Wrisberg and Pein, 2002), physical assistance devices (Wulf and Toole, 1999), and practice schedules (Keetch and Lee, 2007) seems to have a positive impact on learning. However, a limitation of these studies is that they did not explore the effects of self-controlled practice on learning when participants were asked to learn multiple movement patterns (Wu and Magill, 2011). Given that many sports involve multiple movement patterns, it would be interesting to explore these effects.

The study by Wu and Magill (2011) explored this by giving the participants the choice of different time structures and found that individuals who chose their own practice schedule performed significantly better in the 24-hour learning transfer test than individuals who did not choose their own practice schedule. This provides more support for giving adults choice.

In addition to giving participants choice regarding the time structure in which they practice (Wu and Magill, 2011), other research has indicated that giving athletes a choice over the amount of practice they do may also enhance learning (Post et al., 2011). With a sample of 24 participants, Post and colleagues explored the effects of allowing participants to choose the amount of practice they had on a darts-throwing task. The results revealed that the participants who controlled the amount of practice performed better in the retention task (performing the same task again) and a transfer task (e.g. performing a related task). From a coaching perspective, these findings indicate that allowing participants to control the amount of practice they have might reap immediate and longer-term benefits in performance.

Chiviacowsky and Wulf (2002) found that performance improvements occurred in a transfer task, but not a retention task. Chiviacowsky and Wulf argued that performance increments in transfer tasks are a more sensitive measure of learning than performance increases in a retention task. This is because the transfer task requires individuals to adapt a skill that they have previously attempted to learn. It also has implications for transferring skills learned in training into competitive situations. Those who control the amount of practice they do should be more able to adapt their learning to diverse situations, which is important for sports such as golf where golfers may play different courses and even for team sport athletes who might have to play in different weather conditions and against opponents of different standards.

Although these results suggest that coaches should allow all athletes to decide the amount of practice they have, other researchers have found this may have a negative impact, so coaches should be cautious with all athletes. Some athletes' preferred learning conditions, such as the amount of practice one partakes in, might not result in performance increases through enhanced learning (Schmidt and Bjork, 1992). This is because learning should be most effective from maximising the number of practice attempts or sessions (Schmidt and Lee, 2005). Therefore giving an athlete complete control of the amount of practice might not be the most effective way to enhance learning in all situations, as some athletes might decide to have a small number of practice trials (Post et al., 2011). Perhaps coaches and athletes could come to an agreement themselves about the amount of practice an athlete does, as learning progresses. This would give the athlete control, but also allows the coach to make an input using his or her experience.

Enhancing learning

One method employed by coaches to help athletes learn more effectively is through providing feedback. That is, a coach may provide the athlete with knowledge of his or her results about whether a specific movement or skill execution was successful or not. The purpose of such feedback is to enable athletes to correct errors (Wulf et al., 2010). Research by Chiviacowsky et al. (2009) explored how knowledge of results after good trials influenced learning among a sample of 22 adults with a mean age of 65.9 years, on a beanbag-throwing experiment. Knowledge of results for trials after small errors is more effective for enhancing learning than knowledge of results after trials with much larger errors. The authors provided some clues as to why only providing knowledge of results feedback might be so helpful in enhancing learning. For example, being provided with knowledge of results after a successful trial might have a reinforcing role that encourages people to perform the same movement again. Additionally, providing adults with knowledge of their results after successful trials may have a motivational impact on learning (Badami et al., 2011).

Hutchinson et al. (2008) found that feedback that indicated participants had performed above average in comparison to other performers, resulted in increased performance. Enjoyment of the task and increased levels of belief were also higher among athletes who were told they had performed better than average. Lewthwaite and Wulf (2010) also found that social comparison feedback can have more permanent effects on learning. Those who received positive feedback performed better in a transfer test than those who received negative feedback. Furthermore, learners who received information that they were improving at a greater rate in comparison with their peers also performed more effectively than individuals who received information that they were learning at a slower rate than their peers (Wulf et al., 2010). These findings have been attributed to athletes feeling concerned about themselves when they experience negative feedback, which disrupts performance (Lewthwaite and Wulf, 2010) and performers feeling energised when they receive positive feedback, which facilitates learning (Kühn et al., 2008).

The aforementioned studies indicate the importance of coaches providing feedback that it is positive in nature, because positive feedback influences motivation, which in turn is related to performance and learning. For example, if a particular athlete is improving much more than his peers the coach could mention this to the athlete to enhance his or her motivation, but should refrain from making social comparisons if the performer is below average. With regard to learners that perform below average, coaches should focus on the positive elements of an athlete's performance and provide positive feedback to maximise enjoyment and effort.

Although using feedback may increase levels of motivation (e.g. Badami et al., 2011) other research has found that pep talks given by a coach have no effect on motivation (Gonzalez et al., 2011). Indeed, Gonzalez et al. explored the influence of a video clip of a coach giving a pep talk in relation to motivation, inspiration, inspiration to perform, and emotion. The results revealed the pep talk did not have an effect on motivation, but did influence the inspiration to perform. However, one should not automatically dispel the influence of coach pep talks on motivation. This is because in the movie the pep talk was given by an actor and so was not specific to the group of players nor did the players know the coach. As such, the athletes would have known that the pep talk was not directed at them. Future research could monitor the effects of pep talks with coaches that athletes are familiar with as opposed to using video clips of pep talks. Furthermore, other research has suggested that athletes need differing amounts of information and emotion according to the situation (Vargas-Tonsing and Guan, 2007). Therefore, the information and emotional content of the pep talk video clip may not have elicited motivational responses.

Enhancing learning via instructions

A goal of coaches is to teach athletes sporting techniques they can use when they play sport. There is evidence to suggest that the instructions a learner receives influence how he or she will perform under high pressure situations (Lam et al., 2009; Law et al., 2003; Liao and Masters, 2001). It has been suggested that when athletes learn a new task they should have as little information as possible about the mechanics of a particular movement. When an athlete learns a movement with little understanding of the mechanics or processes involved, they are said to have engaged in implicit learning. One method to help an athlete learn implicitly involves analogies (Masters, 2000). According to Masters, an analogy refers to the athlete equating a sport skill with something that is similar, yet unrelated. An analogy reduces the number of rules an athlete has about a particular movement to just one biomechanical metaphor relating to the movement.

With this in mind, Liao and Masters (2001) examined the influence of using an analogy on learning a table tennis topspin forehand shot. This involved one group of athletes thinking about a right-angled triangle when they hit a forehand compared with another group who received 12 instructions. The analogy group had fewer rules, but the performance of the two groups was the same in learning. However, the analogy group's performance was more resistant to the negative effects of pressure and distractions than the group that received 12 instructions. This finding is relevant for athletes who have to play sport with many distractions such as coach communications, team mates, and even an audience, in addition to playing in pressurised competitions. As such, analogy learning may help athletes maintain performance despite experiencing anxiety and having several distractions.

The effectiveness of analogy learning has also been found in another table tennis study using the analogy of the bat travelling along the hypotenuse of a right-angled triangle (Law et al., 2003) and a basketball study (Lam et al., 2009). In the basketball study the players used the analogy of the hand reaching for a biscuit from a biscuit jar. The results of the basketball study found that the analogy group and the group that received coaching allocated equal amounts of attention to the task throughout learning and the trials, but the analogy group had fewer rules or information about the mechanics of basketball shooting in addition to not having their performance influenced by pressure. Despite some literature indicating that analogy training might have a limited influence on performance during learning (Koedijker et al., 2007), the majority of the evidence indicates that analogy learning helps athletes to maintain performance under pressure (Lam et al., 2009; Law et al., 2003; Liao and Masters 2001). A challenge for coaches when working with beginners is to generate analogies that the players can understand and implement when learning, because this has the potential to help athletes circumvent the negative impact of pressure on performance.

Effects of coach behaviour

Researchers explored how supportive a coach is in relation to giving his or her athletes choices among adult athletes and the effects of such behaviour (Zourbanos et al., 2010). Other research examined the factors that influence whether a coach is supportive or controlling (Stebbings et al., 2011).

In addition to coach behaviour being associated with positive evaluations of team experiences (Sheldon and Watson, 2011), how supportive a coach is also influences self-talk (Zourbanos et al., 2007, 2010). Zourbanos et al. (2007) explored the relationship between coach behaviour and statements, and athletes' self-talk. Self-talk refers to the inner dialogue that individuals have regarding thoughts, which influences behaviours and emotions, and may even distract athletes from performing at their best (Meichenbaum, 1977). Zourbanos et al. (2007) found that how supportive a coach was predicted whether the coach would give positive statements to athletes, which in turn predicted positive self-talk among the athletes. Interestingly, the relationship between the coach and positive self-talk explained 32 per cent of the variance of athletes' self-talk, indicating the key role that coaches play in shaping the self-talk content of athletes. The research by Zourbanos et al. (2007) was cross-sectional, so causality cannot be inferred from that study. That is, it is unclear whether positive coach behaviour caused positive self-talk among the athletes or whether positive self-talk among the athletes caused positive coach behaviour.

Zourbanos et al. (2011) published a three-study paper that in part addressed this limitation, with Study 3 of the paper being an experiment to assess the relationship between coach behaviour and self-talk. The experimental study revealed that positive coaching behaviour directly reduced the amount of negative self-talk, whereas the cross-sectional questionnaire-based studies (Study 2 and Study 3) provided support for the notion that positive coach behaviour is related to positive self-talk and negative coach behaviour is related to negative self-talk among athletes. As such, Zourbanos et al. (2007) stated that coaches should adopt a supportive stance toward the athletes they coach by encouraging them, using positive language, giving constructive comments, but avoiding negative verbalisations such as criticism and irrational comments.

Antecedents of coaching behaviour

Understanding why certain coaches provide a supportive versus controlling behaviours may be the key to reducing negative behaviours among coaches and thus has the potential to improve motivation, positive team experiences, and self-talk (Sheldon and Watson, 2011; Zourbanos et al., 2007, 2011). To this end, Stebbings et al. (2011) examined the antecedents of such behaviours among a sample of 443 coaches. It was reported that coaches' psychological well-being predicted coaching behaviour, with the coaches who had higher levels of psychological well-being providing more supportive behaviours and less controlling behaviours. An important implication from this research is that coaches should seek help when they suffer from poor psychological well-being. Providing support to coaches might indirectly improve their supportive behaviours (Stebbings et al., 2011).

CASE STUDY 8.1   COACHING AN EXPERIENCED GOLFER HOW TO DRAW THE BALL USING AN ANALOGY

Peter is an experienced golf coach who played on the European Tour for 12 years, then took up coaching and coached winners on the European Tour. He has been coaching Robert, who is 31 years old and has a handicap of 5, for three months. Peter believes that Robert should learn to shape the ball, such as right to left (known as draw for right-handed players) and left to right (known as a fade for left-handed players) in order to make improvements to his game. Peter discussed his thoughts with Robert, who was very keen to learn this new skill so he could improve his handicap even further. Robert was a former county tennis champion, so Peter used Robert's previous learning experiences by suggesting that a draw is similar to a topspin forehand in tennis, whereas a fade feels like a sliced backhand. This really helped Robert understand the difference between the two. As such, Peter instructed Robert to address the ball with a slightly closed stance, but then once he was in position all he had to do was swing normally and "roll your wrists" on impact. This analogy of "roll your wrists" helped Robert not to get too bogged down in trying to manufacture a right to left ball flight and allowed him just to focus on that simple instruction.

Case study reflection

This case study illustrates how a golf coach used an analogy to illustrate how a new skill, drawing the ball, could be taught. In this example, the instructions that the golfer had were very limited, other than ensuring his stance was correct and then focusing on the movement in his hands.

Summary points

- Andragogy refers to the understanding and supporting of learning among adults.
- Adults become motivated to learn skills when they experience needs and interests, which learning will satisfy.
- Adults may learn more effectively if coaches adhere to the eight principles proposed by Knowles (1995).
- Coaches should provide feedback after successful performances of a skill and positive feedback enhances intrinsic motivation.
- Coaches should provide the smallest amount of instruction as possible when teaching adult athletes a new skill.
- Coach behaviour influences motivation and self-talk among adult athletes.

Practice exam questions

1 Discuss how control may influence learning among adults.
2 Describe how the feedback a coach provides influences learning.
3 Discuss how the instructions a coach provides influences learning.
4 How does the behaviour of a coach influence athletes and what factors influence this behaviour? Discuss.
5 What are the key principles of adult learning and how might these differ from those for child athletes?

Critical thinking questions: applying theory to practice

1 How could a coach incorporate the eight principles proposed by Knowles (1995) within a training session?
2 Describe how a coach could enhance learning feedback within a coaching session.
3 How can a coach enhance the motivation of the adult athletes he or she coaches?
4 How should a coach instruct his or her athletes to maximise learning?
5 Describe how coaches should behave when coaching adult athletes.

Case study questions

1 Although the tennis analogy helped Robert in this instance, what other analogies could Peter have used if it confused Robert?
2 Develop some analogies that you could use in the sports that you coach.
3 What are the advantages of coaches, such as Peter, using analogies?

9

COACHING ATHLETES WITH LEARNING DISABILITIES

The purpose of this chapter is to provide coaches with information on different types of learning disabilities and how this could influence their coaching practice. In particular, this chapter contains information about the following learning disabilities:

• Attention deficit hyperactivity disorder (ADHD)
• Visual-perception disabilities
• Language-processing disabilities
• Fine motor skill disabilities.

Additionally, this chapter also contains information on:

• Attitudes of coaches towards athletes with learning disabilities
• Coaching principles when coaching athletes with learning disabilities
• Increasing compliance
• Managing challenging behaviour.

A learning disability refers to a person's neurological handicap that affects his or her ability to understand what he or she is told or reads. Athletes with learning disabilities may also have difficulties remembering what they have been taught (Smith and Strick, 2010). Within the United States, it is estimated that 10 per cent of school children possess some form of learning disability (U.S. Department of Education, 2007). Beyer et al. (2009) stated that although individuals with learning disabilities receive special care in educational settings, there is little information regarding how coaches can help these individuals in sport settings. Indeed, when a person with a learning disability is outside of an educational setting such as playing sport or going shopping, he or she may not appear any different from their peers (Friend and Bursuck, 2009), which is why learning disabilities are often referred to as "invisible" disabilities (Beyer et al., 2008, 2009).

Typical behaviour of individuals with learning disabilities

Coaching athletes with a learning disability may be challenging due to the behaviour they may display. According to Smith and Strick (2010), individuals with a learning disability may have:

- *A short attention span*: Athletes with learning disabilities are easily distracted from what they are doing, lose interest in what they are doing very quickly, move around from activity to activity very quickly even without completing a task or activity, and cannot pay attention for more than a minute at a time.
- *Difficulty following directions*: An athlete with a learning disability often finds it difficult to understand and follow instructions from the coach. A consequence of this is that the athlete might continually ask the coach questions.
- *Social immaturity*: Athletes with learning disabilities may act younger than their age. Furthermore, they are sometimes unable to process non-verbal information such as facial expressions or body language.
- *Problems with conversation*: Another behaviour common among individuals with learning disabilities is rambling at a rate which others cannot understand. This is often caused by people with learning disabilities struggling to find the right words to express themselves.
- *Inflexibility*: Some athletes with learning disabilities may act in a stubborn fashion and ignore suggestions or help from a coach, regarding the different ways they might complete a task more successfully.
- *Poor planning and organisational skills*: If a coach gives an athlete with a learning disability a task that has many parts or instructions, the athlete may struggle to know where to begin due to an inability to break down the task into manageable segments of movements.
- *Absentmindedness*: An athlete with a learning disability may often forget equipment that might be needed for a session or forget to do additional tasks that a coach might set between sessions, such as additional practice of a certain skill.
- *Clumsiness*: Athletes with learning disabilities may often appear awkward or uncoordinated when they play sport, such as bumping into other athletes, losing control of the ball if they are dribbling in soccer, or struggling to perform certain movements such as catching a ball.
- *Impulsiveness*: Athletes with learning disabilities may also interrupt the coach when he or she is talking, have difficulty waiting for their turn on an activity, and voice a variety of observations that may be completely unrelated to the sport they are playing or practising.

Types of learning disabilities

There are four main types of learning disabilities, although it should be noted that athletes with learning disabilities may have more than one type of disability (Smith and Strick, 2010).

Attention deficit hyperactive disorder (ADHD)

ADHD is an umbrella term for three forms of attention deficit hyperactive disorder (Rief, 2008):

1   *ADHD-I:* Individuals with ADHD-I have problems with their attention span, but they are not hyperactive or impulsive. As such, this form of ADHD is often referred to as the predominantly inattentive type.
2   *ADHD-HI:* Individuals with this type of ADHD are hyperactive and can also be very impulsive, so this form of ADHD is labelled the predominantly hyperactive and impulsive type.
3   *ADHD-C:* Most individuals that are diagnosed with ADHD have the combined type, ADHD-C. These people display significant symptoms of inattention, impulsivity, and hyperactivity.

For the remainder of this chapter, the term ADHD will be used, rather than distinguishing between ADHD-I, ADHD-HI, and ADHD-C. As such, this is inclusive of all three forms of ADHD and is common practice among medical professionals (Rief, 2008).

According to the American Psychiatric Association (2000), ADHD is characterised by the following behaviours.

1   The athlete has difficulty sustaining attention, does not listen to instructions, and has problems completing tasks. Indeed, athletes with ADHD tend not to follow through on instructions and may fail to finish activities such as sprint drills, training matches, or even competitive matches.
2   The second main symptom of ADHD is hyperactivity, which includes behaviours such as excessive fidgeting and an inability to remain still when this would be expected (e.g. sitting in a classroom).
3   The third symptom associated with ADHD is impulsivity, with ADHD sufferers having a tendency to interrupt others by butting in to conversations, blurting out answers to questions before the questions have been completed, and difficulties waiting for their turn during sporting activities.

Coaching children with ADHD may be challenging, especially in larger groups due to the behaviour associated with ADHD not being conducive to group work. However, it is important that athletes with learning disabilities such as ADHD have positive experiences of playing sport and thus continue sport participation. This is because previous research has found that children with ADHD experience more psychological well-being compared with those who do not play sport. Indeed, Kiluk et al. (2009) explored the relationship between sport participation and mood among 65 children diagnosed with ADHD. They found that children with ADHD who participated in sport were significantly less likely to report anxiety or depression symptoms. One factor that may determine whether an individual with learning disabilities, such as ADHD, participates in sport is the attitude of the coach towards athletes with learning disabilities (Beyer et al., 2008; Rizzo et al., 1997).

Visual-perception disabilities

Visual perception refers to the ability of the eyes to gather information, interpret that information, and then translate it into visual attributes such as luminance, colour, motion, and depth (Spaniol et al., 2011). A variety of brain structures are involved in contributing to the images that people see (Morozova et al., 2008). Visual perception such as motion and depth are important in sporting contexts in which athletes have to make decisions about the direction in which a ball is moving, the speed at which it is moving, and whether a ball is accelerating or decelerating, in addition to other competitors or team mates moving.

Smith and Strick (2010) reported that there are a number of behaviours associated with visual perception disabilities that might be apparent when an athlete is playing sport, such as:

- Confusing left and right.
- Poor spatial judgement, so athletes might attempt to run into spaces that simply are not big enough for them to run into.
- Poor sense of direction.
- Difficulty judging speed and distance.
- Poor visual imagery, so an athlete might struggle to see what they should do in a training task such as dribbling round cones.
- Struggling to understand different strategies that a coach might ask his or her team to perform.
- Slowness in reacting to visual information.
- Appearing clumsy.

Language-processing disabilities

Language processing refers to an athlete's ability to read, write, and spell (Taylor and Walter, 2003). Estimates indicate that language-processing disabilities related to reading, writing, and spelling affect 5–10 per cent of all children within the United Kingdom (Stein et al., 2000). The common term for such language-processing disabilities is dyslexia. Reid (2009) suggested that defining dyslexia is a very difficult process and even questioned the need to define this learning disability, because capturing the feelings and experiences of those who have dyslexia in a single statement might be very difficult, if not impossible. There are a variety of definitions regarding dyslexia, but Reid suggests that four main themes emerge from many definitions of dyslexia:

1   Dyslexia is developmental in that individuals with dyslexia find it very difficult to develop literacy (e.g. writing) and language (e.g. punctuation) related skills. As such, athletes with dyslexia may be poor at understanding the instructions that a coach gives them due to under-developed language capabilities.
2   The central theme of dyslexia is related to literacy, which includes word recognition, spelling, decoding abilities, and writing. Within a sport setting, athletes may struggle to decode what a series of instructions means, such as the tactics given by a coach for a soccer match.
3   Different teaching and learning approaches for athletes with dyslexia are required. As such, if a coach knows that an athlete has dyslexia, the coach might want to adjust his style (information on coaching styles and facilitating learning with dyslexic athletes and athletes with other learning disabilities is provided in this chapter).
4   There may also be a number of additional secondary factors associated with dyslexia which include problems organising, sequencing events, and motor skill problems. That is, athletes who have dyslexia might be very disorganised in aspects such as turning up to training sessions with the correct kit, problems comprehending team tactics, or co-ordination problems.

Fine motor disabilities

Motor skills refer to a person's ability to perform a specific movement with precision (Haibach et al., 2011). Indeed, Haibach distinguished between gross motor skills that involve movement created by large muscle groups such as quadriceps, hamstrings, and biceps and fine motor skills, which are created by much smaller muscle groups. Gross motor skills are generally less precise than fine motor skills.

Attitudes of coaches towards athletes with learning disabilities

Rizzo et al. (1997) explored 82 coaches' attitudes towards coaching athletes with mild learning disabilities in youth soccer. They found that a coach's attitude is a critical factor in whether individuals with learning disabilities play sport. Rizzo et al. (2017) found that although some coaches expressed beliefs against coaching athletes with learning disabilities, their attitudes and intentions were in agreement with coaching athletes with learning disabilities.

The authors tried to explain their findings by suggesting that the coaches did not have the opportunity to state that they were undecided in their beliefs about coaching athletes with learning disabilities, but nevertheless, this is a worrying and concerning finding. Rizzo and colleagues also found that as the perceived competence of the coach increased, coaches were more willing to coach a team that included athletes with learning disabilities. The authors cited experience as a reason why coaches did not feel competent to coach athletes with learning disabilities, because only 38 per cent of the sample had previously coached athletes with learning disabilities and 75 per cent did not have a family member with a learning disability, so they may have had little contact with individuals who have a learning disability.

The notion that coach experience might influence a coach's attitude towards athletes with learning disabilities was supported by Beyer et al. (2008), who (1) compared the attitudes of coaches with previous experience of coaching athletes with learning disabilities (ADHD) with those coaches who had no experience, and (2) collected information on coaches' experiences of coaching athletes with ADHD with a sample of 221 sports coaches. These authors found that coaches who had experiences of coaching athletes with ADHD had a more positive attitude to athletes with this learning disability than those who had no experience at all. These positive attitudes were related to their experiences of coaching athletes with ADHD.

Only 26 per cent of the coaches in the Beyer et al. (2008) sample had experience of coaching athletes with ADHD, which is less than in the previous research by Rizzo et al. (1997). Indeed, Beyer et al. argued that because the prevalence of children with ADHD is relatively high, up to 10 per cent of all children (U.S. Department of Education, 2007), it is more than likely that most of these coaches will have coached an athlete with a learning disability, but not known about it. As experience appears to be a crucial factor in shaping a coach's attitude towards coaching athletes with learning disabilities, a way to improve coaches' attitudes and then behaviour may be to give coaches hands-on experience of coaching athletes with learning disabilities, such as ADHD or dyslexia (Rizzo et al., 1997). At the very least, there is a need to improve coach education regarding coaching athletes with learning disabilities, which could involve information on understanding the behaviour and recognising the signs of people with learning disabilities and how coaches should behave (Beyer et al., 2008; DePauw and Gavron, 1991).

Coaching principles when coaching athletes with learning disabilities

Stowe (2000) and Reid (2009) outlined a number of principles that coaches can take on board when they are coaching athletes with learning disabilities to improve the effectiveness of their coaching. These include:

1   *Involve the athlete:* All athletes, but especially those with learning disabilities, need to be involved in the planning sessions so they take ownership. Generally, athletes with learning disabilities will learn more effectively when they are presented with small amounts of information at a time. It may also important to:

a   Tell the athlete what the coach would like him or her to achieve at the start of each coaching session in addition to asking the athlete what he or she would like to achieve.

b   Tell the athletes how they will be coached and explain the rationale for the activities.

c   Regularly ask athletes how they feel they are progressing with certain skills.

2   *Multisensory coaching:* Athletes with learning disabilities, especially dyslexia, require more interactive learning. Coaches could describe feelings and sights when they perform different tasks and encourage athletes to also describe their own feelings when performing different tasks.

3   *Promote logic and not memory:* Athletes with learning disabilities may have problems with their short- and long-term memory, so coaches should teach strategies that encourage athletes to focus on logical processes of different movements as opposed to encouraging athletes to use their memory.

4   *Present material sequentially:* When coaches are teaching different concepts, especially new skills, they should start from the very beginning and build very slowly. It is important that the coach emphasises the importance of the athlete understanding each principle associated with certain tasks (e.g. transfer of weight in tennis serve, hitting the ball at highest point, following through, etc.).

5   *Present material in small units:* For athletes with learning disabilities "less" is usually better, so coaches should present much less information at a time than they would to athletes without learning disabilities.

6   *Review:* Training sessions could start with a review of the previous session, in which the coach describes what he did and can ask the athlete for his or her thoughts on that session.

7   *Provide more opportunities for practice:* Athletes with learning disabilities may need more opportunities for reinforcement than other athletes.

8   *Individualise instruction:* Athletes with learning disabilities often have very different needs. Coaches should bear this in mind and could, for example, encourage athletes to work at their own pace and incorporate this individualised coaching within their coaching plans.

Increasing compliance

Athletes with learning disorders, such as ADHD, are often non-compliant to the instructions they receive (Gudjonsson and Sigurdsson, 2010). This might mean that coaching athletes with learning disorders such as ADHD is difficult for coaches, especially when coaching larger groups. One method that coaches can employ to increase compliance is to make prolonged eye contact with the athlete (Kapalka, 2004). Indeed, if coaches maintain eye contact for a period of around 20 seconds after giving an athlete some instructions, this gives the athlete more time to process what has been asked of them and decide whether they want to comply or non-comply. In addition to maintaining eye contact when providing instructions, Beyer et al. (2009) stated that coaches should stand a little closer than normal prior to giving the instruction. The coach can also ask the athlete to clarify that he or she has understood the instructions that they have been given.

Managing challenging behaviour

Research from non-sport domains found that athletes diagnosed with learning disorders, including ADHD, perform and behave at their best when they receive immediate and frequent feedback (Fiore et al., 1993). Based on these research findings, Anhalt et al. (1998) developed a behavioural management programme that can be adapted for coaches in sport settings. The programme includes consequences for appropriate and inappropriate behaviour and peer-mediated interventions.

Consequences for appropriate behaviour

1   *Labelled praises:* A labelled praise refers to positive feedback in response to a specific behaviour, as opposed to praises that are unlabelled and do not specify which behaviour is being praised. Within a sporting context, the comment "Excellent pass Shawn, the pace of the pass and the direction were brilliant" is an example of a labelled praise, whereas "Good pass, Shawn" is an example of an unlabelled praise.
2   *Happy face or point rewards:* When coaching children with learning disorders, coaches can reward behaviours such as adhering to a task and working well with other athletes. The coach would award the happy faces or points at the end of each training session and awards happy faces for each compliant behaviour observed. It is crucial that the coach explains why he or she has awarded each happy face.
3   *Reward activity:* Coaches could reward athletes who have accumulated the most points or happy faces with the choice of taking part in a reward activity. The reward activity should be a different activity to the tasks within the training session and should be fun.

Consequences for inappropriate behaviour

1   *Sad-face warning signal:* A coach can give a sad-face warning signal if the children behave in a manner that disrupts the coaching sessions. When the coach issues the warning he or she should call out the athlete's name and hold up two fingers, which represent the choices the athlete has. The coach should say something along the lines of "You have two choices. You

can either improve your behaviour and you will not receive a sad face, or you can receive a sad face. It is your choice."

2   *Awarding of sad faces:* Athletes who continue to behave poorly following the warning signal will be given a sad face or have points taken off their score if that system is being used. It is imperative that the voice of the coach remains calm and constant when the sad face is given to minimise the attention given to children for negative behaviour. It has been found that mild punishment behaviours along with rewards tend to improve on-task behaviours and decreases children's disruptive behaviour.

3   *Losing the privilege of the reward activity:* Athletes who behave in an inappropriate manner should not be allowed to take part in the reward activity. Removing privileges can be very effective in increasing target behaviours. The coach sets a clean slate of happy and sad faces after each reward activity, so each athlete knows he or she has a chance of doing the reward activity if they behave well in the next phase of the session.

Peer-mediated interventions

Anhalt et al. (1998) suggested that individuals can be put into groups, with these groups receiving awards for working together. This may be advantageous in sport settings, in which a coach might be coaching a number of athletes or because the coach wants to practise teamwork skills for team sports such as soccer or rugby. In addition to grouping athletes being more suitable in coaching sessions, having athletes work together in what was termed a "cooperative learning environment" has been found to enhance self-esteem, interpersonal co-operation, tolerance of others, and social acceptance. As such, the coach would separate athletes into different groups and would administer the consequences for appropriate and inappropriate behaviour at the group level.

CASE STUDY 9.1   EXPERIENCES OF MANAGING CHALLENGING BEHAVIOUR

The following case study represents the dialogue between Jon, a 24-year-old rugby union coach, and a very talented rugby union player called Chris. Jon is a volunteer coach and has coached Chris for nearly one season. Chris is eight years old, and has been playing rugby since he was four years of age. Within the last six months Chris was diagnosed with ADHD and although he is very keen to play rugby and learn, he can be quite disruptive, rude, and violent to other players. The dialogue in this case study starts after Chris had been very disruptive in a training session when Jon was providing instructions to the group. He spoke to Chris in a calm manner so the other players could not hear what he said:

Jon: Chris, I know you know what you have to do in these drills, but other players don't know what to do. If you talk to other players when I am speaking they won't understand. You have two choices, you can either not listen and receive some minus penalty points or you can listen and not receive any penalty points. [Jon made a conscious effort to hold pro-longed eye contact with Chris.]

Chris: Shane was the person who started talking to me and I wasn't doing anything coach.

Jon: Chris, you have two choices: you can either not listen to me and receive minus penalty points or listen and not receive any points.

Chris: OK I will listen.

However, within two minutes of the warning Chris continued to be disruptive and would not listen and the following dialogue ensued:

Jon: Chris, two minutes ago I gave you two choices and you have continued not listening. I am therefore giving you a minus point. Your score for the session is minus one.

Within the next 10 minutes Chris showed some exemplary behaviour by helping a team mate out who was struggling after he missed a tackle by encouraging him and saying what he did wrong, to which Jon said:

Jon: Chris, that was excellent that you encouraged your team mate after he made a mistake and then gave him some advice. I am awarding you one point for each of those things, so you are now on plus one.

Case study reflection

Coaching athletes with learning disabilities might be very challenging, especially when a coach has a large group of athletes to coach or if he or she is coaching a mixed group of athletes. This could result in coaches spending more time monitoring and managing the behaviour of the athletes with learning disabilities in comparison with those that do not have a learning disability. Therefore, coaches need to try and ensure that all athletes receive the coaching they require and deploy strategies to manage any problem behaviours. Such techniques may make managing troublesome behaviours much easier as they will have less impact on the whole group.

Summary points

- Athletes with learning disabilities may have a short attention span, have difficulty following instructions, be socially immature, have problems conversing with others, and might be poor at planning.
- There are four main types of learning disabilities: ADHD, visual-perception, language processing (also known as dyslexia), and fine motor disabilities.
- Coaches who have limited experience or no experience of coaching athletes with learning disabilities may have a negative attitude towards coaching athletes with learning disabilities.
- Coaches who are more competent are more likely to have a positive attitude towards coaching athletes with learning disabilities.
- Providing coaches with guidance on how to coach athletes with learning disabilities and behaviour management techniques may enhance coaches' attitude towards coaching athletes with learning disabilities.
- Coaches should adapt their coaching when working with athletes with learning disabilities to maximise learning.
- There are a variety of techniques to increase compliance and manage disruptive behaviour that coaches can use.

Practice exam questions

1 Compare and contrast the four main types of learning disabilities.
2 Describe the different types of ADHD and the behaviours associated with each type.
3 Describe how a coach's attitude might be influenced by whether an athlete has a learning disability or not.
4 Describe the principles that coaches should adhere to when coaching athletes with learning disabilities.
5 Describe the behaviours that athletes with learning disabilities might display.

Critical thinking questions: applying theory to practice

1 Describe how coaching training programmes could improve the attitudes of coaches towards athletes with learning disabilities.
2 Compare and contrast coaching instructions among athletes with learning disabilities and athletes who do not have learning disabilities.
3 What are the advantages and disadvantages of awarding happy and unhappy faces in coaching sessions?
4 David has ADHD and is very disruptive. Describe how a coach could manage David's challenging behaviours.
5 Describe how a peer-mediated intervention could be incorporated into a training session with athletes with learning disabilities.

Case study questions

1 Is Chris' behaviour typical of an athlete with ADHD? Discuss.
2 What other techniques could Jon have used?
3 What impact might Chris have on the group's learning and how can this be managed?

10

PROVIDING PSYCHOLOGICAL SUPPORT TO AN INJURED ATHLETE

The purpose of this chapter is to provide the coach with information on how he or she can help athletes whilst they are injured and when returning to sport after an injury. As such, this chapter contains information regarding:

- A definition of an injury
- Psychological responses to injuries
- The role of the coach
- Rehabilitation
- Psychological strategies during the rehabilitation process
- Returning to play
- Preventing fear of re-injury.

A definition of an injury

An injury refers to any incident that happens during training or competition, which requires help from a medical professional, and prevents the athlete from training or competing in his or her sport for a period of at least one day after the injury happened (Kerr et al., 2008). Injuries can be common in sport, so it is important that coaches understand how athletes respond to injuries in order to help them through the challenging period in which they are injured. Further, Ivarsson et al. (2013) even argued that coaches should attempt to reduce the number of stressors encountered by athletes, such as daily hassles and negative life events, because they were linked to athletes sustaining more injuries.

Psychological responses to injuries

Athletes who sustain an injury are likely to experience stress, anger, depression, anxiety, tension, fear, and even mood disturbances (Madrigal and Gill, 2014;

Roiger et al., 2015; Ruddock-Hudson et al., 2014; Udry, 1997). The severity of the injury is likely to influence the psychological responses, with less severe injuries being associated with less psychological disturbances (Nippert and Smith, 2008).

Udry (1997) stated that there are three phases that an injured athlete will pass through:

1   *Information processing phase:* As soon as the injury occurs the athlete tends to focus on:
    - pain caused by the injury;
    - the amount of time he or she will be unable to play for;
    - how the injury occurred;
    - what he or she could have done differently to prevent the injury from occurring in the first place.
    During this phase, the athlete might also start thinking about the consequences of being injured, such as the competitive events or matches that he or she will not be able to play in.
2   *Emotional upheaval phase:* When the athlete receives information from medical professionals regarding the length of time he or she will be unable to play sport for, a variety of negative emotions including anger, agitation, and frustration may be experienced. Athletes might also feel emotionally depleted, isolated from their team mates, and self-pity. Some athletes may be in denial about the injury and think they will be able to return much quicker than the medical professionals suggested.
3   *Positive outlook phase:* During this phase the athlete accepts that he or she is injured. The mood of the athlete starts to improve once he or she starts to see progress in the injured body part in rehabilitation.

According to Udry (1997), the rate at which an athlete passes through each phase is dependent on the severity of the injury, the personality of the athlete, and the progress made during rehabilitation.

The role of the coach

Although some coaches may be tempted to concentrate on uninjured players, the coach plays a very important role in helping injured athletes. Several studies found that the social support for injured athletes may facilitate recovery from an injury, reduce stress, and improve motivation. More specifically, Bianco (2001) found the social support that injured national skiers received from their coach was very important in reassuring the athletes that they would get better, help them maintain a perspective about the injury, encouraging them to focus on future opportunities and adhere to their rehabilitation programme. Mitchell et al. (2014) reported that social support was associated with lower stress levels among injured athletes. Other studies by Gould et al. (1997) and Johnston and

Carroll (1998) reported that athletes believed the social support they received from their coach was instrumental in them recovering.

Information regarding how coaches can socially support their athletes is covered in Chapter 13 of this book. It is important that coaches spend time with injured athletes and reassure them throughout their time being injured. This period involves the rehabilitation period and when the athlete returns to his or her sport. The rehabilitation period can be a very difficult time for athletes, especially if they have a serious injury.

Rehabilitation

The rehabilitation process

Once an athlete receives an injury diagnosis and the appropriate medical treatment (e.g. surgery), the athlete will start his or her rehabilitation. The length of time the athlete will spend in rehabilitation is dependent upon the injury, with this phase varying from a week to several years in extreme cases. The aim of rehabilitation is to help the injured body part heal, so the athlete can return to sport. As such, the athlete may spend long periods of time working on restoring his or her injured body parts.

Taylor and Taylor (1997) stated that in addition to athletes engaging in physical exercises to heal injured parts of their body, they should also take part in mental rehabilitation training. Mental training for injured athletes has the potential to increase an athlete's emotional well-being during the rehabilitation phase to prevent psychological problems when they return to their sport. Although mental rehabilitation can be very effective, Arvinen-Barrow et al. (2014) suggested that psychological care should be subtle as athletes may feel self-conscious when receiving psychological help.

Before the psychological training strategies are taught to athletes, coaches should first provide assurance and information to the athlete about how he or she may feel during rehabilitation and the processes they are likely to go through during their rehabilitation. Taylor and Taylor (1997) identified four stages of the rehabilitation process:

- *Stage 1 – Range of motion*: During the initial rehabilitation sessions, the primary aim is to increase an athlete's range of motion within the injured body part. The coach should reassure the athlete that he or she is likely to experience pain during this phase, because he or she will be performing movements that are unfamiliar and under the control of the physiotherapist. It is therefore essential that coaches encourage athletes to engage in pain management strategies (information regarding how athletes can deploy pain management strategies is presented later in this chapter).
- *Stage 2 – Strength*: When an athlete achieves an 80 per cent range of motion in his or her injured body part, they are considered to be in Stage 2 of the

rehabilitation process. The athlete will be asked by his or her physiotherapist to start testing the injured body part for the first time since the injury occurred to increase its strength. It is likely that the athlete may experience some doubt and apprehension about the ability of the injured area to manage these demands. The coach should reassure the athlete that they may experience worry and negative emotions during this phase, but this is completely normal. Coaches could provide coping training to the athletes to help them get through this stressful period.

- *Stage 3 – Co-ordination*: Once an athlete's strength improves, he or she will be in Stage 3 of rehabilitation. During this phase, the athlete will be instructed by his or her physiotherapist to continue strengthening the injured body part. When the injured body part is strengthened to a sufficient level, he or she will be instructed to engage in more specialised exercises (e.g. balance, agility, acceleration, and speed exercises). It is important that coaches help athletes maintain a positive focus during this phase, because athletes are asked to perform sport-specific exercises, and they are likely to make comparisons with their pre-injury performances. The coach should provide reassurance that performances will improve with time and hard work.

- *Stage 4 – Return to sport*: The final phase of the rehabilitation process is when the athlete returns to sport. Once the injured body part is able to perform at its pre-injury level, the athlete is physically ready to resume training. An athlete's return to competition can be difficult, so the coach plays an important role.

Coaches should be aware that athletes may experience setbacks in rehabilitation, whereas other athletes may become fearful of resting when they are rehabilitating their injured body part.

Setbacks during rehabilitation

When an athlete receives information about the four stages of the rehabilitation process, he or she may perceive that his or her rehabilitation will be very straightforward. That is, he or she may feel that they will make steady progress and then return to sport within the timeframe provided by medical professionals.

In an ideal world the rehabilitation would run smoothly, but Taylor and Taylor (1997) suggested that most athletes experience a setback along the way. An athlete's injured body part might initially respond very well to treatment, but then he or she might not make further improvements for a number of weeks. When an athlete's progress is slower than anticipated or a setback occurs (i.e. the athlete regresses from Stage 2 to Stage 1 after too much pain and soreness), it is paramount that the coach provides encouragement and assurance to the athlete. The coach can do this by sharing his or her experiences with other athletes who had the same injury and went on to make a full recovery despite numerous setbacks. Additionally, Podlog and Dionigi (2010) suggested that coaches could arrange for injured athletes to speak to athletes who sustained the same injury and discuss their worries.

The fear of rest during rehabilitation

Taylor and Taylor (1997) stated that athletes who are especially motivated and disciplined, may have a tendency to spend too much time doing rehabilitation exercises, because of feelings of guilt. The coach should regularly speak to the athlete and the medical professional to check whether this is happening. When this occurs, the coach should speak to the athlete about the importance of rest within the rehabilitation process. The coach can tell the athlete about the importance of rest in boosting recovery (Kindermann, 1988) and that feeling guilty is normal, but that there is nothing to be guilty about.

Psychological strategies during the rehabilitation process

Coaches can provide training in a variety of strategies to help athletes manage the feelings encountered during their rehabilitation. Some of these strategies (e.g. goal setting, mental imagery, and coping training) are mentioned in other chapters in this book, so are not covered in as much detail in this chapter. However, information is provided on how coaches can adopt these strategies so that they can be used with injured athletes.

Goal setting for injured athletes

Setting goals whilst injured involves the athlete been asked to consider objectives, targets, or a desired standard for their injured body part by the coach. The goals an athlete sets should be influenced by the extent of the injury, so the coach could involve the medical professionals within the goal-setting process to ensure the goals set are realistic. Goal setting may be especially beneficial for injured athletes, because Locke and Latham (2002) found that goals have an energising influence that may result in athletes adhering to the programme, such as their rehabilitation programme.

When helping athletes set goals, coaches should apply the SMARTS goal principles (Smith, 1994), which are covered in depth in Chapter 4 of this book. As such, athletes should be encouraged to set goals that are specific (e.g. return to sport stronger than pre-injury level), measurable (e.g. improve quadriceps strength by 5 per cent), action-oriented (e.g. incorporate plans regarding how goals can be achieved), realistic (e.g. improving quadriceps strength by 5 per cent of pre-injury level is realistic, but improving the strength in these muscles by 25 per cent would not be realistic), time (e.g. return to training by 22nd July), and self-determined (i.e. the athlete sets his or her own goals, with little help from the coach; the coach only supports the athlete).

Mental imagery

Mental imagery, which is outlined in depth in Chapter 18 of this book, refers to the process of an athlete using his or her imagination to see themselves performing a movement (e.g. moving the injured body part) or a certain skill (e.g. serve in tennis that the athlete wants to perform when he or she returns to sport). Arvinen-Barrow et al. (2015) reported that psychological skills, such as mental imagery, were used by 27 per cent of injured athletes but of those athletes that used mental imagery 71.6 per cent believed that it helped them recover quicker. As such, it appears that only a small number of athletes are likely to use imagery, so coaches should encourage athletes to engage in mental imagery during their rehabilitation. There is evidence that mental imagery can aid recovery (Durso-Cupal, 1996). Mental imagery can also enhance recovery during rehabilitation by increasing the amount of blood and warmth that flows to the injured body part (Blakeslee, 1980). In order to promote healing, Taylor and Taylor (1997) suggested that coaches could ask athletes to make images associated with the healing process or even create imagery scripts that are associated with healing. Such imagery scripts could encourage athletes to imagine blood flowing to the injured area or ice on the injured area, which will block the pain.

In addition to imagery being useful in aiding injury, Martin et al. (1999) argued that mental imagery also serves a number of other purposes, such as:

- Replacing the physical practice that the athlete can no longer do with mental practice, so the athlete can mentally practise skills he or she had learned prior to being injured.
- Allowing an athlete to see themself in a recovered state.
- Controlling negative disturbances that can occur among injured athletes.

Coping

Coping refers to the thoughts and behaviours that an athlete engages in to manage the stress they are encountering. Being injured and going through a rehabilitation programme can be very stressful (e.g. Nippert and Smith, 2008; Udry et al., 1997), so it is essential that coaches reassure their athletes that it is normal to experience stress and teach their athletes how to cope. Information on coping and how coaches can teach their athletes to cope is presented in Chapter 21 of this book.

In addition to the coping strategies recommended in Chapter 21, research with a sample of injured athletes found that avoidance coping may be a particularly effective strategy that coaches can teach injured athletes, especially those athletes with a long-term injury (Carson and Polman, 2010). There are two forms of avoidance coping:

- *Behavioural avoidance*: Coping strategies classified as behavioural avoidance involve athletes physically removing themselves from stressful situations, such as walking away from another athlete that is frustrating them. The behavioural coping strategies in the Carson and Polman (2010) study included the players taking up a new hobby (e.g. learning a new language), involving themselves around the team (e.g. performing match analysis), continuing outside interests (e.g. learning new recipes), and organising coaching sessions for younger players within the club. Coaches could therefore encourage injured athletes to engage in these behavioural avoidance strategies.

- *Cognitive avoidance*: Coping strategies classed as cognitive avoidance involve attempts to mentally disengage from thoughts surrounding a stressor, such as blocking out the pain of an injury. The cognitive avoidance strategies used by the players included denial (e.g. the players denied that they were experiencing pain during rehabilitation sessions by blocking out thoughts of pain) and players not speaking about their injury (e.g. players would change the topic of conversation so they were not chatting about their injury all the time). Coaches should be aware that some athletes might want to speak about their injury, whereas others will not.

Pain management strategies for rehabilitation

Rehabilitation sessions can be extremely painful for athletes (Carson and Polman, 2010). Coaches can also teach their athletes a variety of pain management strategies, such as abdominal breathing and dissociation (Taylor and Taylor, 1997).

1   *Abdominal breathing*: According to Taylor and Taylor (1997), abdominal breathing is one of the simplest and yet most neglected methods of reducing pain within rehabilitation sessions. Coaches can help athletes heal more effectively by training them in deep breathing techniques, which provide the body with more oxygen than normal. Athletes need more oxygen when they are in pain. As such, coaches could encourage their athletes to inhale through their nose to the count of five and exhale slowly to the count of 10 whilst in rehabilitation sessions.

2   *Dissociation*: Dissociation training involves the athlete being taught to focus his or her attention away from the pain by distracting themself (Taylor and Taylor, 1997). As such, the coach could ask the athlete to count, hum a tune, listen to music, or imagine themself in a favourite location (e.g. beach).

Coaches can encourage athletes to use abdominal breathing simultaneously with dissociation during rehabilitation sessions.

Positive focus

To help athletes maintain a positive attitude during their rehabilitation period, Taylor and Taylor (1997) argued that coaches could ask their athletes to focus on the four Ps:

- *Positive*: The coach could ask the athlete to think about the positive aspects of his or her rehabilitation (e.g. gains made to injured body parts and other areas of performance such as conditioning, strength, or technique).

- *Present*: Coaches could ask athletes to think about the present and not to think a long way ahead nor to dwell on the past.
- *Process*: Athletes could be asked by the coach to think about what they need to do daily in order to enhance their recovery so that the athlete can take confidence that they are doing the right thing.
- *Progress*: Finally, the athlete should be encouraged to write down and then think about these gains.

Basic psychological needs

Wadey et al. (2016) found that athletes' basic psychological needs (e.g. autonomy, relatedness, and competence) were associated with athletes' stress-related growth (i.e. positive changes after a stressful incident, such as being injured, which results in a person performing at a superior level; Park et al., 1996). As such, Wadey and colleagues advocated that individuals such as coaches who spend time with athletes during rehabilitation should ensure that athletes' basic psychological needs are met. Information on self-determination theory and fulfilling athletes' basic psychological needs are presented in Chapter 16 of this book.

Returning to play

Once the athlete has completed his or her physical rehabilitation programme and the injured area has returned to the same level as it was prior to injury, the athlete will be ready to return to full training and then competition. It should be noted, however, that some athletes might never return to playing sport. Arden et al. (2014) reported that less than 50 per cent of athletes who sustained an anterior cruciate ligament knee injury returned to their sport. The main reasons for athletes not returning to the sport were not trusting the knee, fear of a new injury, and poor functional movement in the knee. Indeed, a systematic review echoed these findings as athletes with less fear about getting re-injured were much more likely to return to sport (te Wierike et al., 2013).

Arden et al. (2014) identified an athlete's psychological readiness to return to sport as the strongest factor that predicted whether or not he or she would resume playing sport. Coaches can enhance an athlete's psychological readiness to return to sport by providing information on the five stages that Taylor and Taylor (1997) described, which should help reassure the athlete. Taylor and Taylor stated that returning athletes go through five stages: (1) initial return, (2) recovery confirmation, (3) return of physical and technical abilities, (4) high-intensity training, and (5) return to competition. Providing athletes with an understanding of these stages should make the transition to competing more manageable and less stressful.

1   *Initial return*: The athlete returns to full training, which is potentially very stressful because he or she will find out whether their rehabilitation

programme was successful or not. The athlete will also be excited, because it will be his or her first time playing their sport for a while. The coach should encourage the athlete not to set performance expectations that are too high, as this could lead to disappointment if expectations are not fulfilled.

2   *Recovery confirmation:* During the second stage the athlete receives confirmation that his or her injury has healed or that there are complications. Some athletes will return with few or no problems, but other athletes may experience unexpected pain, swelling, decreased strength, and compensation injuries to other parts of their body. Athletes that experience complications during this phase of their return might experience psychological difficulties, because they may think that all of their efforts in rehabilitation were wasted. The coach should support the athlete and tell him or her that this sometimes happens and that a full recovery will be made.

3   *Return of physical and technical abilities:* In Stage 3, the athlete increases his or her training intensity. They improve their conditioning and spend time practising the technical skills associated with their sport, which could not be performed whilst injured.

4   *High-intensity training:* By the time the athlete is ready to take part in high-intensity training, he or she is in Stage 4, and can focus on improving their conditioning. The injured area will be better or at the same as level as it was prior to being injured.

5   *Return to competition:* When physical conditioning is deemed sufficient, the athlete is ready to compete. He or she may feel both excited and nervous. The coach should tell them that this is to be expected and encourage them to use coping strategies to manage any stress encountered (see Chapter 21).

Preventing fear of re-injury

Even though an athlete may have physically healed when he or she returns to competition, it does not mean that they will not experience any psychological stress from the injury (Taylor and Taylor, 1997). Indeed, Heil (1993) argued that athletes might experience the most stress when they return to their sport, due to fears about re-injury. A fear of being re-injured can cause psychological difficulties such as reduced focus and decreased confidence, in addition to physical difficulties such as muscle tension, which actually increases the likelihood that the athlete will become injured again.

Some athletes may develop a fear of being re-injured when they return to sport (Kvist et al., 2005). This fear can be related to athletes spending a long time away from their sport, which may involve being isolated from team mates (Taylor and Taylor, 1997). Coaches should therefore try to foster continual involvement among injured athletes by asking them to analyse matches, scout opposition, get involved in coaching, and attend social functions.

Research by Ivarsson et al. (2015) suggested that providing athletes with mindfulness training and thus reducing stress levels may reduce the re-occurrence of injuries. This finding supports the work of Ivarsson et al. (2013) who found that daily hassles and negative life stressors were direct predictors of injury. Additionally, mindfulness techniques may also be suitable for when athletes return to their sport. Indeed, Bennett and Lindsay (2016) found that a mindfulness intervention helped an athlete manage the anxiety associated with returning to sport. Information on how coaches can provide mindfulness training is presented in Chapter 23 of this book.

CASE STUDY 10.1   SUPPORTING AN ATHLETE WITH AN ANTERIOR CRUCIATE LIGAMENT INJURY

George is a 59-year-old coach who has coached soccer professionally for 25 years and is now the head coach of a semi-professional side, which play in the sixth-tier of English football. One of his senior players, Maurice, a 32-year-old centre back, suffered an anterior cruciate ligament (ACL) injury and is expected to be out injured for at least nine months. As soon as Maurice suffered the injury, George spoke to him and reassured him that whatever the injury was he would be back playing and that it was not the end of his soccer career. George stayed in regular contact with Maurice and even before Maurice's operation, George asked him to set some goals. Maurice wanted to return to the first team and play at this level until he was 35 years old.

Maurice had a particularly painful rehabilitation, due to a previous injury, so George taught Maurice a variety of psychological skills such as coping strategies, mental imagery, and pain management skills. Maurice found these really helpful. George did not explain the psychological responses to injury phases to Maurice, because Maurice had suffered this type of injury in the past and was aware of how he would feel.

George encouraged Maurice to maintain his involvement in the team. He asked him to scout opponents and provide feedback to the team. Maurice was also asked to attend training sessions when he could, and attend matches so he could keep up to date with team tactics.

Additionally, George also encouraged Maurice to spend time thinking about what he was going to do after his soccer career and he encouraged Maurice to speak to a careers advisor, which he found useful.

Above all, George maintained regular contact with Maurice throughout his injury period and provided continual reassurance that George had a part to play in his team when he recovered from injury.

Case study reflection

Coaches should base the psychological support to injured athletes on their individual needs. In this example, Maurice had previously suffered other serious injuries so did not need information on how he might feel at different stages, because he had experienced all of these feelings before.

Summary points

- An injury prevents an athlete from training or competing in his or her sport for a period of at least one day after the injury occurred.
- Stress, anger, depression, anxiety, tension, fear, and even mood disturbances may be experienced by the athlete after an injury.
- There are there three phases that an injured athlete will pass through: (1) information processing, (2) emotional upheaval, and (3) the positive outlook phase.
- The coach has an important role to play in helping an injured athlete make a successful return to sport.
- Many setbacks can occur during an athlete's rehabilitation.
- Coaches can make an athlete's rehabilitation more manageable by providing information on how they are likely to feel and teach them a range of strategies that can be used.
- An athlete may find returning to sport very stressful and be fearful of re-injuring themself, so the coach should continue the support provided to the athlete during this phase.

Practice exam questions

1 Describe the psychological responses an athlete may have to an injury and their implications.
2 Discuss the role that the coach plays in an athlete's recovery.
3 Outline the four stages an athlete goes through in their recovery and describe what a coach can do to smooth the progression from one stage to another.
4 All rehabilitations are straightforward. Discuss.
5 An athlete's rehabilitation is complete when their injured body part has healed. Discuss.

Critical thinking questions: applying theory to practice

1 Reflect on instances when athletes you coach have experienced an injury. What could you have done better and what would you do now to help the athlete?
2 It is commonly thought that keeping an athlete involved whilst they are injured will be very beneficial. Describe the activities a coach can set an injured player to foster involvement.
3 Critically evaluate whether a coach should spend a large amount of time with injured athletes.
4 How can a coach make an athlete's return to sport smoother?
5 Discuss the role that psychological skills may have in an athlete's rehabilitation programme.

Case study questions

1 How was Maurice likely to be feeling immediately after being diagnosed with an ACL injury?
2 If Maurice had not previously sustained an injury, how could George have explained the psychological responses to injury?
3 Why did George want to maintain regular contact with Maurice? Discuss the benefits of George's approach.

PART V

Relationships, support, and influence within coaching practice

PART III

Relationship support
and influence within
coaching practice

11

THE COACH–ATHLETE RELATIONSHIP

The purpose of this chapter is to provide coaches with information on the complexities of relationships with athletes and factors that influence this relationship. In particular this chapter provides information on:

- A definition of the coach–athlete relationship
- The benefits of the coach–athlete relationship
- The undesirable consequences of a strong coach–athlete relationship
- Describing the coach–athlete relationship
- Factors that influence the coach–athlete relationship
- How coaches can improve the coach–athlete relationship
- Conflict in the coach–athlete relationship and what to do when it happens.

A definition of the coach–athlete relationship

Jowett and colleagues (Jowett and Cockerill, 2003; Jowett et al., 2005; Jowett and Poczwardowski, 2007) defined the coach–athlete relationship as any situation in which a coach's and athlete's thoughts, feelings, and behaviours are interrelated. According to Jowett and colleagues this relationship is a dynamic process, as both the coach and the athlete can influence the quality of this relationship. Additionally, the coach–athlete relationship is thought to change over time and can thus be viewed as a process (Jowett and Poczwardowski, 2007). Sandström et al. (2016) provided support for the notion that the coach–athlete relationship changes over time.

The behaviours, thoughts, and feelings of both the athlete and the coach shape the relationship, because thoughts and feelings from the athlete or the coach influence behaviours, which will in turn affect how either the athlete or the coach responds (Jowett and Poczwardowski, 2007). For example, if a coach believes strongly in the ability of his or her player, he or she will experience positive thoughts and feelings about the coaching sessions that take place. This is likely to influence the coach's behaviours as he or she will be enthusiastic about training and helping the player reach their full potential. In response, the athlete will trust the coach and behave in a manner that is conducive to improving and maximising performance.

The benefits of the coach–athlete relationship

- *Enhanced performance*: Jowett and Cockerill (2003) interviewed 12 Olympic medalists regarding their experiences of the coach–athlete relationship and found that the coach–athlete relationship enabled athletes to perform well and therefore win Olympic medals. Vieira et al. (2015) found that volleyball players who won medals perceived a closer and more committed coach–athlete relationship. Nikbin et al. (2014) found that commitment to one's coach and trust in them were significantly and positively associated with sporting performance.
- *Burnout*: Isoard-Gautheur et al. (2016b) reported that athletes with a stronger perception of the coach–athlete were less likely to report symptoms of burnout.
- *Fear of failure*: Sagar and Jowett (2015) found that athletes with a strong relationship with their coach were much less likely to suffer from a fear of failure when competing.
- *Collective efficacy*: Hampson and Jowett (2014) found that those who perceived a stronger coach–athlete relationship also believed in their ability to be successful as a team.
- *Dropout*: The quality of the coach–athlete relationship also influences intentions to continue playing sport. For example, Gardner et al. (2016) found that athletes who perceive a positive coach–athlete relationship are more likely to enjoy their sport and less likely to drop out.

The undesirable consequences of a strong coach–athlete relationship

Although there are clearly many positive outcomes of an athlete perceiving a strong coach–athlete relationship, one study found a negative consequence. Nicholls et al. (2016a) examined the relationship between the coach–athlete relationship, stress appraisals, and coping among 274 athletes. They found that athletes who reported a highly committed relationship reported higher threat levels and more disengagement-oriented coping. Both threat appraisals (Moore et al., 2012) and disengagement-oriented coping (Nicholls et al., 2016b) are negatively associated with performance. As such, coaches should monitor athletes who are highly committed to them and provide appraisal and coping training.

Describing the coach–athlete relationship

Jowett (2005) suggested that every coach–athlete relationship contains two key elements:

1   *Successfulness*: The successfulness element of the coach–athlete relationship refers to the degree to which the athlete is successful.
2   *Effectiveness*: The effectiveness of the coach–athlete relationship refers to the degree to which the athlete and the coach get on with each other. For example, an effective relationship would include trust, empathy, respect, and closeness between the coach and the athlete.

Based on the notion of success and effectiveness in the coach–athlete relationship, Jowett (2005) argued that there are four types of coach–athlete relationships:

• *Effective and successful*: An effective and successful coach–athlete relationship occurs when the coach and the athlete get on very well and trust each other implicitly. They also have lots of success in terms of the results achieved by the athlete, whether that is winning events or selection into national teams.
• *Effective and unsuccessful*: A relationship in which the coach and the athlete get on very well and trust each other, but have limited sporting success is described as an effective and unsuccessful relationship.
• *Ineffective and successful*: A relationship in which the athlete and the coach do not get on or trust each other, but have an element of success in terms of what the athlete achieves, is described as an ineffective and successful coach–athlete relationship. Even though there is performance success in this relationship in terms of competition results and improvements made, there might be arguments between the athlete and the coach.
• *Ineffective and unsuccessful*: If a coach has a very poor relationship with his or her athlete that yields poor results, it can be classified as an ineffective and unsuccessful coach–athlete relationship.

The most widely cited conceptualisation of the coach–athlete relationship was proposed by Jowett (Jowett, 2005; Jowett et al., 2005). She suggested that the coach–athlete relationship consists of 3+1 Cs: closeness, commitment, complementarity, and co-orientation.

• *Closeness*: Closeness refers to the relationship between the athlete and the coach. If an athlete has a close relationship with his or her coach, it would be characterised by the athlete and the coach valuing one another and supporting each other, in addition to caring for the well-being of each other. On the other hand, coach–athlete relationships that lack the quality of closeness involve the athlete and the coach not caring, valuing, or supporting each other.

- *Commitment*: Jowett and Poczwardowski (2007) defined commitment as the coach's and athlete's intent to maintain the relationship. As such the athlete will want to continue working with his or her coach. There will be intent from both parties to maximise successful outcomes, such as winning competitions and achieving selection onto different teams.
- *Complementarity*: Complementarity refers to how the behaviours between the coach and the athlete correspond to each other. For example, a coach–athlete relationship would be high in complementarity if the coach acts in a caring and encouraging manner, which is reciprocated by the athlete who also acts in a caring manner and is enthusiastic about training sessions with the coach.
- *Co-orientation*: Co-orientation between the athlete and the coach occurs when the athlete and the coach have established a common ground on the views that they both hold, such as how they think it might be best for the athlete to progress. This common ground is achieved via the coach and the athlete discussing their views regarding future accomplishment goals (Jowett and Meek, 2000).

Factors that influence the coach–athlete relationship

Researchers have identified a number of factors that appear to influence the coach–athlete relationship (Jackson et al., 2011; Lafrenière et al., 2011; Lorimer and Jowett, 2009). For example, Jackson and colleagues explored how personality influenced the commitment and trust among 91 athletes and their coaches. Interestingly, the more dissimilar the athlete and coach were in terms of extraversion (e.g. outgoing) and openness (e.g. inventiveness) the less committed and close they were.

Lafrenière et al. (2011) explored how coaches' passion for coaching influenced the athletes' perception of the coach–athlete relationship. They found that harmonious passion (e.g. a strong desire to take part in activities that one loves) predicted whether a coach would support his or her athletes to make their own choices, leading to a high-quality coach–athlete relationship, and the athlete being happier. Conversely, obsessive passion predicted controlling behaviours from the coach, which resulted in a low-quality relationship.

Lorimer and Jowett (2009) explored empathetic accuracy (e.g. the degree to which the coach and the athlete could accurately perceive the psychological condition of one another) and meta-perspective (e.g. how the coach thinks the athlete views the relationship or how the athlete thinks the coach views the relationship), among 121 athletes and coaches. Athletes and coaches who had a positive meta-perspective, such as thinking the other partner is trusting, were more able to accurately predict the psychological condition of the other. In turn, the relationships in which the coach and the athlete could accurately predict the psychological condition of the other were rated as being more satisfying.

How coaches can improve the coach–athlete relationship

Sport psychology researchers such as Mageau and Vallerand (2003) and Rhind and Jowett (2010) provided suggestions regarding how a coach can improve or maintain the relationship with his or her athletes. Mageau and Vallerand outlined the following strategies:

- *Give your player or players some choice – within reason*: Coaches could give their players choices, although it is important to impose rules and limits within the choices.
- *Provide a rationale*: It is important that the coach explains why he or she would like a player to work on certain aspects (e.g. conditioning or technical skills).
- *Acknowledge feelings*: A coach can empathise with a player by demonstrating that he knows how the player is feeling, by acknowledging the player's feelings.
- *Give players the chance to show their initiative*: Coaches could also allow players to use their own initiative by asking them what they would like to work on and then how they would go about doing it, or what tactics they would like to play.
- *Provide feedback that is informative and non-controlling*: Feedback from the coach should allow the athlete to improve and thus be constructive, but be non-controlling. Controlling feedback is when the coach uses his or her comments to control the athlete's behaviour. For example "Your passing was excellent today, if you carry on passing like that in the future I will pick you in every match" is an example of controlling feedback. Whereas "The direction and the weight of your passes was spot on" places more emphasis on information and is not controlling.
- *Avoid ego-oriented behaviour*: It is important that coaches do not compare their players with other players, because this could lead to frustration on the part of the players.

Alternatively, Rhind and Jowett (2010) proposed the COMPASS model of maintenance strategies within the coach–athlete relationship. The acronym COMPASS stands for:

- *Conflict management*: Conflict management includes proactive strategies such as the coach taking steps to avoid conflict in the future by clarifying his or her expression. Also included in conflict management are reactive strategies, such as the coach cooperating with the athlete during discussions about any disagreements, to repair conflict that has already ensued.
- *Openness*: This strategy refers to the coach being open about his or her feelings and also encouraging the athlete to do the same. As such, the coach could encourage the athlete to talk about how he or she is feeling.
- *Motivation*: The coach can show the athlete that he or she is motivated to continue working with the athlete and helping the athlete develop.

- *Positivity*: The coach can demonstrate a positive attitude to the athlete by adapting his or her behaviour to suit the needs of the athlete and also show fairness with them.
- *Advice*: Coaches can maintain the coach–athlete relationship by giving the athlete advice on problems they may be encountering. This advice may be sport-based advice on technical skills and advice on non-sporting matters such as relationships.
- *Support*: A coach can demonstrate support to the athlete by being available for the athlete to discuss both sport and non-sporting matters.
- *Social networks*: The relationship between the coach and the athlete can be improved or maintained by the athlete and the coach spending time with each other away from the sporting environment.

Conflict in the coach–athlete relationship and what to do when it happens

Even though a coach might adhere to the strategies proposed by Mageau and Vallerand (2003) and Rhind and Jowett (2010), conflict may still occur. If conflict does occur between the coach and the athlete, Rahim (2002) suggested a number of strategies that the coach can engage in to manage the conflict. These strategies include:

- *Integrating*: The coach and the athlete have an open and honest exchange regarding their views. It is hoped that this process will allow the coach and the athlete to identify alternative solutions to the issues that are causing conflicts (e.g. training schedules or technical aspects of performance).
- *Compromising*: The coach and the athlete can make a compromise by agreeing that they are wrong and listen to the desires of each other. For example, a tennis coach might want a player to spend more time working on her serve, but the tennis player does not want to. In this instance the compromise could be the player and the coach agreeing that the player will work on her serve, but only do it for half the amount of time that the coach had wanted.
- *Obliging*: The coach could attempt to minimise the different points of view between themself and the athlete through discussion.
- *Dominating*: A coach can dominate by telling the athlete what or she has to do.
- *Avoiding*: In certain circumstances, the coach might avoid confronting the athlete about the issues that cause conflict, and let the conflict persist.

These examples of conflict management provided by Rahim (2002) are very different in nature. Ideally, coaches would want to avoid either dominating or avoiding approaches to conflict management, because these have the potential to be the most disruptive.

CASE STUDY 11.1   MANAGING CONFLICT IN THE COACH–ATHLETE RELATIONSHIP

Mickey is a 29-year-old golf coach with an all-time-high world ranking of 155. He coaches a variety of high-level players, but has been having some problems with Lucy, a player Mickey has coached since she was 14 years old. She is now 16 years old and plays for England. Over the last six months Mickey and Lucy's relationship has become very strained, yet her performances in the last six months are better than ever and she recently won a national age group championship. They disagree on how Lucy can take her game forward, what training activities they do, and even who Lucy trains with. Mickey feels as though every idea he suggests could result in an argument and believes the problems started when Lucy started receiving coaching with the England set-up. As such, Mickey feels the only way forward is to resolve the conflict or face the possibility of terminating their relationship. Mickey knows that he is a strong character and can sometimes be difficult to deal with. He attempted to resolve the conflict by arranging a meeting with Lucy, so they could discuss their views. In this meeting, Mickey encouraged Lucy to be honest at all times and wanted to hear her views regarding what aspects of training she felt were beneficial, what aspects she did not like, how she saw their relationship moving on, and what he could do differently. Following this, Mickey gave his viewpoints. As it turned out, Lucy and Mickey had too many differing views that could not be resolved. For example, Lucy wanted to spend more time working on the take-back phase of the golf swing based on the advice she had received from England coaches, whereas Mickey said she needed to work on her impact position to make more improvements. In the end Mickey and Lucy decided to terminate their relationship, because they had differing opinions on what to work on next.

Case study reflection

Coaches may be very frustrated and upset if a player no longer believes in the advice that is given to them and ultimately decides to use another coach. This is something that happens across all sports. Coaches have to accept that it will happen, especially in sports where the athlete has power over who he or she is coached by.

Summary points

- The coach–athlete relationship is any situation in which a coach's and athlete's thoughts, feelings, and behaviours are interrelated.
- Athletic excellence and personal growth can be facilitated by the coach–athlete relationship.

- There are two key elements to the coach–athlete relationship: (1) successfulness and (2) effectiveness.
- Closeness, commitment, complementarity, and co-orientation are key components of the coach–athlete relationship.
- Coaches can improve the coach–athlete relationship by giving their athletes choices and rationale, acknowledging their feelings, and provide them with non-controlling feedback.
- The COMPASS model can be implemented by coaches to maintain a coach–athlete relationship.
- Conflict in the coach–athlete relationship will arise from time to time. There are a number of steps that coaches can take to manage any conflict.

Practice exam questions

1 What is the coach–athlete relationship, and why is it important that coaches understand more about this relationship?
2 Describe the different types of coach–athlete relationship, with regard to effectiveness and successfulness and their implications.
3 Compare and contrast Jowett's (2005), LaVoi's (2007) and Poczwardowski's (1997) conceptualisation of the coach–athlete relationship.
4 Compare and contrast Mageau and Vallerand's (2003) and Rhind and Jowett's (2010) models regarding improving the coach–athlete relationship.
5 Discuss the factors that influence the coach–athlete relationship.

Critical thinking questions: applying theory to practice

1 Describe how a coach can provide an athlete with more choice and what this would entail in training sessions.
2 Describe and provide examples of controlling and non-controlling feedback and comment on the implications of providing different types of feedback.
3 How can coaches show athletes that they are motivated to work with them?
4 Describe how a coach could integrate with his or her athlete to manage conflict.
5 What are the implications of a coach and an athlete avoiding conflict management?

Case study questions

1 How would you classify Mickey and Lucy's coach–athlete relationship? Justify your answer using theory.
2 Describe Mickey's approach to conflict management.
3 How would you have attempted to manage the conflict in this instance?

12

UNDERSTANDING AND BUILDING TEAM COHESION

This chapter provides information on the factors that coaches should consider when they coach team sports. Coaches who coach individual sports, but within team settings, may also find this chapter useful. Information is provided on:

- A definition of team cohesion
- Conceptual model of team cohesion
- Factors that influence team cohesion
- The importance of team cohesion
- The effects of coach behaviour and leadership on team cohesion
- Team-building strategies
- Factors to consider when planning team-building interventions.

A definition of team cohesion

A widely used definition indicates that team cohesion is "a dynamic process which is reflected in the tendency for a group to stick together and remain united in the pursuit of its instrumental objectives and/or for the satisfaction of member affective needs" (Carron et al., 1998: 213).

Conceptual model of team cohesion

The definition of team cohesion provided by Carron et al. (1998) is related to the proposed four-dimensional conceptual model of team cohesion provided by Carron et al. (1985). As such, Carron et al. (1985) suggested that each athlete, who is a member of a team, holds two specific perceptions about the team he or she plays in. These are:

- *Individual attractions to the group* (ATG): This part of the model holds that individuals have perceptions regarding why others (e.g. a coach or captain) might be motivated to keep them in their team, in addition to the athlete's own personal feelings about the team he or she plays for.
- *Group integration* (GI): Group integration refers to the athlete's perceptions regarding the bonding, closeness, and similarity within a particular team.

The model proposed by Carron et al. (1985) is four-dimensional because both ATG and GI also have a component of either social cohesion (S) or task cohesion (T). Task cohesion refers to the extent to which team mates work together in unison to achieve their team's overall goal. Some athletes might not be motivated to achieve a team objective (e.g. winning the league, reducing the number of suspensions in a season, or avoiding relegation). Social cohesion refers to an athlete's perceptions regarding how well he or she gets on with and likes his or her team mates. As such, group cohesiveness can be represented as four different manifestations (see Figure 12.1), which are (Carron et al., 2007):

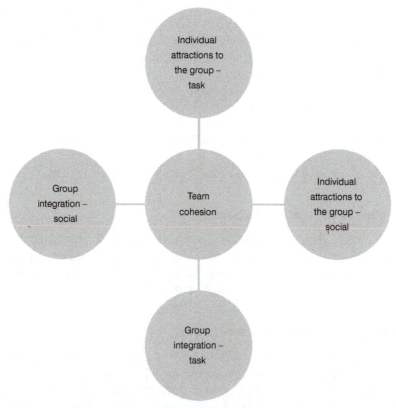

FIGURE 12.1 Team cohesion in sport

1 *Individual attractions to the group-task* (ATG-T): A team that has athletes that score highly in ATG-T would feel strongly about playing for their team and are highly motivated to work hard in order to achieve team goals.
2 *Individual attractions to the group-social* (AGT-S): Teams that have athletes who score highly on AGT-S would be characterised by athletes who feel a strong bond within the team with many members being friends.
3 *Group integration-task* (GI-T): Athletes within teams who score highly on GI-T would feel close to their team mates and motivated to achieve common team goals, which would be reflected in their behaviour.
4 *Group integration-social* (GI-S): Teams with athletes that score highly on GI-S would have athletes that feel a close bond and friendships, who are keen to maintain the level of friendship and closeness that they have.

Factors that influence team cohesion

Research by Eys et al. (2009) identified 10 categories that influenced task cohesion and seven categories that reflected social cohesion (see Table 12.1).

The importance of team cohesion

It is imperative that coaches have an understanding of why this construct is important when coaching teams. Team cohesion has been associated with a variety of desirable outcomes such as:

1 *Enhanced team performance:* A meta-analysis containing 46 studies, by Carron et al. (2002), revealed that there was an effect size of 0.66 for the

TABLE 12.1 Factors that influence task and social cohesion

Factors that influence task cohesion	*Factors that influence social cohesion*
Athletes working together	Athletes knowing one another
Effective communication among team mates	Being friends and getting along with other athletes
Bonding between team mates	Feeling well supported
Team members understanding their team mates' abilities	Engaging in non-sport activities with each other
Athletes being unselfish	Not having any conflict or cliques
Athletes having experiences of attempting to achieve goals	
Being led well by other team mates	
Being in a team full of committed athletes	
Having parity in terms of status with other team mates	
Having a good coach–team relationship	

relationship between team cohesiveness and team performance. Indeed, Filho et al. (2015) reported that team excellence occurs once team cohesion has been established. More recently, however, Benson et al. (2016) found that cohesion did not predict performance, but success actually improved team cohesion. Overall, the weight of evidence suggests that cohesion is linked to team performance.

2 *Increased peer efficacy:* Marcos et al. (2010) explored the relationship between team cohesion and perceived peer efficacy among athletes and coaches participating in semi-professional soccer and basketball. Peer efficacy was conceptualised as each athlete's belief about their team mates' abilities to be successful in completing a task. Athletes who reported higher levels of cohesion also reported higher levels of peer efficacy.

3 *Decreased jealousy:* Research has suggested that team cohesion is negatively associated with jealousy, which refers to an athlete wanting to be another person or wanting what another athlete has (Kamphoff et al., 2005).

4 *Increased effort:* Bray and Whaley (2001) explored the amount of effort exerted by basketball players along with team cohesion. They found that athletes in more cohesive teams exerted more effort than those who felt their teams lacked cohesiveness.

5 *Increased collective efficacy:* With a sample of female and male professional football players, Leo et al. (2015) found that team cohesion was associated with teams' beliefs in their ability to operate as a team and be successful.

There are a number of benefits from higher levels of cohesion, although coaches should be aware of some of the pitfalls associated with highly cohesive teams. For example, in Hardy et al.'s (2005) sample, 56 per cent of athletes reported that there were disadvantages of being in a highly cohesive team, such as problematic communication with other athletes and the potential for social isolation for athletes who are not in the main group. Furthermore, 31 per cent of athletes reported disadvantages of high task cohesion such as communication problems, increased pressure, and reduced personal enjoyment.

The effects of coach behaviour and leadership on team cohesion

Westre and Weiss (1991) explored whether team cohesion was related to coach leadership style and coach behaviour. Higher frequencies of instruction by the coach, social support from the coach, a democratic style of leadership in which athletes had their say over decisions, and positive feedback were associated with more task cohesion among athletes. Based on these findings, Westre and Weiss (1991) advocated a number of strategies that coaches can apply to their coaching to enhance the cohesiveness of their teams. For instance, the coach can facilitate feelings of cohesion by providing regular instruction about skills, strategies, and tactics. Coaches should also provide positive feedback and demonstrate that they support their athletes (see Chapter 13 for more information).

Callow et al. (2009) explored the effects of coach leadership behaviours on cohesion among 309 Frisbee players, who competed at different levels. The authors found that when the coach fostered acceptance of group goals (e.g. the team working together to achieve the same goal), promoted teamwork (e.g. promoting team members working together to achieve a set goal), had high performance expectations (e.g. expecting athletes to achieve high standards), and gave individual consideration to athletes (e.g. recognising that athletes have different needs), there was a positive association with task cohesion. Furthermore, when the coach encouraged athletes to accept group goals and promoted teamwork there was a positive association with social cohesion.

More recent research identified a relationship between coach behaviour and task and social cohesion. De Backer et al. (2011) found that perceived justice by the coach (e.g. the coach rewarding an athlete with appropriate match time based on his or her contribution to the team) and support (e.g. a coach allowing and supporting athletes in making their own choices regarding training) was positively related to task and social cohesion. As such, coaches should be very concerned about their athletes' perceptions of justice (De Backer et al., 2011) and improve their athletes' sense of perceived justice by providing information on the decisions they have made.

Although the aforementioned studies indicate that coach behaviour is related to both task and social cohesion in sports teams (Callow et al., 2009; De Backer et al., 2011; Westre and Weiss, 1991), other research indicates that athletes' perceptions of their relationship with the coach is a more important predictor of group cohesion than coach behaviours alone. Indeed, Jowett and Chaundry (2004) found that behaviours such as supporting athletes, providing feedback, and allowing athletes to have their say accounted for 26 per cent of task cohesion. When the relationship between the coach and the athlete was considered along with coaching behaviour these two factors accounted for 34 per cent of task cohesion. Similarly, considering only coach behaviours accounted for 12 per cent of social cohesion, which rose to 15 per cent when the authors also considered the perceived relationship the athlete had with his or her coach. The results from this study and other studies suggest that coach behaviours are important in influencing cohesion, but that coaches can also enhance cohesion by considering their relationship with the athletes they coach (see Chapter 11 for more information).

Team-building strategies

Team building refers to the process in which a team is enhanced or improved. This may result in enhanced team performance. Bloom et al. (2003) examined expert coaches' perceptions of team building and revealed that coaches planned team-building strategies before the season began, and knew when different team-building activities would take place during the season, such as different training sessions and social activities (team dinners and social gatherings). Another interesting finding was that the coaches wanted control over all team-building activities, but they did not want to be seen as the person who dictated to the players what activities would be undertaken.

- *Team goal setting*: Information on goal setting, and in particular, team goal setting is presented in Chapter 4. A team goal involves athletes having a shared perception regarding what they want to achieve (Martin et al., 2009). It is important that coaches set team goals as well as individual goals, when working with team sport athletes, because team goals are strongly linked to overall team success (Prapavessis and Carron, 1996) and team motivation (Munroe et al., 2002). Martin et al. (2009), in their meta-analysis, found that goal setting was a very effective intervention strategy. However, the effectiveness of team goal setting is influenced by the extent to which team goals are monitored and updated. Cormier et al. (2015) advocated that goals are regularly monitored and adjusted accordingly.
- *Team performance profiling*: Information on how coaches can implement performance profiling techniques is presented in Chapter 5 of this book. Researchers such as Carron and Hausenblas (1998) suggested that team performance profiling is a technique that allows coaches to gather the opinion of their team members before creating a team-building intervention.
- *Athlete integration*: To ensure that athletes feel integrated in their team, coaches can develop activities that encourage athletes to learn about each other, ask athletes to accept that there will be personality differences among group members, and break up cliques. Conducting these integration strategies should allow individual team members to feel a sense of personal belonging to the team (Cormier et al., 2015). Indeed, Cormier and colleagues found that social events were a successful way of integrating athletes.
- *Role development or role clarity*: Ryska et al. (1999) found evidence to suggest that it is important for coaches to develop strategies that help athletes understand and accept their roles within the team. These roles should develop over time. In particular, Ryska and colleagues stated that coaches could can try and develop unique roles for athletes within their team and promote open and continuous dialogue or communication among team mates.
- *Choosing effective team leaders*: Another factor that can influence team cohesion is the qualities of the person that the coach selects as team captain. Indeed, Cormier et al. (2015) reported that this selection is important and that effective team leaders are those that share the same philosophies as the coach, are instrumental in developing a positive team environment, organise social events, and monitor the team environment.

Factors to consider when planning team-building interventions

There are several factors that coaches could consider when designing a team-building intervention, which include:

- *Duration*: The meta-analysis by Martin et al. (2009) revealed that as the length of the intervention increases, so does the effectiveness. Interventions that lasted more than 20 weeks were more effective than team-building interventions that lasted only two weeks. Indeed, Brawley and Paskevich (1997) stated that team-building interventions should be at least a season long. From a coaching perspective, it appears that it takes time for interventions to be introduced to athletes, for athletes to trust an intervention, and for their behaviour to change (Martin et al., 2009). Coaches should understand that team-building interventions are not quick fixes and they will not produce immediate improvements in cohesion or team performance.

- *Less might be more*: The review by Martin et al. (2009) also revealed team-building interventions with fewer component parts (e.g. just goal setting vs. goal setting, role development training, performance profiling, and athlete integration) might be more effective. Martin and colleagues contended that if athletes have fewer activities to focus on, their attention can be directed towards one activity. However, if coaches just use goal-setting techniques they will exclude other activities that could benefit their team. Martin et al. concluded that these findings may be influenced by the team-building interventions being too short in duration. As such, coaches should conduct team interventions over a longer time frame (e.g. one season) and introduce different team-building strategies gradually, and once the coach feels that his or her team members have become familiar with each strategy.

- *Direct versus indirect approaches*: With regard to how a coach can implement team-building strategies, they can be implemented via a direct approach or an indirect approach (Carron et al., 2007). The direct approach involves the coach or the sport psychologist giving the team-building training. The indirect approach is when an individual who has the team-building knowledge passes his information on to an individual such as a coach who runs the team-building sessions.

- *Team building for individual sport athletes playing in a team*: Carron et al. (2007) and Martin et al. (2009) found that team-building interventions may have a greater effect among individual sport athletes who come together to form a team (e.g. tennis players, golfers, or badminton players). However, Martin et al. stated that team sport athletes do benefit from team-building interventions; it is just that the improvements among these athletes might be less. This is because athletes in team sport setting will probably have a higher level of cohesion. However, team-building interventions may be especially useful for newly formed teams. From a coaching perspective, coaches should not get frustrated if they feel their team-building interventions are having little effect among team sport athletes, especially in established teams.

CASE STUDY 12.1   A PLAN TO IMPROVE TEAM PERFORMANCE IN AN ACADEMY RUGBY TEAM

Stuart is a 29-year-old academy manager in a professional rugby league club. He felt that the previous season's academy team was not a cohesive unit and did not perform as a team. Therefore, Stuart implemented a season-long team-building intervention, which he ran himself. Stuart was aware of the need for players to bond outside of rugby, so he planned several social functions during the first half of the season in which players would be able to get together and have some fun. These included paintballing and going out for a meal when they toured Scotland, a pre-season barbeque, go-karting in November, a club Christmas dinner in December, and a night out in January.

With regard to team-building strategies, Stuart planned individual and team goal setting, individual and team performance profiling, athlete integration, and role development sessions. Stuart started off with team goal-setting sessions which involved getting the players together to discuss team goals for the season, followed by individual goal-setting sessions. Stuart did not put a specific time period on how long he worked on goal setting with the players, and only started performance profiling once he felt the players had fully grasped the goal-setting techniques and their behaviours had changed. Furthermore, Stuart planned not to forget about goal setting and performance profiling when he introduced role development training sessions and regularly conducted goal setting and performance profiling across the season. This sent a clear message to players that all aspects of team building were processes that needed constant attention and work.

Stuart also acknowledged his own behaviour as a factor that contributed to his team's poor cohesion in the previous season. After reading books and journal articles, Stuart changed his behaviour. He felt he did not acknowledge the individuals in the group, so he spent more time taking individuals aside to listen to their views and opinions, and any individual needs they may have. This included asking players which areas of their game they felt they needed to work on. One behaviour that Stuart did not change was his desire for players to always give their best, whether in training or in matches.

Case study reflection

Team cohesion is important for the success of most teams, yet it is something that can be difficult to attain. Teams do not become cohesive units over night and the development of team cohesion takes time. In this case study, Stuart used a variety of strategies and addressed the group as a whole and individual players.

Summary points

- Team cohesion is multi-dimensional, dynamic, instrumental, and dynamic.
- Task cohesion refers to the extent to which team mates work in unison together to achieve their team's overall goal.
- Social cohesion refers to an athlete's perceptions regarding how well he or she gets on with and likes his or her team mates.
- Team cohesion is associated with enhanced performance, positive mood, peer efficacy, and effort, but reduced anxiety and jealousy among team mates.
- Coaches' behaviours influence team cohesion, as does a coach's relationship with his or her athletes.
- Team-building interventions should include goal setting, performance profiling, athlete integration, and role development.
- Team-building interventions should be at least a season long.

Practice exam questions

1 Compare and contrast task cohesion and social cohesion.
2 Critically evaluate Carron et al.'s (1998) conceptual model of team cohesion.
3 Discuss the importance of team cohesion.
4 Coach behaviour influences team cohesion. Discuss.
5 What factors should coaches consider when designing team-building interventions?

Critical thinking questions: applying theory to practice

1 How can a coach promote task cohesion among the team he coaches?
2 Reflect on how you have influenced team cohesion within your coaching career.
3 What behaviours should a coach use when coaching beginners compared with higher level athletes?
4 How can a coach ensure that his or her players have high levels of perceived justice?
5 Design your own team-building intervention and justify your plan with supporting evidence.

Case study questions

1 Discuss Stuart's approach to building team cohesion.
2 Discuss how you could provide role development training in the sport you coach.
3 Discuss Stuart's approach to working with both the team and individual players.

13

SUPPORTING ATHLETES SOCIALLY

The purpose of this chapter is to provide coaches with information on the importance of socially supporting athletes and how they can provide social support. This chapter provides information on:

- A definition of social support
- Role of the coach in providing social support
- Benefits of social support
- The multi-dimensional nature of social support
- The different types of social support
- Social support preferences
- Creating a social support network.

A definition of social support

A widely used definition of social support in the sport literature is "an exchange of resources between at least two individuals perceived by the provider or the recipient to be intended to enhance the well-being of the recipient" (Shumaker and Brownell, 1984: 13). Rees (2007), however, suggested that there is little consensus regarding how to define this construct. This is because it is very difficult to encapsulate fully the reasons why a person may support another person. In the definition provided by Shumaker and Brownell, it is inferred that the provider of social support does this to improve the recipient's well-being. Within sport however, there are number of reasons why a coach may give an athlete social support, such as to improve a technical fault in an athlete's technique, to help him cope with stress, or to help him feel part of the team. Although helping an athlete improve technical faults, cope with stress, and making him or her feel part of the team may enhance the athlete's well-being, the coach does not specifically intend to enhance well-being through providing his or her athlete with social support, this is just a by-product. For the remainder of this chapter, social support from a coach will refer to the processes by which coaches attempt to help their athletes. The key aspect is that the coach attempts to help his or her athlete, but the intentions regarding why a coach wants to help his athlete or the reasons why the coach is supporting his or her athlete are not specifically considered, because this makes defining social support unnecessarily complicated.

Role of the coach in providing social support

A systematic review by Sheridan et al. (2014) examined social support among youth sport, across 73 different studies published between 1990 and 2013, and found that coaches were the most prevalent providers of social support to young athletes. Coaches reported providing emotional, esteem, and informational social support. A crucial role of coaches, in addition to providing technical and tactical knowledge to athletes, is to provide different forms of social support.

Benefits of social support

A variety of studies found that the social support provided by a coach has a variety of desirable consequences for the athlete:

1   *Burnout and well-being:* Athletes who receive high levels of social support are less likely to experience symptoms of burnout and report greater well-being. Defreese and Smith (2014) examined perceptions of support among 465 collegiate athletes. Although social support did not act as a moderator of the stress-burnout or burnout–well-being relationship, social support did contribute to burnout and well-being.
2   *Sporting performance:* Sport psychology scholars explored the relationship between social support and sporting performance (Rees and Freeman, 2009, 2010; Rees et al., 2007), and have found evidence to suggest that social support may account for up to 24 per cent of the variance in performance. For example, Rees et al. (2007) explored the relationship between social support, stressors, and performance among a sample of 117 high-level golfers, who completed questionnaires within two days of a competitive round and reported their performance after the round. Overall, social support aided the performance of the golfers.
3   *Career transition:* Adams et al. (2015) found that social support was vital in helping junior athletes make a successful transition from being an athlete competing in junior events to competing within adult competitions. As such, coaches play an important role in helping athletes make this transition.
4   *Self-talk:* Social support from coaches also influences self-talk (e.g. verbalisations that an athlete addresses to himself or herself; Hardy et al.,

2005). Self-talk can involve positive statements or negative statements. Zourbanos et al. (2011) explored the relationship between social support and self-talk and found that social support was positively associated with positive self-talk among athletes.

5 *Overcoming adversity:* Morgan and Giacobbi (2006) explored the experiences of eight highly talented collegiate athletes, the parents of these athletes, and their coaches. Social support from the coaches included helping the athletes with emotional difficulties and low self-esteem. It also involved providing information to athletes, which enabled them to achieve their goals and develop. Indeed, Morgan and Giacobbi stated the social support received by these players from coaches and parents was indispensable. From a coaching perspective, coaches should also encourage the parents of their athletes to provide social support, especially to child and adolescent athletes.

6 *Fun:* Smoll et al. (1993) developed a coaching effectiveness training programme to increase both supportiveness and instructional behaviours of coaches who worked in male youth sport settings. As such, coaches were encouraged to immediately reinforce effort and give encouragement to athletes after they made a mistake. The results indicated that athletes who had been coached by individuals who had received coach effectiveness training reported having more fun and were more attracted to playing in their team, compared with athletes who received coaching from untrained coaches.

7 *Enjoyment:* Researchers with a sample of 1342 athletes from sports such as American football, soccer, and volleyball found that athletes who felt they received positive coach support were more likely to enjoy sport (Scanlan et al., 1993). Positive support included coaches saying things to make the athletes feel good.

The multi-dimensional nature of social support

It is commonly accepted that social support is a multi-dimensional construct (Rees, 2007; Rosenfeld and Richman, 1997). Indeed, Rosenfeld and Richman suggested that support can be classified in one of three broad dimensions:

1 *Tangible:* Tangible social support refers to support that involves a coach assisting his or her athlete to complete a task (e.g. a gymnastic coach helping a gymnast to perform a hand stand by holding the legs of the athlete).

2 *Informational:* A coach's communication with an athlete that involves the coach telling the athlete that he or she is part of a network of communication in which the athlete is free to speak to people in the network is an example of informational social support. That is, the coach provides the athlete with information on the support structures in place.

3 *Emotional:* A coach who comforts and encourages an athlete would be considered as using emotional social support.

The different types of social support

Although social support can be broadly classified as having three broad dimensions (Rees, 2007; Rosenfeld and Richman, 1997), researchers have identified six specific types of social support that coaches could deploy when coaching. As such, Rosenfeld and Richman suggested the following social support strategies that coaches can use:

1   *Listening support:* A coach can provide listening support by simply listening to the athlete without giving the athlete any advice or judging what the athlete tells the coach. This may be difficult for some coaches, especially if they hear information that they are not happy with. It is important that the coach keeps quiet and lets the athlete say what he or she wants to say.

2   *Emotional support:* Coaches can provide emotional support by showing an understanding of the problems an athlete may be encountering. The coach should also demonstrate that he or she cares about the problems encountered by the athlete and comfort the athlete.

3   *Emotional challenge:* Sometimes it may be beneficial for the coach to challenge the athlete, so he or she may evaluate their own attitudes, values, and feelings towards something. This may be important if the coach feels that an athlete's attitude is not aligned to his perception of reality (e.g. an athlete may feel a particular coach does not like him or her, when the coach knows that the coach does like the athlete).

4   *Reality confirmation support:* In order for athletes to confirm that their views are real or reflective of other team mates, coaches can ask players to discuss pertinent factors that athletes might be having problems with together as a group (e.g. managing stress or balancing a busy schedule). This will allow players to listen to other players who have the same problems and shared ideas may generate new ideas for managing problems.

5   *Task appreciation support:* Coaches should recognise the amount of effort athletes put in to certain tasks (e.g. a training session) and express an appreciation for the work that athletes do, whether that is a midfielder in soccer who continually tracks back or a golfer who spends hours practising his or her putting. The coach should always show an appreciation for hard work.

6   *Task challenge support:* A coach can challenge an athlete's way of thinking about a training session activity in order to motivate and stretch the athlete. This may result in more creativity, excitement, and involvement for a particular training activity. For example, a coach could ask athletes to comment upon why a certain training activity is important and the benefits they acquire from participating in certain training activities. Coaches could also ask athletes how they would like to adapt different training sessions or drills to make them more relevant to competitions.

Social support preferences

The strategies outlined by Rosenfeld and Richman (1997) provide coaches with a number of strategies that they can use to enhance the social support they give to athletes. However, emerging research indicates that there are a number of factors that coaches should consider, which may influence how they provide social support.

Horn et al. (2011) explored the relationship between preferred coach behaviour and different psychological characteristics such as motivation and anxiety, among a sample of 195 collegiate athletes. Athletes who were intrinsically motivated (e.g. played sport for the enjoyment of playing) required frequent social support, as did athletes who were highly anxious. From a coaching perspective, coaches should recognise athletes who are intrinsically motivated and anxious, and tailor their coaching to the individual needs of the athletes by providing more frequent social support. The guidelines by Rosenfeld and Richman (1997) state how coaches can provide social support, whereas the research by Horn et al. (2011) indicates the factors that influence how often coaches should provide social support.

Coaches could also consider the age and the experience of the athlete when deciding how much social support an athlete requires. Høigaard et al. (2008) examined preferred coach behaviours in successful (e.g. team winning first 10 games of the season) and unsuccessful (e.g. team losing first 10 games of the season) soccer scenarios among a sample of 88 soccer players of different ages, experience, and skill levels. They found that the younger and less experienced soccer players required more social support from their coach than the older and more experienced players. The authors provided a very interesting explanation regarding why the younger players need more social support from their coach. They suggested that playing in the Norwegian Premier League or First Division is both challenging and stressful, so those who were inexperienced needed frequent social support from their coach. Høigaard and colleagues (2008) suggested that the younger players may rely more on their coach for social support, because they had not established a support network in the team or their private life. Indeed, older players are more likely to be married than younger players and can rely on their wives as a source of social support. It is important that coaches consider the age and personal circumstances of athletes when deciding how frequently to give their athletes social support.

Coaches could also consider the team circumstances when providing social support. Høigaard et al. (2008) found evidence to suggest that athletes require more social support in the unsuccessful performance scenario. Indeed, Høigaard and colleagues suggested that preferring more social support during times of adversity is a natural consequence of athletes having to deal with difficult and stressful situations. From a coaching perspective, it seems imperative that coaches should consider team success when deciding how much support they provide. For example, when a team loses several matches, the coach could increase the amount of social support he or she provides.

Creating a social support network

In addition to coaches providing social support to athletes using the strategies outlined in this chapter, coaches can also set up a social support network that encourages team mates, friends, and parents of the athletes to provide social support. Indeed, Rosenfeld et al. (1989) found that it may be beneficial for athletes to receive social support from their coaches, team mates, friends, and parents, so developing a formal network. Furthermore, the nature of the social support that an athlete receives appears to differ depending on the person providing the social support. Coaches and team mates tended to provide sport-related social support, whereas parents and friends provided non-sport social support.

Coaches could also foster a supporting network within their teams by encouraging athletes to be supportive of one another. One example of how coaches could create a supportive network during training would be to have players lead coaching sessions. This would result in players helping other players when they take on the role of the coach. The coach could praise this type of behaviour and positive communication among athletes.

Although a coach can influence how much support they give athletes and how supportive other players are of each other, they may have less influence regarding how much support parents and friends provide for their athletes. Coaches could speak to the parents of athletes at the start of a season, illustrate the importance of social support, provide information regarding how parents, wives, siblings, or friends can provide social support, and encourage these people to be supportive.

CASE STUDY 13.1   PROVIDING SOCIAL SUPPORT IN DIFFICULT CIRCUMSTANCES

Christine is a 25-year-old badminton coach who started coaching a new player, Louise, two weeks ago. Louise is a 12-year-old aspiring badminton player who left her previous coach because Louise's dad (Eric) felt that her previous coach was not good enough. From the outset of their relationship Christine could see that Louise was quite nervous and lacked confidence in her game. Alternatively, Eric was a robust character with many strong opinions about his daughter and what she needed to work on during training. After several phone calls with Eric, and assessing Louise's levels of anxiety and confidence using a questionnaire, Christine felt she needed to socially support Louise and that her father also needed to do the same. Christine felt more confident about providing Louise with additional social support than she did about asking Eric to change how he supported his daughter. She knew this was going to be a very delicate matter, but thought the benefits would really help Louise.

In Louise's subsequent training sessions, Christine emphasised how supportive of Louise she was and would listen to what she had to say in a non-judgemental way. She demonstrated that she cared about Louise, and really praised her when she put in lots of effort during training. Incidentally, Christine felt that Eric was more concerned with Louise's results. The sessions went well and Louise responded well to Christine's caring behaviour. At the end of a session, Christine asked if she could have a quick word, alone, with Eric and spoke about how she felt Louise's enjoyment and performance at badminton could be enhanced by creating a supportive network that places little emphasis on the outcomes of competitions and more on caring for and supporting Louise regardless of the results that she obtained. This was met with resistance from Eric who asked Christine what she thought he had been doing since she started playing badminton. Christine agreed that he had been very supportive of Louise and then mentioned some additional strategies and provided a rationale for each strategy such as listening and emotional support. When Christine described the listening support strategy, Eric admitted that listening was not his strong point, but agreed that this was something he was going to work on.

Case study reflection

As a coach, providing social support to an athlete may only be half of the solution to really helping an athlete, because the social support an athlete receives away from sports training or competition is also very important. However, speaking to parents about how they could socially support their own child can be a delicate process and thus diplomacy is required.

Summary points

- Coaches may provide social support to athletes for a number of reasons.
- Social support is associated with athletes having more fun and enjoyment, performing better, dealing with adversity, and positive self-talk.
- Social support is multi-dimensional and includes tangible, informational, and emotional support.
- Coaches can socially support their athletes by engaging in a variety of different strategies.
- Coaches should consider the age, experience level, motivation, and how anxious an athlete is when deciding how to socially support the athlete.
- Creating a social support network has the potential to enhance social support in teams.

Practice exam questions

1 What is social support and who provides social support to athletes?
2 What are the potential benefits of providing social support to athletes?

3   Social support is a multi-dimensional construct. Discuss.
4   What factors influence how a coach can socially support his or her athletes? Discuss.
5   Discuss the importance of creating a social support network in team sports.

Critical thinking questions: applying theory to practice

1   Reflect on how you have provided social support within your coaching career.
2   What are the tell-tale signs that an athlete might not be receiving enough support and how may this manifest itself?
3   Describe how a coach can ensure that the support he or she provides is tangible, informational, and emotional.
4   How could a coach's behaviour change after a team has a run of four defeats?
5   How can a coach create a social support network in his or her team?

Case study questions

1   What impact may Eric be having on his daughter's confidence and performances?
2   Consider how Eric might undermine the good work that Christine does.
3   In the longer term, how could Christine help Eric become more supportive to Louise?

14

ENHANCING MOTIVATION AMONG ATHLETES

The purpose of this chapter is to provide information on the factors that underpin an athlete's motivation and how coaches can enhance the motivation levels of their athletes. This chapter contains the following information:

- A definition of motivation
- The differences between extrinsic motivation, intrinsic motivation, and amotivation
- The hierarchical model of intrinsic and extrinsic motivation
- Age-related differences in motivation
- Coach influence on motivation
- Enhancing motivation: RESISTANCE.

A definition of motivation

According to Conroy et al. (2007) motivation refers to "the process of initiating, directing, and sustaining behaviour" (p. 182). Essentially, motivation is concerned with *why* people conduct certain behaviours (Deci and Ryan, 2000). Indeed, Keegan et al. (2009) found that coaches can influence motivation through their instruction and assessment of athletes.

The differences between extrinsic motivation, intrinsic motivation, and amotivation

1   *Intrinsic motivation:* An athlete is said to be intrinsically motivated when he or she wants to perform an activity for the satisfaction gained from performing the activity (Ryan and Deci, 2007). There is evidence to suggest that winning

teams display higher levels of intrinsic and extrinsic motivation (Blegen et al., 2012) and females are more intrinsically motivated than males (Clancy et al., 2016), inferring that coaches might need to work harder with males than females to instil intrinsic motivation.

2   *Extrinsic motivation:* Athletes are extrinsically motivated when they perform an activity for expected rewards or outcomes, such as winning money or accolades (Vallerand, 2007).

3   *Amotivation:* An athlete is amotivated when he or she does not have any intent or energy towards performing a specific action (Ryan and Deci, 2007). For example, an athlete who plays football but does not really enjoy or want to play football, would be classified as being amotivated.

The hierarchical model of intrinsic and extrinsic motivation

Vallerand (2001) proposed that intrinsic motivation, extrinsic motivation, and amotivation occur at three levels: (1) situational, (2) contextual, and (3) global. An athlete may experience differing levels of intrinsic motivation, extrinsic motivation, or amotivation across different situations. For example, a soccer player might be intrinsically motivated in one match, but amotivated in the next match after suffering a heavy defeat. Athletes also experience differing levels of motivation across different contexts. An athlete might be intrinsically motivated to play sport, but extrinsically motivated in his or her Saturday job (i.e. only works for the money he or she earns). Finally, motivation occurs at the personality level. Given that personality is relatively stable, some individuals may be categorised as those who are generally intrinsically, extrinsically, or amotivated across many situations. A key premise of Vallerand's (1997) model was that global motivation influences contextual motivation, which in turn affects situational motivation. Additionally, situational motivation can also have an impact on contextual motivation.

Age-related differences in motivation

It is important that coaches consider the age of the athletes they coach, because there are some age-related motivational differences among athletes of different ages. Nicholls (1989) argued that children aged between 4 and 10 years are not able to differentiate between ability and effort. This means that children between the ages of 4 and 10 years believe that athletes who try hard will perform well and have high ability. However, in a child's later years he or she will begin to distinguish between effort and ability and will eventually realise that ability is not always related to effort and that sometimes athletes will perform very well even though they may not put in as much effort as other children.

As children get older, around 11–12 years of age, there is a tendency for some athletes to want to demonstrate their superior ability over other children at performing certain tasks. Not only do they want to show that they are more able, they want to do so by exerting the same or less physical effort than other children. Harwood et al. (2008) therefore argued that coaches should make a strong effort to create mastery motivational climates for children aged from 11 to 12 years so that children do not have the opportunity to demonstrate their superior ability over other children. Even though children under the age of 12 years are unable to discriminate between effort and ability, it could be argued that coaches should foster a mastery motivational orientation for all children. This is because the benefits of this motivational orientation include enjoyment, competence, and intrinsic motivation (Ames, 1992).

Adult athletes are motivated to play sport for pleasure, fun, competition, and improved health benefits (de Franco Tobar et al., 2013). Further, older athletes' motivation is influenced by the feedback they receive. Badami et al. (2011) explored whether providing adults with feedback after good trials compared to bad trials influenced intrinsic motivation (e.g. performing a certain behaviour for their own satisfaction and enjoyment). Indeed, Badami and colleagues found that individuals' motivation was higher when feedback was given after good trials, as opposed to when it was given after poorer trials. Feedback after good trials also increased perceived competence. Coaches working with adult athletes could enhance learning, intrinsic motivation, and perceived competence by only providing their athletes with knowledge of results after successful performances. The motivational impact of feedback, as alluded to by Chiviacowsky et al. (2009), should not be overlooked. This is because the extent to which feedback provides a positive or negative emotional state directly influences performance among learners and psychological well-being (Hutchinson et al., 2008; Lewthwaite and Wulf, 2010; Wulf et al., 2010) and motivation (Badami et al., 2011).

Coach influence on motivation

Scholarly activity indicated that coaches directly influence intrinsic motivation levels among athletes (Amorose and Horn, 2000, 2001; Weiss et al., 2009). Generally, athletes are more likely to be intrinsically motivated if they perceive their coach provides feedback positively, socially supports athletes, provides athletes with choices, and places an emphasis on training (Amorose and Horn, 2000, 2001). Coaches who are kind and supportive towards their athletes promote motivation, which in turn facilitates enjoyment and thus reduces dropout (Gillet et al., 2012) and promotes performance (Gillet et al., 2010). How a coach communicates with his or her athlete also influences motivation levels (Buning and Thompson, 2015).

There also appears to be differences between children and adolescent athletes with regard to the impact that a coach can have on motivation. Black and Weiss (1992) explored the relationship between motivation and coach behaviour among a sample of 312 athletes who were divided into three age groups: (1) 10–11 years of age, (2) 12–14 years of age, and (3) 15–18 years of age. Interestingly, the findings revealed that coach behaviour was not related to intrinsic motivation among the 10–11-year-old athletes, but intrinsic motivation correlated with how the coach behaved among the athletes who were aged 12–14 and 15–18 years. There were other age-related findings, as the swimmers within the 12–14 years group who received more information after a positive performance were more intrinsically motivated. However, the swimmers that were the most intrinsically motivated among the 15–18 years group also felt that they had more information after a positive performance in addition to receiving praise from their coach. This study reveals the importance of coaches providing information to athletes.

In order to maximise intrinsic motivation among athletes aged between 12 and 14 years, coaches should focus their efforts on providing regular feedback after an athlete performs well. Older adolescent athletes also require regular feedback after they have performed successfully, but it is important that coaches also provides these athletes with praise regarding their accomplishments. Although the research by Black and Weiss (1992) found that coach behaviour did not influence motivation among athletes aged between 10 and 11 years, other research by Theeboom et al. (1995) revealed that coaches can increase the intrinsic motivation of their athletes by manipulating the coaching environment (see Chapter 15 for creating an optimal motivational climate). It would therefore be incorrect for coaches who work with athletes aged between 10 and 11 years to dismiss how they behave, because they think it does not have an impact on intrinsic motivation; it clearly can.

Bengoechea and Strean (2007) found evidence to suggest that coaches influence the motivation of adolescent athletes aged between 13 and 17 years in a variety of different ways. Indeed, these authors identified five motivational roles that coaches may play, which included:

1   *Providers of support:* The adolescent athletes reported that they benefited from their coaches and other people acting in a supportive manner, which enhanced motivation, self-perception, and emotions. In particular, the results suggested that coaches had the most impact on adolescents by adopting an approach in which the athletes felt that their coach was "backing them". The athletes reported that this approach allowed them to make their own decisions.

2   *Sources of pressure and control:* Coaches were also found to be a source of pressure. Athletes reported worrying about meeting the expectations of their coach. Bengoechea and Strean (2007) suggested that if coaches create pressure to perform certain activities (e.g. compete at particular competitions) the athletes may feel they have little or no choice, which reduces intrinsic motivation. However, the results also suggested that not all controlling behaviour by a coach has a negative impact on motivation. Some of the adolescents reported that, at times, they lacked motivation to take part in the least enjoyable aspects of their sport. However, they knew they were important for their own performance or for that of the team. As such the athletes may need or expect some form of controlling behaviour.

From a coaching perspective, if the coach has to use controlling behaviour, it is essential the coach states the perceived benefits of the athlete engaging in particular training (e.g. hill sprints). Indeed, Vallerand (2001) argued that exerting controlling behaviour may produce positive outcomes, but coaches should be cautious when adopting this approach. For instance, coaches could try and increase intrinsic motivation by trying to make tasks more enjoyable before resorting to controlling behaviours.

3   *Sources of competence-relevant information:* Athletes were motivated by coaches who increased their perception of being competent through providing feedback. Unlike children, as adolescents progress through their teenage years they tend to rely less on others to generate feelings of competence and tend to rely on judging competence based on their achievement of personal goals and skill improvement (Horn et al., 1993). However, adolescents don't exclusively use internal feedback and do also rely on feedback from coaches as a source of competence. It is therefore important that coaches provide feedback that emphasises competence in adolescent athletes such as "You are really getting to grips with the forehand stroke and are hitting excellent strokes now".

4   *Socialisation of achievement orientations:* Coaches play an important role in developing the environment an athlete is in, which has been referred to as being either:

   a   Mastery (Ames, 1992), task (Nicholls, 1989), or learning (Dweck, 1986). Athletes in this type or environment are concerned with improving and judge their accomplishments based on the improvements made or the amount of effort exerted, or;

   b   Performance (e.g. Ames 1992; Dweck 1986) and ego (Nicholls, 1989). In this second type of environment the athlete's main desire is to be better than other athletes. As such, an athlete would judge his or her performance based on his or her standing in relation to other athletes.

   The Bengoechea and Strean (2007) study found that the coach is pivotal in determining the environment or motivational climate among adolescent athletes, through stating how success is measured (e.g. improvements or effort vs. comparisons with other athletes or outcome such as winning). Coaches can maximise motivation by creating an environment in which athletes' success is judged on how they improve and the amount of effort exerted. Adopting this stance does not mean that coaches cannot introduce a competitive element within their coaching, because many adolescents enjoy an element of competition. However, coaches could place less emphasis on who wins matches in training or competitions and focus on improvements made and what athletes can do to improve further.

5   *Models to emulate:* Adolescent athletes also observe their coaches and take on board some of the behaviours of the people they are observing, which can increase motivation (Weiss, 1995). As such, if a coach demonstrates a positive attitude to improving and exerting maximal effort in training and during competitions, athletes may also adopt this approach.

Enhancing motivation: RESISTANCE

Enhancing intrinsic motivation has the potential to benefit athletes, because intrinsically motivated athletes experience less anxiety than those who are extrinsically motivated (Weiss and Amorose, 2008). The research by Bengoechea and Strean (2007) suggested that a coach can influence and thus enhance motivation by developing a mastery or task motivation climate. An intervention study conducted by Harwood and Swain (2002) examined the effects of a season-long (a) player, (b) parent, and (c) coach intervention on goal involvement responses, self-regulation, competition cognitions, and goal orientations among four adolescent tennis players. Each participant received four 90-minute educational sessions and the set of coaches and parents received two 90-minute educational sessions. The different sessions focused on motives for playing tennis and also included a series of personal tasks so the tennis players could become familiar with the aims of the intervention.

Furthermore, Harwood and Swain (2002) created the RESISTANCE acronym, which represented the 10 factors in tennis that could reduce an athlete's intrinsic motivation. The RESISTANCE acronym stands for:

- *Rating*: Athletes were made aware that it was not their rating or ranking that produced their performance, but the effort they exerted.
- *Esteem*: Players were encouraged to separate themselves from the outcome, so if they lost they were less inclined to think of themselves in a negative fashion.
- *Seeding*: Players were encouraged to pay little attention to their seeding or their opponent's seeding, as they were told that rankings do not determine results, performance does.
- *Importance*: All matches were of the same importance and no match is more important than another match.
- *Score*: The score by which a player beats another player or the score by which a player gets beaten is not important.
- *Team*: Team mates were encouraged to play like the player who had earned and deserved his or her place on a team.
- *Audience*: The main concern of an audience is to watch players try their best and give maximal effort at all times during a match.
- *No justice*: The players were encouraged to think rationally and understand that one bad call from a referee does not determine the outcome of a match, as the performance for the rest of the match determines the outcome.
- *Comparison*: Players were asked to not base what they thought they had achieved solely on making comparisons with other players (e.g. one player might have reached a semi-final, but compares himself only with the player who made the final. The player who made the semi-final could focus on the improvement he made in different areas of the game to reach the semi-final and think about what he can do to improve his technique to reach future finals).

- *Endorsements*: Players were encouraged to worry less about designer labels, and were told that fashion has never won anyone a match, performance wins matches.

Harwood and Swain (2002) successfully developed the RESISTANCE intervention to increase task involvement (e.g. the desire to improve) in relation to enhancing pre-competitive task goals and reducing ego involvement (e.g. the desire to show superior ability).

CASE STUDY 14.1   INCREASING MOTIVATION BY APPLYING THE RESISTANCE PRINCIPLES

Huw is a 29-year-old full-time badminton coach who has just started coaching the county under-16 team. There are two players on the squad who also play for their national team, with several other players aspiring to achieve national honours. Huw is concerned that some of the players are a little too occupied with their rankings and how their rankings compare with other players and focus too much on the score of matches. He often hears players talking about the scores before matches in terms of predicting how much they will beat an opponent by and he felt that some players were too concerned with the outcomes of matches (e.g. selection to the national squad, invitation to national competitions, chance to earn a scholarship years down the line). As such, Huw wanted the players to become more intrinsically motivated.

In order to enhance intrinsic motivation levels, Huw adapted the RESISTANCE principles and used parts of the guidelines which he felt would benefit his players the most. He spoke to the players as a group and individually. Competition draws would often be published online, before the competition took place, which gave the players opportunities to see who they were playing and view recent results of the opponents. Huw was concerned that this was having a detrimental impact on performance, as he felt some players were beaten before they turned up, whereas others relaxed too much if they were playing an unseeded player, and perceived an easy draw. As such, Huw discussed the concept of how players are seeded and how when players are in developmental stages they are of little importance as some players might be unseeded because they have not played the required number of competitions or they may have been injured. As such, Huw wanted his team to focus more on their individual performance and try as hard as they could for every point within every match, rather than on the opponent's seeding.

The players in Huw's squad compared themselves with each other based on achievements, such as competitions won or national/international representation. Huw wanted the players to focus more on judging achievements by using self-referenced measures, such as how much improvement has been made over the course of a specific time period (e.g. month, season, two years). In order to facilitate this, Huw created a progress sheet which included the key attributes to be successful in badminton and players completed these sheets on a regular basis to monitor improvement.

One of the international players on Huw's squad recently suffered a dip in form since being selected for his national team. As such, Huw spoke to this player individually to identify some of the reasons. The player, Mark, said that he always wanted to be picked for his country, but seemed to lack the desire and motivation now he'd achieved this goal. Huw encouraged Mark to play like he did to get into the squad and they worked on setting some new goals.

Case study reflection

Huw believed that the players on his squad were externally motivated and focused too much on their own rankings, their opponent's ranking, and the scores of matches. As such, Huw wanted to engender an emphasis on intrinsic motivation for playing sport so encouraged players to focus less on the importance of rankings and making comparisons with others players, as he felt these were the most important aspects to address for his squad. Coaches can pick and choose elements from an intervention which they feel will benefit their players the most, and this can vary from player to player, even within the same team.

Summary points

- Motivation is concerned with *why* people conduct certain behaviours (Deci and Ryan, 2000).
- Motivation is associated with enjoyment, dropout rates, and performance.
- Female athletes may be more intrinsically motivated than male athletes.
- Coaches directly influence motivation through their behaviour and communication, although the impact of the coach appears to vary depending on the age of the athlete.
- Coaches can enhance motivation by applying the RESISTANCE principles to their coaching practice.

Practice exam questions

1   Compare and contrast intrinsic and extrinsic motivation and the implications of these types of motivation for athletes.
2   Motivation changes across the lifespan. Discuss.
3   Discuss how coaches influence motivation levels.
4   To what extent can motivation be changed? Discuss.
5   Critically evaluate the RESISTANCE programme.

Critical thinking questions: applying theory to practice

1   Describe how a coach can implement the RESISTANCE principles into a coaching session.
2   Reflect on how you have influenced the motivation of athletes in your coaching practice.
3   How can a coach enhance motivation among adolescent athletes?
4   How can a coach enhance motivation among adult athletes?
5   How can a coach enhance motivation if he or she is coaching adult and adolescent athletes within the same group?

Case study questions

1   What signs indicated that the players were extrinsically motivated, and what other signals could a coach identify?
2   Huw used certain aspects of the RESISTANCE guidelines. What are the strengths and weaknesses of this approach?
3   How could Huw monitor the effectiveness of the RESISTANCE principles that he included in training?

15

CREATING THE OPTIMAL MOTIVATIONAL CLIMATE

The aim of this chapter is to provide information on how coaches can shape the coaching environment and the impact that this has on athletes. Information is provided on:

- A definition of the motivational climate
- Mastery/task-involving motivational climates
- Performance/ego-involving motivational climates
- Impact of the motivational climate on athletes
- Manipulating the motivational climate
- Using TARGET to create a mastery motivational climate for athletes.

A definition of the motivational climate

A motivational climate refers to the way in which coaches influence athletes' motivation through their coaching practices (e.g. providing feedback, structuring practices, and providing recognition; Ames, 1992). According to researchers (e.g. Keegan et al., 2009; Treasure, 2001) the way in which the coach emphasises or determines success versus failure determines the motivational climate and there are two main types of motivational climates, mastery and performance motivational climates (Amorose, 2007).

Mastery/task-involving motivational climates

Mastery motivational climates are often referred to as task-involving climates. In a mastery or task-involving motivational climate the coach focuses on encouraging the athletes to learn, make personal improvements in the activities they are undertaking, and exert maximal effort in all activities. In this coaching environment, the coach provides tasks that challenge the athlete towards self-improvement, but these tasks are not unrealistic in the level of challenge that is set. The coach also rewards the athlete or athletes based on progress and improvement. Athletes are evaluated based on the amount of effort that they put into a task and are praised for trying as hard as they can. Finally, in mastery motivational climates, the coach develops activities that promote maximal co-operation among athletes.

Performance/ego-involving motivational climates

Performance/ego-involving motivational climates are sport settings in which the coach emphasises and rewards winning. As such, coaches in this environment only praise the athletes that win in both training and competition. Within this environment there is also an emphasis on players outperforming other players, so a coach would set tasks that encourage competition between players and allow players to be ranked. An example of this type of task would be a sprint task in which the coach keeps all of the times and produces a rank order. In addition to rewarding winning, Amorose (2007) reported that coaches in this environment punish mistakes by shouting at athletes or giving them physical tasks such as press-ups and promote rivalries between athletes.

Impact of the motivational climate on athletes

Scholars found that the climate a coach develops influences motivation. Athletes in a mastery motivational climate are likely to be more intrinsically motivated whereas athletes in a performance motivational climate are more likely to be extrinsically motivated (Amorose, 2007). Further, athletes of low ability who are in a mastery motivational climate are more likely to enjoy playing sport (Jaakkola et al., 2016). Mastery motivational climates are also associated with enhanced team cohesion (McLaren et al., 2015), fulfilling the psychological needs of athletes (Hodge and Gucciardi, 2015), increased behavioural engagement (Curran et al., 2015), self-esteem, competence, and intention to continue playing sport (Atkins et al., 2015), and decreased anxiety (Smith et al., 2007). In contrast, performance motivational climates are associated with less enthusiasm and vigour (Curran et al., 2015), enhanced cortisol responses (indicative of stress) and shame (Hogue et al., 2013), and anti-social behaviour (Hodge and Gucciardi, 2015). Overall, mastery motivational climates are associated with a variety of positive outcomes, so it is important that coaches understand how to manipulate the sporting environment.

Manipulating the motivational climate

Several studies attempted to manipulate the motivational climate (e.g. Hassan and Morgan, 2015; Hogue et al., 2013; McLaren et al., 2015; Smith et al., 2007; Theeboom et al., 1995; Treasure, 1993) and then assessed the effects of manipulating the environment on different outcomes, such as athletes' perceptions of coach behaviour, cortisol levels, anxiety, or group cohesion.

Treasure (1993) conducted a 10-week intervention to create one of two conditions: (1) a mastery motivational climate or (2) a performance motivational climate among child soccer players. TARGET stands for *Task* (e.g. design of learning), *Authority* (e.g. location of decision making), *Recognition* (e.g. use of incentives), *Grouping* (individual vs. cooperative work), *Evaluation* (e.g. use of feedback), and *Time* (pace of instruction). The mastery motivational climate group were coached in accordance to the TARGET principles. Treasure (1993) found that the motivational climate could be manipulated, because the soccer players in the mastery motivation climate group perceived that they were in a motivational climate, whereas the athletes in the performance group perceived that they were in a performance-oriented climate. The study by Treasure (1993) is important, because it suggests that coaches have the potential to shape the motivational climate. More recently, Hassan and Morgan (2015) examined the effectiveness of the TARGET-based intervention among four coaches and their 43 athletes. In support of the TARGET programme, videos of coaching sessions revealed that coaches demonstrated more mastery coaching behaviours (e.g. rewarding athletes who improve the most) and athletes were more likely to perceive that they were in a mastery motivational climate.

Theeboom et al. (1995) conducted an intervention study that examined the effects of a motivation climate training programme (e.g. mastery vs. performance) on enjoyment, perceived competence, intrinsic motivation, and motor skill development among Wushu athletes. This study consisted of child athletes who were aged between 8 and 12 years, who were randomly assigned to one of two groups: (1) mastery-oriented group, or (2) performance-oriented group. The results revealed that the children in the mastery-oriented group scored higher than the performance-oriented group in enjoyment and had better motor skills. Furthermore, Theeboom et al. (1995) also interviewed the athletes and found that those in the mastery-oriented group seemed to have higher levels of intrinsic motivation and perceived competence than the performance-oriented group.

The effects of the Mastery Approach to Coaching (MAC; Smoll and Smith, 2008) on motivational climate has been tested in two studies (Smith et al., 2007; McLaren et al., 2015). The key premise of MAC is that coaches are encouraged to provide positive reinforcement, give corrective instructions in a positive manner, offer accurate technical advice to athletes, and help athletes learn from mistakes. First, Smith et al. (2007) examined the effects of MAC on anxiety, with a sample of 216 athletes and their 37 coaches. Athletes who played for MAC-trained coaches reported higher perceptions of mastery-climate coach behaviours than athletes who played for coaches in the control group. The MAC intervention had a positive impact on anxiety, relative to the athletes who played for untrained coaches. Second, a study by McLaren et al. (2015) examined the effects of mastery motivational climate intervention on perceptions of group cohesion among coaches from 21 teams and 243 athletes based at these teams. The coaches were divided into three groups: (1) intervention condition, who received a 1.5-hour session on mastery approach coaching behaviours and the book *Coaches who never lose* (Smoll and Smith, 2008); (2) attention-control condition, who received advice on how coaches can regulate anxiety and optimise athletes' experience; and (3) the control group. The intervention positively impacted on perceptions of group cohesion when data was analysed at the end of the season-long study.

In contrast to the aforementioned studies, which successfully manipulated the motivational climate over a prolonged period, Hogue et al. (2013) adopted a different approach, by assessing the effects of a motivational climate intervention over a much shorter time-frame (i.e. 60 minutes after a juggling session). Participants were assigned to a task-involving juggling climate (e.g. emphasis on improvement, peer coaching, and group improvement tasks) or an ego-involving group (e.g. praise given to best performers, ranking the jugglers, and encouraging competition between the jugglers). Athletes who were in the ego-involving motivational climate group experienced greater cortisol responses, anxiety, stress, and shame in comparison with the task-involving motivational climate jugglers. Furthermore, jugglers from the task-involving motivational climate reported higher levels of enjoyment, self-confidence, effort, and excitement regarding juggling again.

Collectively, these studies indicate that an athlete's perception of the motivational climate can be manipulated. Coaches are instrumental in changing an athlete's perception of the motivational climate. Creating a mastery motivational climate has the potential to result in a variety of desirable consequences, such as reduced anxiety, stress, and shame, in addition to maximising enjoyment, intentions to continue playing sport, and group cohesion.

Using TARGET to create a mastery motivational climate for athletes

Task

A crucial role of the coach is to design activities that his or her athletes will participate in, such as practice drills, tactics, or even learning activities. It is crucial that the coach asks athletes to conduct tasks that are varied and diverse in nature. A scholar found that tasks that have variety and diversity are more likely to foster interest and develop learning (Nicholls, 1989). Additionally, coaches should devise tasks that are meaningful to the athlete. For example, if an athlete can see how a task is related to his or her sport, the task is more likely to be viewed as meaningful.

Authority

Authority refers to the degree in which the coach involves athletes in decision making regarding the activities that will be carried out (Treasure, 2001). Indeed, authority is very important, because Ames (1992) suggested that decision making is related to positive motivation patterns. Therefore, the more choices athletes have, the more positively motivated they will be. However, when coaches give athletes choices, it is essential that the choices are of tasks that are similar in difficulty levels.

This is because some athletes may opt for tasks that are very difficult, whereas other athletes will select tasks that are very easy if they are worried that they will be compared with other athletes and they have low perceptions of ability (Ames, 1992). Furthermore, Ames stated that if choice is motivated by fear, such as the fear of performing poorly compared with others, then it is unlikely to enhance personal control. Indeed, the coach should ensure when he or she gives athlete choices that all choices are of an equal difficulty. This will ensure the athlete chooses the activity for reasons of personal interest as opposed to fear of performing poorly.

Recognition

Treasure (2001) stated that it is very important to reward athletes and provide incentives to perform, because these incentives or rewards might be viewed by athletes as being more important than the activity itself. However, coaches have to be very careful how they administer rewards or incentives, because they can have a negative effect. For example, Lepper and Hodell (1989) found that awarding a whole group of children, who had various abilities and differing levels of interest, created less motivation. This might have occurred because the children knew they would receive an award regardless of how much effort they put in to a task. Additionally, rewards can also decrease motivation if athletes perceive that the reward is a bribe for them to perform certain behaviours. In order to create a mastery motivational climate, coaches should reward athletes who improve or those who demonstrate maximum effort, as opposed to those who put in little effort. This will ensure that feelings of satisfaction and pride are a result of the improvement an athlete makes or the effort they put in as opposed to comparisons with other athletes.

Grouping

According to Ames (1992), how a coach determines how groups are formed, keeps athletes apart from one another, or decides how athletes move from one group to another, is a key factor in determining the motivational climate of a group. Indeed, if coaches select groups based on ability, such as a group of the most talented athletes, a group of athletes with average ability, and a group of athletes with the least ability, there might be a tendency for the coach to give more (1) instructional time, (2) opportunities, (3) encouragement, and (4) attention to the most talented group of athletes (Treasure, 2001).

Coaches might be tempted to group individuals based on ability if they have a group of individuals with different abilities (Treasure, 2001). However, to create a mastery motivational climate, coaches should avoid creating homogeneous ability groupings. This will prevent older children making social comparisons. Rather, coaches should group individuals randomly to form heterogeneous ability groupings and regularly change groupings or move athletes from one group to another to avoid social comparisons and foster a mastery motivational climate (Marshall and Weinstein, 1984).

Evaluation

How a coach evaluates the athletes he or she coaches is one of the most important factors that determines whether athletes perceive they are in a mastery or performance motivational climate (Treasure, 2001). Research has revealed that when athletes compare themselves with other athletes based on ability, it negatively influences motivation and may result in a sense of decreased self-worth (Treasure, 2001). As such, coaches should make evaluations related to the individual by commenting on progress towards the goals of an athlete, the improvement made, or the amount of effort in comparison to other training sessions or matches, thus avoiding peer comparison evaluations. Providing these types of evaluations will encourage athletes to focus on their own ability to improve and foster a mastery motivational climate.

Timing

Timing is related to the other five dimensions of the model (i.e. task, authority, recognition, grouping, and evaluation). That is, time is related to the task, so coaches should consider what they are asking their athletes to do and the amount of time that they are giving them to complete a specific task. With regard to authority, athletes should be able to control which tasks they do first. It is imperative that the coach spends the same amount of time with each group, as opposed to spending the majority of time with only one group (Keegan et al., 2009). Coaches should be aware of timing, because some athletes may need more time than others to develop the skills that are required to play sport, but as Treasure (2001) stated: athletes "who need the most practice and playing time are the ones who receive the least" (p. 93). It is important that coaches consider time when they evaluate athletes and provide feedback at the appropriate times, such as after successful attempts or when an athlete has demonstrated improvement.

CASE STUDY 15.1   CREATING A MASTERY MOTIVATIONAL CLIMATE IN CHILDREN'S SOCCER: APPLYING MAC AND TARGET PRINCIPLES

This case study represents a coach's attempt to create a mastery climate in a group of children he coached. Steve has been coaching this group of twenty 10-year-olds for the last month and they play in a local league. Steve is concerned by the children being too pre-occupied with results and league table position, so made an attempt to encourage the players to focus on improvement and not the results of matches. Snippets of dialogue between Steve and some of his players are included in this case study for illustrative purposes.

Initial instructions at start of session

Steve: In today's training session I would like you to practise improving your
first touch, because this is really important in soccer matches and it
would be excellent if you can all improve this element of your game.
I have set up four different drills and have laid out cones for each drill.
In Drill 1 you receive the ball along the ground and then trap it and
pass it back to your partner with your left foot, whereas in Drill 2 you
receive the ball at knee height and try to cushion it by raising your
foot and then pass it to your partner with your right foot. In Drill 3
you receive the ball at chest height and try to cushion it with your
chest and pass the ball back to your partner, whereas in Drill 4 you
sprint down the line at full speed and receive the ball into your feet
and cushion it whilst running, get the ball under control and dribble
to the line at full speed. Each person will have a go at each drill. I
would like you to decide which drill to go on and start performing. I
will show you how each drill works by giving a demonstration. Does
anyone have any questions?

Training commences and Steve makes a number of comments

Steve: Well done Ashley, for sprinting down the line as fast as you could and
then controlling the ball.
Ashley: Thanks coach.
Steve: Mike, that is excellent you are really improving your technique and
can cushion the ball much better now.
Mike: I don't think I am improving as I can't trap the ball as well as some of
the others.
Steve: No Mike, you really are getting better. You could improve even more
by making sure you keep your eye on the ball as sometimes you lift
your head up more. Try that now Mike. [Steve gives demonstration.]
Mike: I see what you mean, I will try that now.
Steve: That's it Mike.

End of first round of drills

Steve: Stop everyone. Now decide which drill you want to perform next
and stand by the cone ready to start. I am really pleased with the
effort everyone is putting in and want you all to continue putting in
maximal effort. Start now!

All drills completed

Steve: Well done everyone, you've all now had a go at each drill. I would like us all to spend the next 30–40 minutes in match practices. I would like the people who have just completed Drills 1 and 4 to participate in some 2 versus 1 matches. I would like those that have just completed Drills 2 and 3 to play some 4 versus 4. For the first few minutes I want everyone to practise controlling the ball, so everyone has to take at least two touches. After each goal is scored I want each of you to swap bibs with the closest person to you on the other side.

Steve: Great Stevie, I can see you are all putting in maximum effort. Jonny, that was a really good first touch and it allowed you some time to look up and make a great pass. Well done!

Final speech

Steve: Well done today, does anyone have any questions they would like to ask?

Danny: I struggled to get a good touch with my left foot, but I am good at doing it with my right foot and I can't seem to get better.

Steve: Most of us have a tendency to be better with one foot or another. I think you are making improvements with your left foot, but it is just taking a bit longer than your right. I think that if you keep on practising you will continue getting better with your left foot. Are there any other questions? I am looking forward to the game on Sunday, see you then lads.

Case study reflection

In this case study, Steve was trying to adhere to the MAC (Smoll and Smith, 2008) and TARGET (Treasure, 1993, 2001) principles. Steve developed a variety of tasks that were meaningful to soccer matches, he gave the players choice, he rewarded effort and improvement verbally, regularly switched the groups in the match to reduce social comparison, and provided accurate technical demonstrations of the skills he asked the players to perform and carefully timed what he did.

Summary points

- The motivational climate relates to the ways in which coaches exert their influence on players' motivation through their coaching practice.

- Mastery/task-involving motivational climates are associated with a variety of desirable outcomes such as enhanced enjoyment, engagement, and perceived competence.
- Performance/ego-involving motivational climates are linked to anti-social behaviour, enhanced stress, and shame.
- Motivational climates can be manipulated by providing training to coaches, such as MAC or TARGET principles.

Practice exam questions

1 Compare and contrast the factors that determine whether a coaching environment will be perceived as a mastery or a performance motivational climate.
2 Identify the positive outcomes of a mastery motivational climate.
3 Identify the negative outcomes of a performance mastery climate.
4 Discuss the role of the coach in shaping the motivational climate.
5 Compare and contrast the MAC and TARGET motivational climate interventions.

Critical thinking questions: applying theory to practice

1 Discuss how coaches could implement the MAC principles within their training sessions.
2 Consider your last coaching session and reflect on your coaching behaviours. Describe some of the mastery and performance motivational behaviours that you displayed.
3 Design a one-hour coaching session for your sport that includes elements of the MAC and TARGET principles.
4 Discuss some of the difficulties of implementing all of the TARGET principles within your coaching practice.
5 In order to improve the TARGET intervention, what changes would you recommend and why?

Case study questions

1 Why was Steve concerned about his athletes focusing too much on results?
2 Discuss the ways in which Steve emphasised improvement within the session.
3 Discuss the effectiveness of Steve's instructions.

16

APPLYING SELF-DETERMINATION THEORY AND RESEARCH TO ENHANCE COACHING PRACTICE

The purpose of this chapter is to provide information on how coaches can maximise their coaching effectiveness by utilising self-determination priniciples. This chapter will also contain information on the types of coaching behaviours that are thought to enhance motivation, in addition to coaching behaviours that may negatively impact on athlete motivation. In particular, this chapter contains information on:

- Self-determination theory
- The importance of self-determined motivation
- Basic psychological needs
- The role of the coach in shaping an athlete's motivation
- Coaching strategies to fulfil an athlete's basic psychological needs
- Controlling coaching behaviours.

Self-determination theory

According to Deci and Ryan (1985, 2000), self-determination theory (SDT) is concerned with how and why people participate in different activities, such as sport, exercise, or other recreational activities (e.g. art classes, chess, or gardening). Indeed, the reason why athletes participate in sport can be classified on a continuum of self-determination (Occhino et al., 2014; see Figure 16.1). The most self-determined form of motivation is intrinsic motivation, which occurs when athletes play sport because they enjoy it and have a strong interest in their chosen sport or sports. At the other end of the continuum is amotivation, which occurs when the athlete has no motivation to play sport.

FIGURE 16.1   Self-determined motivation continuum

In between amotivation and intrinsic motivation are four types of extrinsic motivation (i.e. external regulation, introjected regulation, identified regulation, and integrated regulation). The least self-determined type of extrinsic motivation is external regulation. According to Ryan and Deci (2007), an athlete exhibits this form of motivation when he or she plays sport to attain rewards (e.g. medal for finishing first) or avoiding punishment (e.g. coach shouting at player). The next least self-determined form of extrinsic motivation is introjected regulation. An athlete is motivated to play sport to experience pride but to avoid feelings of anxiety or shame by not participating has an introjected form of extrinsic motivation. Although still a form of extrinsic motivation, identified regulation is relatively self-determined. Ryan and Deci suggested that an athlete who plays sport because they value the benefits associated with playing sport (e.g. enhanced energy, enhanced health, and building new friendships) is behaving through identified regulation. The most self-determined form of extrinsic motivation is integrated regulation. It is still extrinsic, because the athlete is playing sport for reasons other than enjoyment or fun (e.g. wanting to win at sport), but shares some of the characteristics of intrinsic motivation as playing sport becomes part of the athlete's life and makes them feel better or fulfils psychological needs (Ryan and Deci, 2007).

The importance of self-determined motivation

Why is an athlete's level of self-determined motivation important? A number of studies revealed positive outcomes for athletes who participate in sport for self-determined reasons, in comparison with those who participate in sport for non-self-determined reasons. For example, Vallerand and Rousseau (2001) found that those who participate in sport for more self-determined reasons are more likely to perform better and persist in adversity for longer.

Basic psychological needs

According to Duda (2013), a key construct of SDT is "basic psychological needs". Basic psychological needs are important because when these are met an athlete is more likely to be intrinsically motivated, whereas when an athlete's needs are not met, he or she is less likely to be intrinsically motivated and have a poorer experience (Ryan and Deci, 2007). Further, fulfilling one's basic psychological needs is essential for maximising well-being, self-motivation, and social development (Ryan and Deci, 2000). According to SDT, there are three basic psychological needs:

1 *Autonomy:* The need for autonomy represents an athlete's need to decide what, how, and when he or she does something. As such, it represents an athlete's need to be the origin of their own actions (Amorose, 2007).
2 *Competence:* The need for competence reflects an athlete's need to feel that he or she is effective in meeting any demands (Duda, 2013), thus viewing their behaviour (i.e. playing sport) as being effective (Amorose, 2007).
3 *Relatedness:* The need for relatedness includes an athlete's need to feel cared for by significant others such as a coach or team mates (Duda, 2013) and a secure sense of belonging (Amorose, 2007).

The self-determination theory predicts that athletes will participate in sports that satisfy these basic psychological needs (e.g. autonomy, competence, and relatedness). Indeed, activities or sports that enhance autonomy, competence, or relatedness will results in athletes playing the particular sport for more self-determined reasons (Amorose, 2007; Ryan and Deci, 2000). However, when an athlete's basic psychological needs are not met, or are thwarted, athletes are more likely to play sport for less self-determined reasons such as external rewards or to avoid feeling guilt or shame in addition to experiencing decreased well-being (Bartholomew et al., 2010). As such, there is a direct association between the extent to which an athlete's needs are met, the type of motivation they have and the playing experiences – whether these are positive or negative (Vallerand and Ratelle, 2002).

The role of the coach in shaping an athlete's motivation

In their motivational model of the coach–athlete relationship, Mageau and Vallerand (2003) stated that the coach is the most important person in determining an athlete's motivation. In the subsequent years there have been a number of studies that explored this contention. For example, Amorose and Anderson-Butcher (2007) examined 581 athletes' perceptions of their coaches, how this was associated with their basic psychological needs, and motivation type. In support of SDT theory (Deci and Ryan, 1985, 2000; Mageau and Vallerand, 2003), coaching behaviours that were perceived as autonomy supportive coach behaviours (e.g. satisfying athlete's psychological needs) predicted intrinsic motivation, promoted continued engagement in sport, and enhanced athletic performance (Occhino et al., 2014). Isoard-Gautheur et al. (2012) found that autonomy coaching styles were linked to athletes' perceived competence and autonomy, but not to relatedness. Further, autonomy, competence, and relatedness were positively linked to self-determined motivation. That is, if handball players perceived their three psychological needs as being met, they were more likely to report playing handball for self-determined reasons. More recently, Amorose and Anderson-Butcher (2015) found that positive motivational responses increased as autonomy supportive coaching behaviours increased, and the most positive motivational outcomes were associated with athletes who perceived high levels of autonomy supportive coaching behaviours but low levels of controlling coach behaviours. Indeed, controlling coach behaviours were positively associated with amotivation, external regulation, and introjected regulation.

The studies by Amorose and Anderson-Butcher (2007, 2015) and Isoard-Gautheur et al. (2012) were cross-sectional so could not assess the effects of coaching styles over time on basic psychological needs and motivation. In order to address this limitation, Paige Pope and Wilson (2012) examined perceptions of coach support, basic psychological needs, and motivation across two waves (i.e. mid- and late-season) among rugby union players. Perceptions of greater support from the rugby players' coach were associated with players perceiving that their psychological needs were met, and playing rugby for self-determined reasons. Furthermore, when coaches were perceived as providing more support and basic psychological needs were met, the rugby players exerted more effort.

More recent research regarding the relationship between support and motivation among athletes has focused on the support provided by parents and coaches combined. For example, Amorose et al. (2016) explored the independent and interactive perceived support from coaches and parents on self-determined motivation among 335 high-school athletes. They found that autonomy support from coaches, fathers, and mothers related to self-determined motivation both independently and interactively. Indeed, a high-level of self-determined motivation was associated with at least two of the three agents (e.g. coach, mother, or father) providing autonomous support. Gaudreau et al. (2016) suggested that coach autonomy support is especially important when a young athlete perceives that they receive little support from their parents. Gaudreau and colleagues tested two hypotheses: (a) synergistic socialisation interaction (i.e. high levels of support are required from parents and coaches for optimal sporting outcomes) and (b) compensatory-protective interaction (i.e. coach autonomy support is important for an athlete to achieve optimal sporting outcomes when the athlete receives little support from their parents). In support of the compensatory-protective interaction hypothesis, Gaudreau et al. (2016) found that autonomy coaching support was more strongly related to psychological needs satisfaction, flow, sport motivation, and athletic achievement among athletes who received less support from their parents.

Overall, there is a significant body of evidence that links an athlete's perception of their coach's behaviour with basic psychological needs and motivation levels. In particular, autonomy supportive behaviours are associated with an athlete's psychological needs being met and more self-determined forms of motivation, whereas controlling coach behaviours are associated with psychological needs thwarting and less self-determined forms of motivation. In order to maximise coaching effectiveness, coaches could adopt or learn autonomy supportive coaching behaviours and refrain from controlling coaching styles. Evidence from non-sport domains indicates that teachers can learn to become more autonomy supportive to their students (Reeve, 1998), so it is plausible that coaches could also learn to adopt autonomy coaching styles, yet refrain from displaying controlling coach behaviours.

Coaching strategies to fulfil an athlete's basic psychological needs

In order to promote self-determined motivation, well-being, flow, and sports performance, coaches need to satisfy their athletes' basic psychological (e.g. autonomy, competence, and relatedness) needs. Amorose (2007), Mageau and Vallerand (2003), and Reeve (2009) provided some excellent suggestions, which formed the basis of an SDT intervention for coaches (i.e. Langan et al., 2015).

Techniques for coaches to enhance competence

- *Challenge the skills and abilities of athletes*: Coaches could design sporting drills that are difficult but attainable by the athletes if they exert their maximum effort. Amorose (2007) suggested that coaches and athletes could agree tasks and the difficulty before the drill starts.
- *Design meaningful, interesting, and skill-building drills*: Drills that coaches design should be congruent with athletes' goals (e.g. score goals, concede fewer baskets, make more tackles etc.). As such, athletes should be able to see how the drills relate to their goals and are meaningful to their sport. Further, the drills should be interesting so the athletes don't get bored, which can be achieved by adding a competitive element, which can be self-referenced, and involve athletes building upon their skills and thus promote skill development.
- *Provide choice within specific rules or limits*: Mageau and Vallerand (2003) suggested that athletes should be given options within set drills or tasks. For example, the coach can say the objective of a soccer drill is for the attackers to score a goal against the defenders, but it is up to the attackers how they attempt to score their goal.
- *Provide constructive feedback*: Amorose (2007) suggested that feedback from a coach could emphasise what the athlete could do to improve his or her performance, progress in his or her sport, or master particular challenges.

Techniques for coaches to enhance autonomy

- *Give athletes control*: Amorose (2007), Mageau and Vallerand (2003), and Reeve (2009) reported that coaches could relinquish control and give more control to the athletes, i.e. where possible, allow them to have input into the structure of training, match preparations, or travel arrangements. This may give the athletes a sense of ownership and empowerment, which could foster self-determined motivation.
- *Provide leadership and initiative opportunities*: Enabling athletes to experience a sense of autonomy is important, and this can be achieved by coaches providing their athletes with opportunities to lead others (Amorose, 2007) or use their own initiative (Mageau and Vallerand, 2003).
- *Goal setting*: Coaches could encourage athletes to set their own goals and devise strategies that will enable them to achieve their goals (Amorose, 2007). Advice on goal-setting strategies is presented in Chapter 4 of this book.

Techniques for coaches to enhance perceptions of relatedness

- *Develop the coach–athlete relationship*: The coach–athlete relationship is key to an athlete's psychological needs being met (Amorose, 2007; Mageau and Vallerand, 2003), so coaches could work on developing their relationship with players and managing any conflict when or if it arises. Information on improving the coach–athlete relationship and managing conflict is presented in Chapter 11 of this book.
- *Promote positive relationships with other players*: Coaches who work in team sports could devise activities that foster camaraderie among players to ensure that all players feel valued. This could also be achieved by not encouraging competition among team mates, or placing very little emphasis on the results of such competitions. Team-building activities may also help athletes feel a sense of relatedness. More information on team building and team cohesion is presented in Chapter 12 of this book.
- *Listen and acknowledge*: Coaches should listen to what their athletes say and acknowledge their feelings, rather than disregarding such feelings (Amorose, 2007).
- *Involve parents*: Amorose (2007) suggested that coaches should play an active role in involving an athlete's parents, especially among younger athletes. This is supported by more recent research (e.g. Amorose et al., 2016; Gaudreau et al., 2016), which demonstrated the importance of autonomy support from parents. As such, coaches could provide information to parents regarding how they can be more supportive to their children and better fulfil their basic psychological needs.

Controlling coaching behaviours

In order to fulfil athletes' basic psychological needs, coaches can deploy autonomy supportive coaching styles and behaviours. Additionally, they should also refrain from engaging in controlling coaching styles or behaviours. Bartholomew et al. (2010) described controlling behaviours that coaches should avoid. In particular, they identified six controlling behaviours:

- *Tangible rewards*: Coaches should refrain from using tangible rewards (e.g. medals, doing extra training sessions if a target is not achieved) to promote or manipulate a particular behaviour. These rewards decrease intrinsic motivation and put pressure on athletes.
- *Controlling feedback*: This occurs when coaches provide feedback that includes information about how a coach expects an athlete to behave (e.g. "Great footwork. I want you to do this in every match for the rest of the season and you might keep your place in the side"). Controlling feedback can also contain information pertaining to the coach demonstrating his or her power over the athlete, such as selection or de-selection.

- *Excessive personal control*: Coaches may try to force their opinions on their athletes, despite the athletes holding different opinions. For example, a coach might believe his or her team conceded five goals in the last match due to the players not understanding the defensive formation, whereas some of the players might believe it was due to their lack of conditioning. In instances where the coach exerts excessive personal control, he or she will ignore the thoughts and opinions of the players.
- *Intimidation behaviours*: This involves a coach verbally abusing players, threatening physical punishment, and/or personally attacking individual players. The aim of such behaviour is to humiliate and belittle players.
- *Promoting ego involvement*: Ego involvement refers to athletes judging their competence in comparison with other players, which can be caused by coaches regularly pitting athletes against one another and rewarding those who outperform the others. This form of coaching behaviour can threaten an athlete's self-esteem and result in athletes being motivated to protect their self-esteem.
- *Conditional regard*: This involves a coach offering attention, affection, and support when an athlete plays in a desired manner (e.g. wins a match, is aggressive in tackles, or is vocal to other team mates), but withdraws attention, affection, and support when the athlete does not perform desired behaviours. Further, some coaches may try to make athletes feel guilty if a particular behaviour is not displayed (e.g. "If you keep missing tackles, you're going to get me sacked").

The key to becoming more effective in fulfilling athletes' psychological needs is being aware of any controlling coaching behaviours and refraining from using these, in addition to increasing the use of behaviours that promote autonomy, competence, and relatedness. Although this may appear easy, Ahlberg et al. (2008) reported that this was particularly challenging, and required constant effort and reflection.

CASE STUDY 16.1 FULFILLING THE BASIC PSYCHOLOGICAL NEEDS OF A TEAM

Mikey is a 36-year-old accountant, who has just started coaching his son's under-15 team. The reason why Mikey started coaching his son's team is because the previous coach was asked to leave after shouting and upsetting the players. As such, some of the players left the club. Mikey is a Level 2 coach and coached a team whilst he was at university. He also undertook some reading in an attempt to adopt a different approach to the previous coach. In addition to shouting at players, the previous coach would punish players by making them do extra fitness training or humiliating them in front of other team mates. The previous coach was also very "up and down" with the players. Some days he would turn up to matches in a very jovial mood and be nice to players even if they made mistakes, but other days he would be in a foul mood and be very nasty to the players, so the players never knew what to expect. Some players often ended up in tears at training sessions and matches.

Mikey wanted to bring fun back to training and matches, so purposefully adopted a different approach. First and foremost, Mikey wanted a much better relationship with his players and started off each training session by spending 5–10 minutes listening to the players' thoughts and opinions of what they could do to improve as a team and also any concerns they had. This seemed to go down well with the players. Mikey also spoke to the parents and asked them not to berate players from the sidelines in matches and wanted any comments made on the touchline to be supportive of the players and the team. Mikey also asked players to adopt this approach during matches and training too.

In his new role, Mikey wanted the players to take ownership of training sessions and tactics, because for too long they had just followed instructions from the previous coach, so Mikey was not sure the players understood the reasons for employing such tactics and performing certain drills in training. As such, Mikey asked the team to think about what they needed to work on in order to improve and asked them to suggest drills and practice sessions to achieve these goals. The players really enjoyed this and Mikey believed that it helped them increase their understanding of tactics and their ability to solve problems during matches. Mikey had some input into the drills too, and offered advice on how they could be more meaningful and realistic of match situations. As the players suggested the areas they needed to work on and some of the drills to achieve this, the players had a good understanding of the rationale for each drill they took part in.

Finally, because the previous coach had knocked the confidence of some of the players, Mikey wanted to improve this and devised training sessions that challenged the players, but allowed the players to be able to complete certain tasks. As the players' skills and tactical awareness increased over the following weeks, Mikey gradually increased the task difficulty.

Case study reflection

Mikey took over the team in difficult circumstances and was aware of the inappropriate coaching styles of the previous coach and the effects this had on the players. As such, Mikey approached coaching differently in an attempt to undo some of the psychological damage caused by the previous coach. In particular, Mikey listened to the players more, gave them more input into training and tactics, and set increasingly difficult training tasks that challenged the players, but gave them a sense of achievement and confidence in their abilities when they were successful.

Summary points

- Self-determination theory (SDT) is concerned with how, why, and when people participate in different activities, such as sport.
- The most self-determined form of motivation is intrinsic motivation, which occurs when athletes play sport because they enjoy it.
- There are four types of extrinsic motivation: external regulation, introjected regulation, identified regulation, and integrated regulation.
- There are three basic psychological needs: (1) autonomy, (2) competence, and (3) relatedness.
- Coaches are instrumental in whether or not an athlete's basic psychological needs are fulfilled and the type of motivation.
- Coaches can adopt a variety of behaviours to fulfil their athletes' basic psychological needs and refrain from engaging in controlling behaviours to prevent needs thwarting.

Practice exam questions

1 Critically evaluate the self-determination theory.
2 Describe the importance of the basic psychological needs.
3 Discuss the role of the coach in fulfilling or thwarting an athlete's psychological needs.
4 Discuss how basic psychological needs are associated with motivation.
5 Discuss the importance of self-determined motivation.

Critical thinking questions: applying theory to practice

1 Reflect on your own practice and discuss your own coaching behaviours that may enhance autonomy.
2 Discuss ways in which you may have enhanced or undermined competence among players you have coached.
3 Discuss how you could enhance relatedness among players you coach.
4 Design your own SDT intervention for enhanced coaching effectiveness and provide a rationale for each component.
5 What advice would you provide to prevent coaches from thwarting an athlete's basic psychological needs?

Case study questions

1 Identify the coaching style adopted by the previous coach and justify your answers with supporting evidence.
2 Evaluate Mikey's approach to coaching, identifying the strengths and weaknesses of such an approach.
3 Describe other behaviours or strategies that Mikey could employ to fulfil the basic psychological needs of the players on his team.

17

PROMOTING ANTI-DOPING ATTITUDES AMONG ATHLETES

The purpose of this chapter is to provide information on doping, how coaches may influence attitudes towards doping and what they can do to reduce favourable attitudes towards doping and doping susceptibility. More specifically, this chapter contains information on:

- A definition of doping
- The doping problem in sport
- Physical health consequences of doping
- Mental health consequences of doping
- Why do athletes dope?
- The role of coaches in shaping attitudes towards doping
- Advice for coaches on promoting anti-doping attitudes among their athletes.

A definition of doping

According to the World Anti-Doping Agency's most recent code (WADA, 2015), doping is defined as the occurrence of anti-doping rule violations. WADA distinguish between (1) substances (e.g. anabolic agents, peptide hormones, diuretics) and methods (e.g. blood manipulation and gene doping) that are prohibited at all times, (2) substances and methods prohibited in competition (e.g. stimulants, narcotics, and cannabinoids), and (3) substances prohibited in particular sports (e.g. alcohol, beta blockers). Such prohibited substances and methods are often referred to as performance-enhancing drugs (PEDs). PEDs are added to WADA's banned list if they meet at least two of the three criteria: (1) there is evidence that the substance/method may enhance performance, (2) using the substance or method poses a health risk, and (3) the substance or method violates the spirit of sport (Bird et al., 2016).

The doping problem in sport

According to the White Paper on Sport (European Commission, 2007), commissioned in regards to European member states, the use of PEDs in sport represents a threat to European sport. This is because doping undermines the key principles of sport: (a) open and fair competition among athletes, and (b) it poses a threat to an athlete's physical (Johnson, 2012) and mental health (Lindqvist et al., 2014).

Although some coaches may view doping as only occurring within elite sport, and think that they do not have to worry about doping if they do not coach elite athletes, this viewpoint is inaccurate. A report by ESPAD (2011), containing students from 36 European countries, revealed that some athletes within grassroots sport also take PEDs. These worrying findings might be due a lack of awareness of what constitutes a doping offence among grassroots athletes, no/very little testing within low-level sport, and athletes being unaware of the dangers that PEDs can pose to both physical and mental health (Nicholls et al., 2015).

Physical health consequences of doping

Anabolic androgenic steroids (AAS), which account for nearly half of all doping offences in grassroots sport (European Commission, 2007), are associated with numerous and serious ill effects on the liver, heart, kidneys, and reproductive system in males (e.g. reduction in testicular size, sperm count, and sperm motility) and females (e.g. menstrual abnormalities and virilisation). These illnesses may be irreversible and can ultimately lead to premature death due to supraphysiological intakes (Bird et al., 2016). These are just the side effects for AAS, there are serious side effects for all banned substances and methods.

Mental health consequences of doping

In addition to numerous serious physical side effects, PEDs are also associated with many undesirable psychological health consequences. For example, AAS are widely accepted as being associated with adverse mental health (Bird et al., 2016), including extremely aggressive behaviour (Lumia and McGinnis, 2010) and a two-to-fourfold increased risk of suicide among former athletes (Lindqvist et al., 2014).

Why do athletes dope?

Donovan et al. (2002) developed a model, called the Sport Drug Control Model (SDCM), to explain why athletes might take PEDs (see Figure 17.1 for an adapted version). Perceived threat, perceived benefit, morality, legitimacy, friends and family, and personality are factors that they identified as influencing an athlete's attitude towards doping. The central premise of this model is that attitudes towards doping directly influence whether an athlete will comply or

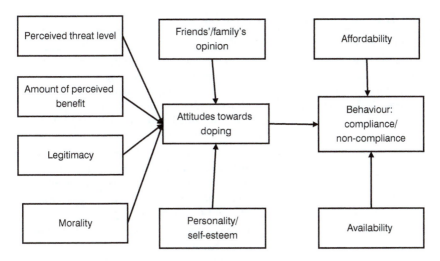

FIGURE 17.1 An adapted version of Donovan's SDCM

not comply with rules associated with performance-enhancing drugs and thus engage in or refrain from doping. Compliance and non-compliance is influenced by affordability and susceptibility.

Perceived threat

According to the authors of the SDCM (Donovan et al., 2002), the athlete evaluates the level of threat associated with taking performance-enhancing drugs, in relation to (a) enforcement and (b) health. It is the perceived level of threat that will influence an athlete's attitudes towards taking performance-enhancing drugs (see Table 17.1).

In addition to athletes evaluating whether they may get caught and the ramifications of testing positive for performance-enhancing drugs, athletes also evaluate the threat of taking performance-enhancing drugs on their health (see Table 17.2).

- *Perceived benefit*: Unlike the appraisals of threat, in which athletes focus on the possible harms that taking performance-enhancing drugs could cause, athletes appraise how they could benefit from taking performance-enhancing drugs. As such, athletes consider whether they can win without taking performance-enhancing drugs, the rewards of winning (e.g. prize money, sponsorships, or a higher salary), how effective performance-enhancing drugs are in enhancing performance, and the availability of the drugs. In his biography, Dwayne Chambers (2009), the banned sprinter, commented that he legitimised his use of performance-enhancing drugs based on his contract with a leading sportswear company. It was stipulated in his contract that he would lose some of his funding if he slipped out of

TABLE 17.1 Threats associated with enforcement

Enforcement	Evaluation
The likelihood of a test occurring either after a competition or outside of a competition (i.e. training)	If an athlete believes it is unlikely that he or she will be tested either after a competition or outside of competing, the athlete will perceive little threat of being caught. If he or she thinks a drugs test is likely to be carried out during a particular period, threat levels will be higher.
Perceived imminence of testing	If an athlete believes that he or she is going to be tested soon, then there is a greater chance that PEDs would be detected in a test. This would enhance threat levels and therefore reduce the likelihood of an athlete doping.
Perceived likelihood of drugs being detected	If an athlete thinks he or she is taking a PED that is undetectable due to advancements in testing being slower than the development of new drugs or methods, he or she will perceive less threat compared with taking a performance-enhancing drug which many other athletes have been caught taking.
Perceived severity of testing positive for performance-enhancing drugs	An athlete may consider the potential penalties of testing positive for performance-enhancing drugs. These may include the athlete not being able to achieve his or her goals due to suspensions, financial losses from not being able to compete due to a suspension, and being ostracised by coaches, friends, competitors, supporters, and/or sponsors. All of these factors influence threat levels.

TABLE 17.2 Threats to health associated with PEDs

Health	Evaluation
Likelihood of ill-health effect	The athlete makes a judgement regarding how likely it is that taking performance-enhancing drugs will cause a health problem (e.g. increase risk of heart disease, fertility problems, or reduced lifespan etc.).
Imminence of ill-health effect	Athletes evaluate when any ill-health effects may occur. If an athlete perceives that such ill health effects are not likely to occur for many years, then the perceived threat is thought to be lower.
Reversibility of ill-health effect	An athlete may evaluate whether any ill-health effects will be reversible or not. If an athlete perceives that the side effects are irreversible, he or she is less likely to dope.
Severity of ill-health effect	The athlete may also evaluate how severe any ill-health effects may be.

the world's top three 100 metre sprinters. Despite taking a cocktail of PEDs, Chambers felt that the improvement in his personal best from 9.97 seconds when clean to 9.87 seconds after a year after being on a doping regime, could have been achieved naturally and without cheating.

- *Legitimacy*: Legitimacy refers to the extent to which organisations (e.g. WADA, UKAD etc.) are viewed as being valid organisations and have power within the process of doping control. As such, this construct refers to the perceived authority of anti-doping organisations to monitor and punish doping offences (Nicholls et al., 2015).
- *Morality*: An athlete's attitude towards taking performance-enhancing drugs is affected by his or her own personal morality. For some athletes, taking performance-enhancing drugs would be completely out of the question, because they oppose them so much, whereas others may not be opposed to taking performance-enhancing drugs.
- *Friends'/family's opinion*: Friends and family play a strong role in influencing an athlete's attitudes towards taking performance-enhancing drugs. If an athlete's family and/or peers support the use of taking performance-enhancing drugs, then it is likely that the athlete will have an attitude that supports doping.
- *Personality/self-esteem*: The athlete's personality also influences their attitude towards doping. Seligman (1991) identified optimism as a factor that might influence whether an athlete will take performance-enhancing drugs. Optimism refers to whether an athlete believes in his or her ability to be successful and has implications for athletes attributing to failure. Optimists attribute any failures to external sources (e.g. weather, illness, referee, or crowd), whereas a pessimistic individual attributes failure to internal sources (e.g. technique or fitness). Pessimists are thought to be more predisposed to taking performance-enhancing drugs, because they believe that failure is something that is permanent and related to themselves.
- *Affordability*: In order for an athlete to be able to take performance-enhancing drugs, they need to be affordable so that the athlete can purchase them.
- *Availability*: In addition to the athlete being able to afford the performance-enhancing drugs, they need to be able to get hold of them.

Two studies (Gucciardi et al., 2011a; Jalleh et al., 2014) quantitatively examined the SDCM and one study (Nicholls et al., 2015) qualitatively examined this model. With a sample of elite Australian athletes, Gucciardi and colleagues found some support for the SDCM, as benefit appraisals, threat appraisals, and morality (cheating) were strongly related to doping attitudes. Friends'/family's opinions, self-esteem, and legitimacy, however, were not associated with doping attitudes. Jalleh et al. (2014) found some similar but also contrasting findings to Gucciardi et al (2011a). In Jalleh's study, legitimacy, friends'/family's opinions, and morality were related to doping attitudes. It should be noted that Gucciardi et al. (2011a) and Jalleh et al. (2014) included Australian athletes, so the SDCM is yet to be tested among athletes of different nationalities or indeed younger athletes.

Nicholls et al. (2015) qualitatively explored the relevance of the SDCM (Donovan et al., 2002) in relation to adolescent athletes who participated in sport within the United Kingdom, Australia, Hong Kong, and the United States. These authors interviewed coaches who lived and worked in these countries, regarding their opinions about adolescent athletes' attitudes towards doping. On the whole, Nicholls et al. (2015) found support for the SDCM, but also found some subtle differences, which led to them creating the Sport Drug Control Model for Adolescent Athletes (SDCM-AA; see Figure 17.2 for an adapted version).

Factors such as stress levels, nationality, ethnicity, competitive level, and maturation were identified as influencing attitudes towards doping among adolescents, but were not in the original SDCM. In particular, the coaches argued that adolescent athletes who experienced sustained stress may be more likely to have a favourable attitude towards doping. Adolescent athletes competing at lower levels may also have a more favourable attitude towards doping due to (a) a lack of testing, (b) a lack of education, and/or (c) wanting to reach the elite level. Both ethnicity and country of residence were also found to influence doping attitudes, as an Australian coach commented that some ethnic groups can have a natural size advantage over other groups, which may mean a more favourable attitude towards doping among those who want to try to get bigger. Another coach felt there were differences in attitudes towards doping among athletes from different countries. Finally, maturation levels were viewed as a factor that might influence doping, as those who are more physically immature may see doping as a way of reducing the advantage of their physically mature counterparts.

The role of coaches in shaping attitudes towards doping

A study by Morente-Sánchez and Zabala (2015) examined coaches' knowledge, attitudes, and beliefs about doping. These authors found that although most of the coaches were not tolerant of doping among their players, 84.9 per cent of the coaches had no knowledge about which drugs were on the prohibited list, yet 39.2 per cent recommended that their players used supplements. This lack of knowledge is very worrying, because coaches could unwittingly recommend that their athletes take banned substances which may have a variety of undesirable health consequences. Further, recommending that athletes take supplements could also lead to athletes doping in the future, because Backhouse et al. (2013) reported that taking nutritional supplements can lead to athletes developing favourable attitudes towards doping. Anti-doping education rarely features on coach education syllabuses, and there is a strong focus on coaches learning about technical and tactical components of sport (Chesterfield et al., 2010).

Despite some coaches possessing very little knowledge of doping (Morente-Sánchez and Zabala, 2015), there is evidence that coaches are key personnel members within an athlete's entourage who may facilitate widespread doping

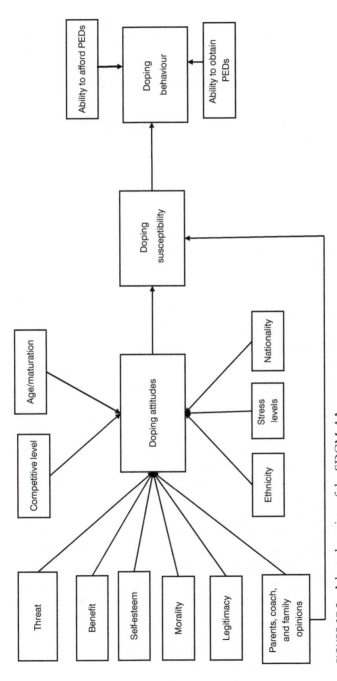

FIGURE 17.2 Adapted version of the SDCM-AA

among athletes (Ungerleider, 2013). There is also evidence, however, that coaches may act as a protective mechanism against doping, and thus reduce doping among the athletes they coach. For example, Erickson et al. (2015) interviewed 10 athletes regarding the factors that are likely to prevent athletes from using PEDs, and found that a strong attachment to a coach was likely to serve as a protective factor. Indeed, these authors stated that coaches influence decision making, effort exerted, and commitment to sport. As such, coaches play a vital role in influencing whether athletes will dope or not.

Advice for coaches on promoting anti-doping attitudes among their athletes

There are a number of strategies that coaches can engage in to reduce favourable attitudes towards doping, and ultimately reduce doping behaviours. These include:

- *Building a strong coach–athlete relationship*: Erickson et al. (2015) indicated that secure attachments between the coach and the athlete serves as a protective mechanism against doping. As such, coaches concerned that their athletes might be at risk of doping should make a conscious effort to improve the coach–athlete relationship. Scholars (e.g. Mageau and Vallerand, 2003; Rhind and Jowett, 2010) provided useful guidelines, which are outlined in Chapter 11 of this book.
- *Education*: Coaches should educate athletes regarding the possible ill-health effects of doping – of which there are many – so the athletes are under no illusion about the consequences of doping. Table 17.3 could be presented to athletes.
- *Motivational climate*: Coaches should ensure that there is no pressure within the sporting environment for athletes to dope. This comes from the head coach, to medical staff, physiotherapists, and other players. That is, coaches and other staff should support athletes and reward improvement. This can be achieved by creating a task-oriented motivational climate rather than an ego-oriented motivational climate. See Chapter 15 for information on how to create the optimal motivational climate.
- *Emphasising improvement*: Coaches should provide information to his or her players to illustrate how they can become better. For example, performance profiling is an excellent psychological tool, which allows coaches and athletes to identify all of the improvements that they can make (see Chapter 5 of this book for more information). This can show the athlete that there are other ways than doping to enhance his or performance.
- *Emphasising an organisation's values*: Finally, a coach can state that taking a performance-enhancing drug is cheating and should be regarded as such. That is, the coach states his views and the organisation's (e.g. sport club or governing body) position on doping and how it is unacceptable.

TABLE 17.3 The possible health consequences of doping

Side effects for males	Side effects for females
Reduced sperm count	Facial hair
Infertility	Body hair
Reduced testicle size	Decrease or loss of breasts
Baldness	Swelling of clitoris
Development of breasts	Deepened voice
Increased risk of prostate cancer	Hair loss
Splayed teeth	Acne
Forehead overgrowth	
Acne	

CASE STUDY 17.1   THE POWER OF THE COACH

Trevor is a 20-year-old rugby union player, who combines studying for a university degree with playing for a Premiership club's academy team, and plays as a hooker. He is yet to make his first team debut, but is a regular for the reserve side. He recently had a chat with the club's head coach because his contract was due to expire at the end of the season, in three months' time. The conversation was as follows:

Coach: I like you as a player, you've got a great skill set, a good attitude, and you are popular with the boys. In order to offer you a contract extension, you are going to have to get bigger and more powerful. I know you are still young, but you can see yourself that some of the younger players are bigger than you, and I am just not sure that you are going to be big enough to play in the premiership.

Trevor: I know some of the boys coming through are pretty big and some of the first teamers are able to dominate me at scrum time. I just do not know what to do. I've always done everything the strength and conditioning coaches ask me to do, but it just does not seem to have any effect.

Coach: Are you taking anything, supplement wise?

Trevor: Just the protein shakes.

Coach: Have you thought about taking other supplements, to try to give you an advantage?

Trevor: I've thought about it, and looked stuff up on the internet as I know some of the other boys are taking stuff, but that kind of thing scares me.

Coach:	Don't let it scare you, it's all legit stuff and it won't harm you.
Trevor:	What about the testers?
Coach:	You academy boys never get tested, and besides, I know of a product that is not on the banned list, as the testers don't know about it. It's good stuff and could be just what you need.
Trevor:	I'm not sure.
Coach:	It depends how much you want a professional career. It's your choice, but if it were me, I know what I would do. Anyway, let me know, if you want some you'll have to go to the gym on Stillingwold Road. Some of the other boys are on it, and it works wonders. Keep this chat to yourself though, as we don't want other people interfering in our business.

Case study reflection

Coaches have a very strong role in influencing the behaviour of the athletes they coach, as the case study suggests. Trevor displayed an unfavourable attitude towards taking supplements that may be banned and could result in a positive test. The coach tried to persuade Trevor that taking an unknown supplement might help his chances of securing a professional contract. Whether Trevor would go on and implement his coach's advice is unknown, but it is likely that some players would listen to their coach and take the supplement, despite not knowing the risks of doing so. It is important to note that most coaches will not be in favour of PEDs, but coaches are a source of influence on their athletes.

Summary points

- Doping represents a violation of anti-doping rules, and includes banned methods and substances.
- Methods and substances may be banned at all times, in competition, or in particular sports.
- Doping violations can occur at all levels of sport.
- There are many physical health consequences associated with doping, which include damage to the liver, heart, and kidneys.
- Taking PEDs can result in a number of mental health problems such as aggression and athletes being more at risk of committing suicide.
- The SDCM model and the SDCM-AA both attempt to explain why athletes dope.
- Coaches influence whether or not athletes will dope.

Practice exam questions

1   Discuss whether doping in sport should be allowed.
2   Discuss the dangers of doping.
3   Critically evaluate the Sport Drug Control Model (Donovan et al., 2002).
4   Discuss the differences and similarities between adult and adolescent athletes in regard to factors that influence doping attitudes.
5   Discuss the role of the coach in influencing whether an athlete will decide to dope or not.

Critical thinking questions: applying theory to practice

1   Discuss ways in which a coach may cause an athlete to dope.
2   Discuss how a coach might prevent an athlete from doping.
3   How could you use the Sport Drug Control Model and the Sport Control Drug Model for Adolescent Athletes to form a doping intervention?
4   If you were devising anti-doping education aimed at coaches who coached (a) adult athletes and (b) adolescent athletes, what differences would there be, and why?
5   Reflect on the ways you might have promoted anti-doping attitudes within your own coaching practice.

Case study questions

1   Discuss what other strategies the coach could implement to help Trevor increase his bulk and power.
2   Discuss the influence of the coach on Trevor.
3   Discuss the impact of coaches who encourage their players to take supplements.

PART VI

Developing mental skills among athletes

18

MENTAL IMAGERY

The purpose of this chapter is to provide information on mental imagery so that coaches can provide imagery training. This chapter includes information on:

- A definition of mental imagery
- The content of mental imagery
- The 4 Ws of mental imagery
- The benefits of mental imagery
- Theoretical models of imagery
- Imagery perspective
- Imagery ability
- The PETTLEP approach
- Different types of imagery content
- Providing athletes with mental imagery training
- Optimising mental imagery training.

A definition of mental imagery

Mental imagery represents "those quasi-sensory and quasi-perceptual experiences of which we are self-consciously aware and which exist for us in the absence of those stimulus conditions that are known to produce their genuine sensory perceptual counterparts" (Richardson, 1969: 2–3). That is, mental imagery refers to the process of an athlete using his or her imagination to see themself performing a movement (e.g. running) or a certain skill (e.g. catching a high ball in rugby or heading the ball in soccer).

The content of mental imagery

The title "mental imagery" might infer that it only includes images of what an athlete wants to achieve. This would only be partially correct, as a very important part of mental imagery is the feelings that athletes create. Coaches should make sure, when they develop mental imagery programmes, to also include a number of other elements when asking athletes to engage in mental imagery. Munroe et al. (2000) found that in addition to visual images, imagery would be more effective if coaches included:

- Feelings of performing a particular skill (e.g. bodily feelings associated with kicking the ball, such as the leg muscles contracting and the feeling in the foot)
- Noises associated with the task (e.g. the noise made when a cricketer strikes a ball for six runs)
- Smells associated with the image (e.g. the smell of the freshly mown grass on the golf course).

By asking athletes to incorporate visions, feelings, noises, and smells within their mental images, coaches have the potential to make imagery more realistic and thus more beneficial for the athlete.

The 4 Ws of mental imagery

Munroe et al. (2000) explored where, when, why, and what athletes imagine among a sample of 14 elite sports performers from seven different sports. This information is particularly useful for coaches who wish to design imagery interventions. Athletes engaged in imagery during competition and training, but imaged more prior to competing. The athletes used imagery to help them learn new skills or tactics, to regulate their arousal levels, or to improve confidence. Finally, the athletes imaged a variety of different things such as their surroundings and making technical corrections.

The benefits of mental imagery

According to Martin et al. (1999) more than 200 studies have been published on the topic of mental imagery. These studies have revealed that mental imagery can influence a variety of constructs:

- *Performance*: Sport performance in a particular skill can be enhanced by an athlete imaging that same skill being performed (Driskell et al., 1994; Pain et al., 2011).
- *Skill acquisition*: Beauchamp et al. (1996) reported that imagery can enhance how people acquire skills. From a coaching perspective, mental imagery may be particularly useful for athletes who are learning new skills.

- *Confidence*: Mental imagery can enhance the confidence of athletes. For example, Callow and Walters (2005) and Nordin and Cumming (2005) found that positive imagery and facilitative imagery, respectively, enhanced self-confidence. That is, imagery associated with athletes being successful helped confidence levels.
- *Flow*: Pain et al. (2011) explored the effects of an imagery intervention and music among soccer players and found that both imagery and music helped athletes access the flow state. Flow is associated with enjoyment and fun, and highly regarded as a positive psychological state.
- *Concentration*: A study by Calmels et al. (2004) revealed that softball players, who were trained in mental imagery, could make sense of more external stimuli without being overloaded.
- *Injury*: Ievleva and Orlick (1991) found that imagery can help speed up recovery when athletes are injured, reduce the level of skill deterioration, and help them cope with pain.

Mental imagery appears to have a number of benefits, so it is a useful psychological skill that coaches could train their athletes in.

Theoretical models of imagery

It is important that coaches understand how a mental imagery intervention might help an athlete's sporting performance. This is because athletes might ask their coach how mental imagery influences performance. Four different theories have been proposed, which attempted to explain how mental imagery may influence performance:

1 *The psychoneuromuscular theory*: This theory, which was developed by Carpenter (1894), states that the muscles used in the performance of skills such as goal kicking in soccer, forehand in table tennis, or a putt in golf become innervated when the athlete imagines themself performing the particular skill.
2 *Symbolic learning theory*: This theory was proposed by Sackett (1934), who stated that mental imagery helps athletes' performance by enabling them to understand and acquire the different movement patterns required to execute tasks associated with sports performance (e.g. tennis serve, golf swing, or lay-up in basketball). That is, imagery acts as a coding system in which the individual becomes familiar with the sequence of movements that make up a skill.
3 *Bioinformational theory*: This theory, which was proposed by Lang (1977), indicates that movement patterns are stored in the long-term memory and that engaging in mental imagery strengthens the memory of these movement patterns. Lang suggested that images are stored as stimulus propositions (i.e. relevant stimuli associated with performing a movement, such as spectators

being present or the smell of the sporting arena) and response propositions (i.e. the athlete's responses to the stimuli, such as the athlete experiencing tension in his stomach when he thinks about the crowd, or the feelings of excitement when the athlete smells the gymnasium in which he or she is used to playing volleyball).

4   *Triple code model:* Ahsen (1984) proposed the triple code model as an explanation of how imagery facilitates performance. In this model, Ahsen argued that mental imagery provides a sense of reality to the athlete, which enables him or her to interact as though they are interacting with the real world. This then stimulates physiological responses (e.g. increased heart-rate), so imagery provides meaning to the athlete so that when they perform the movements for real, they will know what it means. Essentially, this model proposes that imagery prepares the athlete to perform by creating a sense of reality.

There is some evidence to support each of the different theories. From a coaching perspective, most athletes may be more interested in knowing that imagery will enhance their sporting performance or psychological well-being rather than the mechanisms by which imagery works.

Imagery perspective

When a coach asks an athlete to engage in mental imagery, the athlete is likely to have one of two different views in his or her head. These two views are referred to as internal imagery and external imagery.

- *Internal imagery:* Athletes who see their images internally will have images that represent what they would see through their own eyes when they perform a particular skill. For example, a golfer hitting a putt will see the ball and the club head from the same view as though he or she were stood over the ball and about to hit the putt.
- *External imagerys:* With external images, the athletes sees himself or herself, as through the lens of a camera.

On the whole, athletes tend to have a preference for either internal or external imagery, although some athletes can interchange between internal and external images (Murphy, 1990). A coach can find out the imagery perspective of an athlete by simply asking the athlete to describe what he or she sees when they image, and whether the images are as though the athlete was looking through their own eyes or whether they were looking at themselves as though through a camera.

With regard to the effects of internal or external imagery on sporting performance, coaches should be aware that neither internal imagery nor external imagery is more beneficial to the performer than the other. Therefore, coaches should encourage athletes to use the perspective they are comfortable with, even if this means that some athletes will interchange between perspectives, as many Olympic athletes interchange on a very frequent basis (Murphy, 1990).

Imagery ability

Imagery ability refers to an athlete's proficiency in engaging in mental imagery. Athletes who are able to create very detailed pictures, smells, noises, and feelings in their mind are regarded as having high imagery ability. Conversely, athletes who struggle to create pictures, smells, noises, and feelings are regarded as having low imagery ability.

Imagery ability is very important because it determines the extent to which an imagery intervention will be effective. For example, Robin et al. (2007) found that tennis players with high imagery ability benefited more from imagery training than players with low imagery ability. As such, coaches need to consider the imagery ability of their athletes and understand that imagery interventions may be more effective for some athletes compared with others. Additionally, the benefits of imagery interventions may take longer to come to fruition for some athletes compared with others.

Sport psychologists have measured the imagery ability for many years. A questionnaire that can be used to assess an athlete's imagery ability is the Test of Ability in Movement Imagery (TAMI) (Madan and Singhal, 2013). The TAMI instructs participants to imagine five body movements and then select the final body position from different images. As such, there is a correct answer for each question, and scores cannot be inflated by athletes (Madan and Singhal, 2014). Although imagery ability is very important in determining the effectiveness of any intervention (Robin et al., 2007), coaches should understand that imagery ability can be improved with practice. That is, the detail in images and the control an athlete has over his or her images can improve with practice (Rodgers et al., 1991).

The PETTLEP approach

Holmes and Collins (2001) created some guidelines that coaches can use when developing imagery interventions for their athletes, with the view of making these interventions more effective. This approach is grounded in cognitive neuroscience in that the authors believe the brain stores memories that are accessed when (a) athletes perform different sports and (b) they imagine themselves playing sport. As such the PETTLEP approach indicates that coaches should ensure that their imagery interventions contain key elements, which form the PETTLEP acronym. This stands for physical, environment, task, timing, learning, emotion, and perspective.

- *Physical*: Coaches may have the view that asking athletes to lie on a couch or bed and close their eyes whilst they are engaging in mental imagery is beneficial. However, the PETTLEP approach disagrees with this and suggests that the athlete should be physically involved, because this makes mental imagery more realistic. Murphy et al. (2008) identified two particular methods by which coaches could include an element of physicality into imagery interventions. First, an athlete could perform the imagery in the kit that he or she normally performs in and hold a piece of equipment. For example, a hooker in rugby union who wants to practise line out throwing, would wear his match kit, hold the ball, stand on the sideline from which throws are taken, and then engage in mental imagery. Athletes may feel self-conscious performing imagery in their kit, but coaches should emphasise the importance of imagery being as realistic as possible. Additionally, athletes could also incorporate movement into their imagery, although coaches should ensure that it is safe for athletes to engage in imagery whilst moving. For example, a tennis player could perform the movements associated with a serve whilst closing his or her eyes and mentally imaging the serve.

- *Environment*: In order to make imagery training more realistic, coaches should ensure that imagery scripts include information regarding details of the environment that their athlete performs in. Furthermore, coaches could provide athletes with photographs or videos of different competition venues which the athlete can look at before engaging in mental imagery. This may be particularly useful for athletes who will be performing at new venues.

- *Task*: Coaches should ask the athlete to describe what he or she focuses on when performing the skill and whether they have any typical thoughts when performing skills. Once these have been collated by the coach, he or she can include these in imagery scripts, so that the athlete thinks about the same things whilst imaging as he or she does when performing the task in real-life.

- *Timing*: Athletes should be encouraged by their coach to image in real time, so that the imaging of a task corresponds to the athlete actually performing the task. Therefore, coaches should discourage athletes from engaging in slow-motion imagery or imagery that is speeded up.

- *Learning*: As athletes progress in their chosen sport, they will become more proficient by learning new skills. As athletes learn new skills, their memories will also change over time as a function of learning and practice. Coaches should therefore regularly update imagery scripts or imagery training so that it takes into account learning that has taken place by the athlete. That is, imagery scripts should closely reflect the athlete's current stage of learning (Murphy et al., 2008).

- *Emotion*: Participating in sport can evoke a variety of pleasant (e.g. happiness) and unpleasant emotions (e.g. anger; Nicholls et al., 2010), and this should be represented in imagery scripts. This will make imagery scripts more realistic and has the potential to strengthen the memory of athletes. However, Murphy et al. (2008) suggested that emotions associated with successful performances should be included in imagery scripts, whereas inappropriate emotions should not be included as they may negatively influence performance. One might assume that pleasant emotions such as happiness may have a positive influence on performance, whereas unpleasant emotions negatively influence performance. However, this is not always the case as unpleasant emotions might have a positive effect on performance (Hanin, 2010). Coaches could therefore speak to athletes prior to designing the imagery intervention to identify emotions that the athlete perceives as being facilitative to performance. This may vary dramatically across different athletes, which is why imagery scripts should be individualised.

- *Perspective*: Coaches should not prescribe either the internal or external imagery perspective, but merely allow the athlete to use perspective or perspectives that they feel comfortable with. It is important that coaches encourage athletes to imagine the feelings that they normally experience when performing the task. Although not specifically stated by Holmes and Collins (2001), coaches could also encourage athletes to imagine noises and smells to increase the reality of the mental imagery even further.

The PETTLEP approach to mental imagery training is a useful guide for coaches, which is supported by research. Smith et al. (2007) found support for many aspects of the PETTLEP model. Indeed, Smith and colleagues found that athletes who imagined in the clothes they wear when competing, whilst at the competition venue performed better in comparison to athletes who imagined in non-sport clothing or at their home wearing non-sport clothes.

Different types of imagery content

In addition to the guidelines presented in the PETTLEP approach (Holmes and Collins, 2001), coaches should also consider the needs of the athlete and devise the imagery intervention based on those needs. Martin et al. (1999) proposed an applied imagery model that contained five types of imagery, along with explanations regarding when coaches could train their athletes in each specific form of imagery.

1 *Cognitive specific* (CS): Imagery that includes an athlete rehearsing different skills such as a goal kick in rugby union, a forehand in tennis, or a short-corner push in hockey is regarded as cognitive-specific imagery. Coaches can use CS imagery to help athletes learn new skills and enhance the performance of skills such as a backhand in tennis. Additionally, Martin et al. (1999) suggested that CS imagery can be used by athletes when they are in rehabilitation to help them maintain their skill level prior to sustaining their injury.
2 *Cognitive general* (CG): CG imagery includes imagery that relates to strategies an athlete might use when playing sport. This would include a rugby player imaging himself lining up in a defensive formation to defend an opponents'

attacking lineout or a hockey player imaging his or her tactics for an attacking short corner. CS imagery training can be given by coaches who want to help their athletes learn new tactics and enhance the performance of athletes when performing certain tactics.

3   *Motivational specific* (MS): Images that involve athletes seeing themselves winning important competitions, receiving a trophy from an official, or standing on a podium with a medal around their neck are classified as MS imagery. This type of imagery can be used by coaches to help athletes formulate goals relating to outcomes (e.g. results of competitions), performance (e.g. specific standards of performance), and processes (e.g. technical components associated with different skills).

4   *Motivational general-arousal* (MG-A): Imagery that includes how an athlete feels is considered MG-A imagery. As such, images that involve athletes with an increased heart-rate, sweaty hands, a nervous stomach, worry, and even being relaxed are considered MG-A images. This type of imagery will be useful for athletes who want to regulate their arousal levels. The coach should speak to the athlete to discover whether the athlete needs help in regulating his or her arousal, such as psyching the athlete up prior to competition or calming the athlete down before competition.

5   *Motivational general-mastery* (MG-M): Images of athletes coping effectively, feeling confident, and mentally tough are classified as MG-M images. If a coach thinks an athlete lacks confidence, he or she could provide the athlete with MG-M imagery training. This form of imagery might also be useful for athletes who struggle to maintain a positive attitude during competition.

Empirical evidence in the sport psychology literature provides varying degrees of support for the applied model proposed by Martin et al. (1999). For instance, only MG-M should be related to confidence. However, other studies have found that more than one imagery type is related to confidence (Callow and Hardy, 2001). From a coaching perspective, this is not a damning finding and means that although an imagery intervention may be geared towards helping an athlete learn a new skill, it is likely the intervention will improve the athlete's confidence level. As such, the model proposed by Martin et al. (1999) provides a useful framework for coaches when they design individualised imagery interventions.

Providing athletes with mental imagery training

The easiest way for a coach to help his or her athlete engage in mental imagery is to provide him or her with an imagery audio-file or an imagery script so that the athlete can create his or her own audio-file. Athletes can record the script onto a mobile phone or a voice recorder and then transfer it onto an MP3 player.

The imagery script provided in this chapter is generic, and is for an athlete who wants to improve his or her confidence. It is important that athletes have individualised imagery scripts depending on their needs. However, coaches could adapt and modify the imagery script based on the needs of their player. For instance, if a coach is working with an athlete who has problems controlling his or her anger, images relating to the athlete controlling his or anger could be included in the script, where the current script is focused on confidence and mental toughness.

Instructions

Before athletes start imaging, they should be made aware by the coach that they should be wearing the clothes they compete in, hold a piece of equipment associated with their sport (e.g. basketball, golf club, or tennis racquet, etc.). Ideally, they should be at a training venue or competition venue when engaging in the script. If a footballer is imaging himself or herself taking penalties he or she should be standing by the penalty spot in front of the goal.

Generic imagery script

"Imagine that you are about to perform a skill that is associated with your sport such as [insert your skill here]. As you partially exhale see yourself performing a [insert your skill]. When you have exhaled to the point where you feel comfortable, perform your skill again in your mind, feeling confident and mentally tough as you do so. Focus your thoughts on the things that you normally think about when performing your skill. Notice what you would normally feel when performing this skill. Feel the confidence in your body and the excitement about the challenge of performing. Notice the sense of ease and lightness whilst you are performing this skill. Almost as if performing [insert your skill] is effortless. Practise [insert your skill] several more times."

30 second pause in script

"Good, now rehearse [insert your skill] in different scenarios, in competitions and in environments that are realistic of where you perform. Make the skills you rehearse relevant to when you perform these skills in matches. See and feel yourself performing [insert your skill] successfully. As in competitions, there will be other people around such as coaches or other competitors. Imagine these others present, but don't let them rush you. Notice how the focus of your concentration shifts from a broad focus as you are looking around to a very narrow focus, as you prepare to execute [insert your skill]. Imagine feeling that you have the ability to meet any challenges you are faced with during your competition. Practise [insert your skill] now making it as realistic as possible. Notice the sounds, smells, and feelings in your body as you mentally image the skill. Take some time to mentally practise these skills."

2 minute pause in script

"That's fine. Now imagine you are about to perform [insert your skill] and you are feeling a little nervous, because you want to perform well. You can stop your worrying by taking a breath and imagining yourself performing with confidence and mental toughness."

30 second pause in script

"Imagine yourself feeling confident in your preparation and focused on your next competition."

20 second pause in script

"You imagine that your pre-competition warm-up goes very well and you remind yourself that you are ready to face the challenge of unexpected obstacles. You notice how confident you feel in your ability to re-focus after any distractions and remind yourself that you are mentally tough. You feel energised and ready to compete."

End of script

Optimising mental imagery training

- It is important that athletes realise that mentally imagery is a skill. Like all skills, athletes should be told that good quality imagery practice will help them improve their imagery ability and thus the impact this has on their sports performance.
- The generic imagery script provided in this chapter will last around eight minutes if it is unaltered. Coaches should ask athletes to listen to the script twice a day for the first week and then once a day for the following week. After this period, coaches could ask their athletes to use the script prior to competition.
- Athletes should be told and encouraged to listen to the imagery script before training sessions.

Summary points

- Mental imagery refers to the process of an athlete using his or her imagination to see themself performing a movement or a certain skill.
- Mental imagery includes visions, feelings, noises, and smells associated with executing a skill.
- There are numerous benefits associated with mental imagery, which include increased performance, confidence, and concentration.

CASE STUDY 18.1   HELPING A BADMINTON PLAYER MANAGE HIS ANXIETY

Christine is a 45-year-old badminton coach who has been coaching badminton players for almost 20 years. She is currently coaching a club-level player called George, who is keen to play in competitions. George is a 51-year-old accounts executive, who has recently complained to Christine that he suffers with anxiety during competitions. George's symptoms are manifested as worry, sweaty palms, increased heart-rate, tension in his stomach, and his muscles feel heavy. When hearing this information, Christine asked some questions regarding George's feelings, such as instances that trigger these feelings. George said that he experienced those negative feelings when he wanted to win an important point or in matches that were very tight.

Christine told George that a mental imagery intervention was something that could benefit him. She explained what would be involved and asked for George's feelings and he was keen to receive some imagery training. Prior to the training starting, Christine asked George to complete the TAMI (Madan and Singhal, 2013) and found that George had moderate imagery ability, so could benefit from the intervention.

The imagery intervention was guided by the PETTLEP principles, so when George received the imagery audio-file, he was asked to listen to it in his match kit, at match venues, whilst holding his badminton racquet. At first, George felt self-conscious doing this, so he arranged to arrive at match venues early so no one could see him engaging in the imagery.

George's intervention involved MG-A images, as George imagined controlling his emotions and successfully recovering. George listened to the script before matches and training sessions for over a month and commented that he really benefited to the extent that he no longer needed to listen to the audio-file as he naturally engaged in imagery. With regard to his performance, George felt that he had made small improvements, but the biggest and most welcome improvement was how he felt.

Case study reflection

In this instance, the intervention had a positive effect on the negative emotions and the symptoms that George experienced, but less impact on George's performance. Sometimes psychological interventions, such as imagery, may have little or no impact on performance. Just because an intervention may not influence sport performance, it does not mean it has been ineffective. Indeed, interventions that improve the psychological well-being of athletes, regardless of how they affect sport performance, should be considered successful.

- It does not matter whether an athlete engages in internal or external imagery.
- It is important that coaches consider the imagery ability of an athlete before initiating imagery training.
- The PETTLEP (Holmes and Collins, 2001) and the applied model of mental imagery (Martin et al., 1999) are useful guidelines for coaches who want to develop an imagery intervention for their athletes.

Practice exam questions

1 Compare and contrast the different theories of mental imagery.
2 Describe the 4 Ws of mental imagery, as proposed by Munroe et al. (2000) and their implications for sports performance.
3 Discuss the potential benefits of providing imagery training for athletes.
4 Imagery perspective matters. Discuss.
5 To what extent is imagery ability important? Discuss.

Critical thinking questions: applying theory to practice

1 Describe the imagery training you would provide for a golfer who is new to the sport and justify your choice with evidence.
2 One of your players has experienced a drop in confidence. Describe what you would do and how you would help the player with mental imagery.
3 Critically evaluate the PETTLEP (Holmes and Collins, 2001) approach to imagery in relation to developing imagery interventions.
4 Discuss the importance of matching the imagery type with an athlete's needs.
5 How would you describe to an athlete how mental imagery improves performance if they asked you to do so?

Case study questions

1 What could Christine have done if George had a low score on the TAMI?
2 Create an MG-A script that was used to help George.
3 If the imagery intervention had little impact on George, what else could Christine have done?

19

MENTAL TOUGHNESS TRAINING

This chapter provides coaches with information regarding how they can develop the mental toughness of their athletes. In particular, this chapter provides information on:

- Defining mental toughness
- Conceptual models of mental toughness
- Gucciardi et al.'s (2008) model of mental toughness among Australian footballers
- The development of mental toughness
- Overview of mental toughness interventions
- Mental toughness training for coaches.

Defining mental toughness

Defining and conceptualising mental toughness is quite a contentious issue (Andersen, 2011), which resulted in several heated arguments within the sport psychology literature (see Clough et al., 2012; Gucciardi et al., 2012, 2013 for such arguments and counter-arguments). Gucciardi et al. (2015) suggested that it is normal for scholars to disagree with each other, especially when a new area of research emerges in the literature and there is uncertainty regarding what a construct (i.e. mental toughness) is and what it is not. Given the lack of agreement regarding conceptualising and defining mental toughness, it would be inappropriate to present only one definition of mental toughness.

Clough and Strycharczyk (2012: 1) defined mental toughness as "The quality which determines in large part how people deal effectively with challenge, stressors and pressure ... irrespective of prevailing circumstances." Alternatively, Gucciardi et al. (2015: 28) defined mental toughness as "a personal capacity to produce consistently high levels of subjective performance (e.g. sales or grade point average) despite everyday challenges and stressors as well as significant adversities", whereas

Hardy et al. (2014: 70) defined it as "the ability to achieve personal goals in the face of pressure from a wide range of different stressors". Although there may be differences in the conceptual models proposed by these authors regarding what mental toughness is, there are some similarities within the definitions such as achieving one's goals or performing well despite encountering stressors or pressure.

Conceptual models of mental toughness

There are three prominent conceptual models of mental toughness. The 4 Cs model of mental toughness (Clough et al., 2002), the model proposed by Gucciardi et al. (2008), and the neuropsychological model of mentally tough behaviour (Hardy et al., 2014) are described in this chapter.

The 4 Cs model of mental toughness

According to Gucciardi et al. (2011b) the 4 Cs model of mental toughness is the most dominant in terms of peer reviewed research. This model, which is grounded in Kobasa's (1979) theory of hardiness, suggests that mental toughness consists of challenge, commitment, control, and confidence.

- *Challenge*: This refers to athletes viewing sporting situations (e.g. being 1–0 down in a soccer match) as being changeable. Athletes high in challenge would perceive competitive events as an opportunity rather than a threat.
- *Commitment*: Athletes who score highly on this quality have a tendency to involve themselves in sporting situations, rather than alienate themselves from an encounter.
- *Control*: This relates to athletes feeling and acting as if they are in control of the sporting situation.
- *Confidence*: An athlete who scores highly on this construct will have a strong sense of self-belief and an unshakable faith concerning his or her ability to achieve success. This model has received criticism from sport psychology researchers, who have suggested that the model represents hardiness, with the addition of confidence. As such, (Connaughton et al., 2008a) argued that it does not encapsulate mental toughness. More recently, however, Weinberg and Butt (2011) suggested that mental toughness and hardiness share a common thread.

Gucciardi et al.'s (2008) model of mental toughness among Australian footballers

The model proposed by Gucciardi et al. (2008) is grounded in Kelly's (1991) Personal Construct Theory (PCT). PCT indicates that individuals try to make sense of themselves and their environment by developing theories about the world. Gucciardi and colleagues identified three dimensions of mental toughness, which included:

1   *Characteristics:* 11 characteristics of mental toughness were identified (self-belief, work ethic, personal values, self-motivation, tough attitude, concentration and focus, resilience, handling pressure, emotional resilience, sport intelligence, and physical toughness).
2   *Behaviours:* Athletes who are mentally tough prepare well for competitions, recover well from injuries, and perform consistently at sport.
3   *Situations:* Within Australian Rules football there are (a) general and (b) competition situations in which athletes demonstrate mental toughness. The general situations included athletes being mentally tough when going through their rehabilitation programme and when they prepared for sport. Athletes also demonstrated mental toughness in dealing with competition pressures (e.g. match environment, competing whilst fatigued, and experiencing decreases in confidence).

The neuropsychological model of mentally tough behaviour

This theory (Hardy et al., 2014) is grounded in Gray and McNaughton's (2000) revised Reinforcement Sensitivity Theory (rRST), which originated from neuropsychological research, with Hardy viewing mental toughness as a behaviour. Hardy and colleagues believed this theory was relevant to mental toughness as reward sensitivity was associated with only mild reactions to threatening situations (Perkins and Corr, 2006) and high performance (Perkins et al., 2007). Conversely, punishment sensitivity was associated with unfavourable appraisals of one's ability to manage pain (Muris et al., 2007), avoiding threatening situations (Perkins and Corr, 2006), and performing poorly (Perkins et al., 2007). Interestingly, the cricket players in the Hardy study who were rated by their coach as being the most mentally tough were insensitive to rewards, but sensitive to punishment. Hardy argued that mentally tough players are able to identify any threats much quicker than their less mentally tough counterparts, which gives these players more time to initiate effective strategies and behaviours to deal with pressurised situations and thus maintain their performance. This is somewhat supported by Nicholls et al. (2016c) who revealed that the most mentally tough athletes were more aware of unsupportive coach behaviours than the less mentally tough athletes. Furthermore, Gucciardi et al. (2016) reported a link between behaviour and mental toughness, in that behavioural persistence was associated with mental toughness on a 20 metre shuttle run. As such, the findings of Nicholls et al. (2016) and Gucciardi et al. (2016) provide some support for Hardy's neuropsychological model of mental toughness.

The development of mental toughness

Researchers also examined how athletes become more mentally tough throughout their career. Bull et al. (2005) were among the first to reveal that mental toughness developed over time, but Bull and colleagues did not explore how mental toughness developed in an athlete's career (Connaughton et al., 2008a). Nevertheless, the Bull et al. study paved the way for more rigorous studies that explored how mental toughness develops.

Connaughton et al. (2008b) interviewed seven athletes regarding how the 12 attributes, proposed by Jones et al. (2002), developed in the early, middle, and later years of an athlete's career. They found that during the early years an unshakeable self-belief in achieving goals, an unshakeable belief that the athlete possesses the unique qualities and abilities to make him or her better than their opponents, and an insatiable desire to succeed were developed. In an athlete's later years, switching sport focus on and off as required, remaining fully focused on the task at hand in the face of competition-specific distractions, not being adversely affected by others' performances, and remaining fully focused in the face of personal life distractions developed.

The next study to explore how mental toughness developed was by Gucciardi et al. (2009b), who took a different perspective to Connaughton et al. (2008b), by asking Australian football coaches for their perceptions regarding the development of mental toughness. The coaches said that early childhood experiences, football experiences, coach–athlete relationships, coaching philosophy, training environment, and specific strategies influenced the development of mental toughness. Interestingly, Gucciardi and colleagues found that coaches could hinder the development of mental toughness of their players. This could happen if the coach let their desire for success, rather than the development of the athlete, overrule what they did.

Thelwell et al. (2010), who reverted to the strategy adopted by Connaughton et al. (2008a), asked the athletes to provide information on how they felt their mental toughness developed. Thelwell and colleagues interviewed 10 gymnasts and created four dimensions regarding how mental toughness is developed:

1 Sport process (e.g. training, competition, and club)
2 Sporting personnel (e.g. coach, team mates, competitors, and sport psychologists)
3 Non-sporting personnel (e.g. parents, siblings, and significant others)
4 Environmental influences (e.g. training environment, family environment, modelling, and the country the gymnast was from).

Connaughton et al. (2010) further advanced our understanding regarding how mental toughness develops by examining the perceptions of athletes, coaches, and sport psychologists within one study, across three specific career phases: (1) initial involvement to intermediate level, (2) intermediate level to elite level, and (3) elite to Olympic/world champion level, based upon the four dimensions proposed by Jones et al. (2007). Similar to Connaughton et al. (2008a), each phase was associated with the development of different characteristics. For example, in the initial involvement to intermediate level the attitude/mindset of the athlete and training dimension (e.g. using long-term goals for motivation) developed.

The environment, parents, coaches, enjoyment of activities, and competitive training were all crucial in helping athletes develop mental toughness. With regard to the intermediate level to elite level, characteristics from the training, competition dimension, and post-competition dimension developed during this stage of the athlete's career.

Mahoney et al. (2014) examined the development of mental toughness from the perspective of adolescents; their work was grounded in Bronfenbrenner's (2005) Bioecological Model. Mahoney et al. (2014) reported that the development of mental toughness involved the influence of significant others (i.e. coaches, parents, and/or peers having an impact during performances), supportive social processes (i.e. activities in one's life that increase learning, understanding, and abilities), curiosity (i.e. being interested in learning and picking things up from one's environment), and critical incidents (i.e. encounters that offer the chance for athletes to receive feedback).

More recently, scholars specifically examined the role of coaches in building mental toughness among their athletes. Coaches can have a positive (e.g. Philippe et al., 2016; Weinberg et al., 2016) or negative impact upon athletes (e.g. Owusu-Sekyere and Gervis, 2016). Philippe et al. (2016) interviewed 17 rugby players about the role of coaches in developing mental toughness. They found that the expertise of the coach (e.g. sharing experience and knowledge of mental toughness), instruction (e.g. coaching teaching psychological skills), and development (e.g. coach actively developing mental strategies among the players) were important. Weinberg et al. (2016) interviewed 15 sport psychologists, who revealed that coaches were instrumental in developing mental toughness, by putting athletes into pressurised situations, and teaching their athletes coping strategies. Although it is apparent that coaches may have a positive influence on developing mental toughness, caution is warranted because Owusu-Sekyere and Gervis (2016) found that such pressurised environments created by coaches may be a form of emotional abuse (e.g. humiliation, intimidation, forced physical effort). Worryingly, the coaches in Owusu-Sekyere and Gervis' study believed that creating pressurised situations in training was a legitimate coaching practice. As such, coaches need to carefully consider how they create pressure within training, so that athletes do not perceive emotional abuse.

Overview of mental toughness interventions

Three interventions aimed to enhance mental toughness among athletes. The first study to attempt to enhance mental toughness was by Sheard and Golby (2006). They explored the effects of a seven-week psychological skills programme on swimming performance and positive psychological development, including mental toughness among 36 national swimmers. The intervention included goal setting, mental imagery, relaxation, concentration, and thought stopping training. The authors reported some increases in swimming performance at competitive meets and a significant increase in mental toughness scores.

More recently Gucciardi et al. (2009a) explored the effects of a specific mental training intervention and a general psychological skills training programme on mental toughness, in comparison with a control group. The mental toughness training intervention comprised of seven sessions and included an introduction (Session 1), training in personal and team values (Session 2), work ethic, attitude, and self-motivation (Session 3), self-belief, concentration and focus (Session 4), resilience (Session 5), emotional intelligence (Session 6), and sport intelligence and physical toughness (Session 7). Gucciardi and colleagues found that athletes in the mental toughness training group and the psychological skills training group experienced an increase in mental toughness after their respective training programmes.

Bell et al. (2013) conducted a two-year mental toughness cricket intervention with high-level cricketers, which was delivered over 46 days. Unlike the previous interventions by Gucciardi et al. (2009a) and Sheard and Golby (2006), which were focused primarily on teaching athletes a variety of different psychological skills, Bell's intervention provided the cricketers with opportunities to practise under pressurised and threatening situations. Different drills and tasks (e.g. batting against pace, batting against spin, and indoor fitness tests) were made threatening by the authors creating consequences for poor performance (e.g. performing the task again, missing a training session, or cleaning the changing room). Players were also taught a variety of different coping strategies, which helped them cope with the stress due to the threat. Unlike the previous mental toughness interventions, where the athletes rated their levels of mental toughness, the coaches rated mental toughness in the Bell study. Bell and colleagues (2013) found that coaches rated cricketers in the mental toughness group as significantly more mentally tough, in comparison with the control group, after going through the training programme.

Mental toughness training for coaches

This section provides information on how coaches can help improve their athletes' mental toughness. These guidelines are based on models of mental toughness (e.g. Jones et al., 2007), research examining mental toughness (Nicholls et al., 2008), and existing mental toughness interventions (e.g. Bell et al., 2013; Gucciardi et al., 2009a).

Coach behaviour

Before engaging athletes in different psychological interventions to help athletes build their mental toughness levels, it is important that the coach considers his or her behaviour and the training environment. Research by Gucciardi et al. (2009b) found that coaches play a pivotal role in the development of an athlete's level of mental toughness. As such coaches should carefully consider their behaviour and ensure that:

- More emphasis is placed on players improving as opposed to the outcome of competitions. This refers to the motivational climate, which is discussed in detail in Chapter 15 of this book. Essentially, coaches should attempt to develop a mastery climate as opposed to a performance climate, so the role of the coach is to provide the athletes with tasks that focus on self-improvement and refrain from comparing athletes with other athletes (Amorose, 2007). If less emphasis is placed on results, athletes should be able to adjust to either winning or losing better, because outcomes are less important in a mastery motivational climate.
- Athlete's weaknesses are not over-exposed by the coach. Research indicates that athletes prefer positive feedback rather than negative feedback (Chiviacowsky et al., 2008b). However, if athletes do not know what their weaknesses are they may never work on any shortcomings and thus explore their full potential. Therefore, coaches have to be very careful how they present criticism to athletes and could present criticism in a positive manner that motivates the athlete to work on his or her weaknesses.
- The training environment challenges athletes. It is also crucial that coaches create an environment that pushes players to try their hardest, so when they play competitive matches they will be used to performing in challenging situations.

Sport intelligence

Gucciardi et al. (2008) found that sport intelligence, which refers to how athletes perceive training and understand competition processes such as tactics, are crucial factors in mental toughness. Coaches can play a strong role in helping athletes increase their sport intelligence. With regard to training, coaches can explain why certain training principles are important and relevant to matches. Sport intelligence in competition can be increased by coaches providing more detailed information on individual roles within a team, team tactics, and other processes that are related to competition, which will be sport specific.

Coping effectiveness training

Qualitative research by Jones et al. (2002) and quantitative research by Nicholls et al. (2008) reported that coping was highly associated with mental toughness. Despite this strong association, coping training has only featured in one mental toughness intervention (i.e. Bell et al., 2013). Furthermore, in Weinberg and Butt's (2011) chapter on how mental toughness can be developed, they only advocated the use of one coping strategy (e.g. cognitive restructuring). This strategy was not associated with mental toughness in the Nicholls et al. (2008) paper.

Appraisal training

Clough et al. (2002) stated that mentally tough athletes view sport as a challenge (i.e. focus on what can be gained) as opposed to a threat (i.e. focus on what can be lost). Therefore, coaches can provide athletes with appraisal training, and teach athletes to perceive situations as a challenge rather than a threat. Coaches can do this by encouraging athletes to focus exclusively on what can be gained from challenging situations. More information on how coaches can teach athletes to appraise stress more effectively is presented in Session 2 of coping effectiveness training in Chapter 21 and in Chapter 22.

Enhancing optimism and reducing pessimism

Research findings infer that mental toughness is positively related to optimism, but negatively related to pessimism (Nicholls et al., 2008). Seligman (2006) suggested that coaches could teach their athletes to be more optimistic by applying the ABCDE acronym of learned optimism to their coaching. This acronym stands for:

- *Adversity*: During times of stress, such as when an athlete makes a mistake (e.g. missing a tackle, dropping a ball, or missing a penalty), the athlete has encountered difficulty or adversity.
- *Beliefs*: It is likely that the athlete will dwell on the mistake that he or she has just made, which can shape their beliefs. For example, if an athlete has dropped a ball, they might believe that they are not very good at catching.
- *Consequences*: All beliefs have consequences. For example, if an athlete believes he or she is poor at catching, they might try to avoid situations in which they have to catch, such as having a preference to stand where the ball is less likely to go to.
- *Disputation*: In order to help athletes remain optimistic during adversity, it is important that coaches dispute any negative beliefs that might occur. The coach has to identify negative beliefs among athletes and can do this by speaking to them to find their views on different matters.
- *Evidence*: Coaches can dispute negative beliefs by using evidence. If an athlete drops a catch, the coach could say "Unlucky with the catch, you've caught some great catches this year and I am sure you will get the next one."

In addition to maximising optimism, it is also important that coaches reduce pessimism. Seligman (2006) also provided useful information regarding how coaches can do this, using the 3 Ps:

- *Personal*: An athlete who is a pessimist believes that his or her misfortune (e.g. not being selected for a team or dropping a high catch) lies within themself rather than being external. Therefore, misfortune is thought to be personal. As such, athletes should be encouraged to attribute their misfortune to external sources (e.g. dropped the ball because of the wind or moisture on the ball).

- *Permanent*: Pessimistic athletes also believe that their misfortune is permanent (e.g. "I am never going to be selected for the team"). Coaches should encourage athletes to view all setbacks as being temporary and state that with practice to improve techniques, setbacks will not occur regularly.
- *Pervasive*: Pessimists also believe that their misfortune is pervasive and expect to experience misfortune in all parts of their life (e.g. sport, education, and relationships, etc.). Coaches should encourage athletes to think positively and rationally – just because one area of an athlete's life is not going to plan, other parts of his or her life should not be affected.

Concentration

Coaches can enhance the concentration of their athletes, which identified Clough et al. (2002), Gucciardi et al. (2008), and Jones et al. (2002) as being an important mental toughness characteristic, by encouraging athletes to use cue words (Miller and Donohue, 2003). The coach could ask the athlete to focus on technical cue words (e.g. follow through, body position, watch ball) or motivational (e.g. confident) when they are performing. Coaches could also encourage athletes to develop routines, which should be learned in practice and then transferred to competition (Schack et al., 2005). It is also important that the routines are individualised for the performer (Cotterill et al., 2010).

Goal setting

Jones et al. (2007) found that athletes use goals for a source of motivation. A goal refers to an objective, target, or desired standard that an athlete wants to achieve in relation to a specific task or sport, and within a specific time limit (Locke and Latham, 2002). Information regarding how coaches can help athletes set goals is provided in Chapter 4.

Summary points

- Establishing an agreed definition of mental toughness has proved troublesome in the sport psychology literature.
- Mental toughness appears to develop throughout an athlete's career.
- Coaches play a vital role in the development of an athlete's mental toughness.
- Mental toughness can be developed through interventions.

CASE STUDY 19.1   MENTAL TOUGHNESS IN SWIMMING

Linda is a 57-year-old swimming coach, who has coached Janine for the last nine years, which included Janine competing at two Olympic games. Janine is now 26 years old and wants to compete at one more Olympic games in four years' time, before pursuing a career in banking. Linda has suspected that Janine lacks mental toughness as she tends to focus on the negatives, lacks confidence, and struggles to cope among other things. As Janine knows that she is attempting to swim at one more Olympics, she wants to give everything and is dedicated to improving psychologically as well as technically.

Linda recently assessed Janine's level of mental toughness using a mental toughness questionnaire, to see if she had low levels of mental toughness. Linda spoke to Janine about what she felt she needed and they planned a mental toughness training programme. This included coping effectiveness training, confidence, and practising skills under pressurised conditions. This was because Janine had always used goal setting very effectively and did not have problems concentrating, so they did not need to include this in the training programme. However, they did spend one session discussing Janine's long-term, medium-term, and short-term goals.

As Janine felt her ability to cope with stress needed more urgent work, they started the coping effectiveness training first. This involved Linda working with Janine to help her understand more about stress, how to cope, and who to turn to for support. For the most part, they had weekly sessions. Linda felt that Janine struggled with certain concepts of coping effectiveness training because they had less time in some weeks, so they spent more time working on parts she did not understand as well. Once Janine had finished the coping effectiveness training, she felt she needed a break before starting the performance under pressure drills and confidence training.

Case study reflection

As mental toughness encapsulates a broad range of characteristics (e.g. coping, confidence, concentration etc.), helping an athlete become more mentally tough is something that could take time, so coaches should be patient.

Practice exam questions

1   What are the strengths and weaknesses of the 4 Cs model of mental toughness?
2   Critically evaluate Hardy et al.'s (2014) model of mental toughness.
3   Discuss the strengths and limitations of Gucciardi et al.'s (2008) model of mental toughness.

4   What similarities exist between the models of mental toughness proposed by Clough et al. (2002), Gucciardi et al. (2008), and Hardy et al. (2014)?
5   Mental toughness changes across an athlete's career. Discuss.

Critical thinking questions: applying theory to practice

1   Reflect on your own coaching practice, and consider how you may have facilitated the development of mental toughness among athletes.
2   Discuss the role of the coach in shaping an athlete's mental toughness.
3   What challenges may coaches face when they try to implement optimism training? Discuss.
4   Devise your own mental toughness intervention for an athlete you have coached in the past who you feel lacked mental toughness.
5   What are the implications of a coach who never points out his athlete's weaknesses? Discuss. |

Case study questions

1   In addition to asking Janine to complete an assessment of mental toughness, how else could Linda assess Janine's mental toughness levels?
2   To what extent does the approach by Linda rely on Janine being self-aware? Discuss this and the implications for devising a mental toughness training programme.
3   It appeared that Janine became overloaded with the coping training she received. How could coaches avoid their athletes experiencing this?

20

MAXIMISING SPORT-CONFIDENCE

The purpose of this chapter is to provide information on the factors that coaches could consider when they want to enhance the confidence of athletes. Specifically, information is provided in relation to:

- A definition of sport-confidence
- A conceptual model of sport-confidence
- An evaluation of the sport-confidence model
- Sources of sport-confidence among team sport athletes
- The benefits of sport-confidence
- Sources of sport-confidence among individual athletes
- Confidence profiling
- Developing sport-confidence.

A definition of sport-confidence

Vealey and Chase (2008) defined sport-confidence as "an athlete's belief or degree of certainty that she or he has the abilities to perform successfully in sport" (p. 71). This definition is grounded in self-efficacy theory (Bandura, 1977), so it is similar in some ways to self-efficacy, but different in that sport-confidence is related exclusively to competitive sport.

A conceptual model of sport-confidence

Vealey and Chase's (2008) sport-confidence model predicted that there are three main sources of confidence for athletes, in addition to those proposed by Vealey (2001) in the original model. These are physical skills and training (i.e. the extent to which the athlete believes that he or she has the ability to execute sport-specific physical skills), cognitive efficiency (i.e. the extent to which an athlete believes that he or she can focus appropriately when playing sport), and resilience (i.e. successfully coping with stressful events; Compas et al., 2001). Sport-confidence levels influence how an athlete will behave, think, and feel. This then influences how the athlete will perform. As such, sport-confidence is critical to how athletes perform, even when factors that are uncontrollable (e.g. weather or opponents) and the physical capabilities of the athlete are accounted for (Hays et al., 2009).

An evaluation of the sport-confidence model

There is evidence to support the accuracy of Vealey's (Vealey, 2001; Vealey and Chase, 2008) sport-confidence model. For example, the sport-confidence model predicts that athletes who are more confident will have a better sporting experience. In support of this contention, Vealey et al. (1998) found that athletes who were confident reported less cognitive and somatic anxiety symptoms and were more intrinsically motivated. Koehn et al. (2013) also assessed some of the key assumptions of Vealey's sport-confidence model. They found that confidence levels were associated with positive experiences, as confidence was linked to flow. Further, the factors that Vealey (2001) predicted as being sources of confidence (e.g. demonstration of ability, physical and mental preparation, and being comfortable with one's environment) were indeed related to confidence levels.

Sources of confidence among team sport athletes

Despite receiving support from Koehn et al. (2013), a potential limitation of Vealey's (Vealey, 2001; Vealey and Chase, 2008) confidence model is that it does not distinguish between factors that influence confidence levels among athletes who participate in individual and team sports (Houston and Newton, 2011). Indeed, Houston and Newton argued that identifying sources of confidence in team sports is just as important as it is for athletes who compete in individual sports. In order to address this gap in the literature, Fransen et al. (2015) explored sources of confidence among team sport athletes who participated in football and basketball. They found that team performance and positive coaching were factors that were associated with high levels of team confidence. Conversely, negative expression and communication by team mates and the coach were factors that were associated with low levels of confidence. As such, this study demonstrates the importance of coach behaviour on influencing confidence levels.

The benefits of sport-confidence

It is important that coaches understand the benefits of sport-confidence, because this may provide them with extra motivation to ensure their athletes are confident. The benefits of athletes with high sport-confidence include:

- *Enhanced sporting performance*: A meta-analysis by Woodman and Hardy (2003) revealed that there was a significant relationship between sport performance and confidence ($r = 0.24$).
- *Effort*: Weinberg et al. (1980) revealed that confident athletes were more likely to exert effort than athletes who are not confident. In addition to highly confident athletes exerting more effort to pursue their goals, they will also persist longer at trying to achieve their goals. This is important from a coaching perspective, especially if an athlete is making technical changes to their game, because these may take time. A confident athlete is more likely to complete any technical changes, whereas an unconfident athlete might give up.
- *Psychological momentum*: Psychological momentum refers to an athlete's perception regarding whether a goal is being achieved (Vallerand et al., 1988). Being confident influences momentum, and momentum influences the likelihood of an athlete winning or losing (Miller and Weinberg, 1991). The most confident players are able to reverse negative momentum. This is because they have a never-say-die attitude and refuse to give up.

Sources of sport-confidence among individual athletes

Once coaches understand how athletes derive their sport-confidence, they can help shape an athlete's sport-confidence. A study by Hays et al. (2007) examined the sources of sport-confidence among a sample of 14 world class athletes, and identified nine sources. These included:

1 *Coaching:* The coach played two pivotal roles in determining how confident an athlete was. For example, some athletes gained confidence from the advice that their coach had given them, whereas others found confidence from receiving social support. As such, coaches should be aware of their role in influencing confidence levels among athletes. Coaches should ensure that their instruction is appropriate and that they are also supportive to maximise confidence levels among athletes.
2 *Preparation:* Athletes felt confident when they were physically and mentally prepared for competing in their sport. For instance, athletes felt they were able to perform at their best when their physical preparation in training had gone well. Mental preparation, which included the athletes setting themselves goals, mental imagery, and developing strategies was also important.
3 *Performance accomplishments:* Performing well in previous competitions was a source of confidence for the athletes, with one of the athletes being highly confident because he had not lost to a particular team in four years.
4 *Social support:* Athletes rated the support they received from their family, partners, or friends, especially during competitive periods, as a source of confidence.
5 *Innate factors:* Some athletes believed they had a genetic advantage that made them resilient to the effects of stress, which gave them an inner belief and acted as a source of confidence.

6 *Competitive advantage:* Athletes gained confidence from seeing their opponents perform poorly in other competitions.

7 *Experience:* Using one's previous experience was an important source of confidence for some athletes, because they knew what to expect and gained confidence from it.

8 *Trust:* Trust was an important source of confidence for some athletes and involved the athletes trusting other team mates or support teams.

9 *Self-awareness:* Being aware of one's self was an important source of confidence for some athletes, because they knew exactly what they wanted.

In addition to these nine global themes, Hays et al. (2007) identified a number of individual differences among athletes that could not be classified within these dimensions. These were enjoyment, commitment of team mates, and whether the athletes felt that it was meant to be that they would do well, which Hays et al. (2007) referred to as omens.

The age of the athlete also influences sources of sport confidence, which is something coaches need to be aware of. Wilson et al. (2004) found some subtle differences to Hays et al. (2007), with a sample of masters athletes, aged between 50 and 96 years (the sample in the Hays et al. study was aged between 21 and 48 years). Although there were some similarities between the two studies, such as preparation, coaching, and social support, the masters athletes rated physical self-presentation, watching others perform, and mastery as sources of confidence. It should be noted that physical self-presentation and vicarious experience were reported as additional sources among the Hays et al. (2007) study. It was apparent from the Hays et al. study that there are individual differences in sources of confidence. Coaches need to investigate and harness these differences to make confidence training more effective. One such method of assessing sport-confidence and sources of sport-confidence among athletes is called confidence profiling (Hays et al., 2010a).

Confidence profiling

Confidence profiling (Hays et al., 2010a) has recently been introduced in the psychology literature. The confidence profile originates from Butler's (1989) performance profile, which is grounded in Kelly's (1991) PCT. Information on performance profiling and Kelly's PCT is presented in Chapter 5, so will only be discussed briefly here. PCT implies that an athlete will attempt to make sense of himself or herself and his or her environment by developing theories about the world. These theories vary from person to person, because individuals differ regarding how they perceive situations and interpret them. Confidence profiling was designed to be an applied method of assessing confidence, so it is very appropriate for coaches to use. Research that has used the confidence profile (Hays et al., 2010b) found that this instrument increased the athlete's awareness of the factors that enhanced and decreased confidence.

The processes involved in confidence profiling by Hays et al. (2010a) have been adapted in this chapter and involve four stages: (1) athletes rate the constructs that they believe confident athletes possess; (2) athletes rate their confidence in self-selected qualities; (3) athletes rate where their source of confidence came from; and (4) the final process involves the athlete plotting the information on a confidence profile:

- *Stage 1*: During the initial stage, after explaining the concept of confidence profiling, the coach asks the athlete to "Write down what you need to be confident about to be successful in your sport". An example of a completed list is presented in Table 20.1 and relates to what a soccer player might think is important to be confident about to be successful in soccer.
- *Stage 2*: The coach then asks the athlete to identify the 12 most important characteristics it is important to be confident in, and asks them to provide a meaning. As such, the coach would ask the player to "Rank the 12 most important qualities it is important to be confident in, with 1 being the most important and 12 being the least important on the list". The coach would then ask the athlete to "Describe what each item on the list means by completing the table". An example of a completed table that identifies the 12 most important characteristics it is important to be confident in is presented in Table 20.2.
- *Stage 3*: The athlete is then asked to rate where the sources of confidence come from for each of the 12 most important characteristics, which have previously been identified by the athlete. The coach would ask the athlete to "Write down where being confident in the important qualities come from". An example of a completed source of confidence sheet is presented in Table 20.3.

TABLE 20.1 Important attributes to be confident about

Having a good first touch
Stamina
Trust from coach
Speed
Skill
Good training sessions
Get on well with team mates
Enjoy matches
Good at defending
Able to pass well
Can play when things get tight
Not afraid to take chances
Feel mentally good
Don't have aches or pains during matches
Comments from coach during matches

TABLE 20.2 Qualities and meanings

Rank order	Qualities an athlete needs to be confident in to be successful at sport	Meaning
1	Speed	Being able to run really fast
2	Stamina	Being able to run for the whole match at a good level
3	Good training sessions	Things go well in training, which makes you feel good going into matches
4	Trust from coach	Knowing that the coach believes in you
5	Comments from coach during matches	What the coach says or shouts during matches or at half-time break
6	Not afraid to take chances	Even though a game is close, doing what it takes to win a match
7	Get on well with team mates	Being friendly with other team mates
8	Enjoy matches	Like the feeling of playing in matches
9	First touch	Being able to control the ball well when I first get it, which gives me time
10	Good at defending	Not letting other players get past
11	Able to pass well	Passes go to right player
12	Feel mentally good	In right frame of mind to play well

- *Stage 4*: Finally, the athlete is asked to plot (a) the 12 most important factors to be confident in, (b) their current ratings between 1 and 10, with 10 being the most confident they could be and 1 being the least confident they could be, and (c) the sources of sport-confidence for each category in the specified box. Figure 20.1 represents a completed confidence profile for the soccer player.

As with normal performance profiling (Butler, 1989), confidence profiling (Hays et al., 2010a) should be conducted on a regular basis. This helps athletes and coaches monitor the effects of any confidence training that a coach may provide, as in accordance with Hays et al. (2010b).

Developing sport-confidence

Once a coach establishes that his or her athlete could benefit from a sports confidence training programme, an intervention can be developed. Feltz et

TABLE 20.3 Sources of sport confidence

Qualities an athlete needs to be confident in to be successful at sport	Sources of sport confidence
Speed	Amount of training, effort in training, legs feeling good
Stamina	Performance on fitness tests, time spent in training working on endurance
Good training sessions	Coach comments, what other team mates say
Trust from coach	Selection for team, extra responsibilities
Comments from coach during matches	Coach told me I was doing well
Not afraid to take chances	Feedback from coach during matches, praise from team mates
Get on well with team mates	Spending time together away from soccer
Enjoy matches	Positive comments from coach during matches, parents being positive
First touch	Coach feedback, comments from other players, more time in matches
Good at defending	Time spent practising defensive formations
Able to pass well	What other players say, coach comments during matches, parents' comments during matches
Feel mentally good	Getting support from parents

al. (2008) provided an excellent framework that coaches can adopt, although coaches should adapt the guidelines based upon the needs of their athlete and the ability of the athlete.

Instructional strategies

A coach can enhance the sport-confidence of the athletes he or she coaches by the way instruction is provided and the drills that are used within training sessions (Hays et al., 2007; Vargas-Tonsing et al., 2004). Normally, a coach would give athletes instructions to help them master specific techniques or tactics (e.g. putting in golf or attacking formations in basketball). Coaches should also try to build confidence in athletes' ability to complete tasks. Feltz (1994) suggested that coaches must take a methodical approach and go through each component of a skill. For example in putting, the coach could break the skill into its component parts: stance, spine angle, position of ball in the stance, grip, ball strike, and follow through. The coach should be enthusiastic about the athlete's ability.

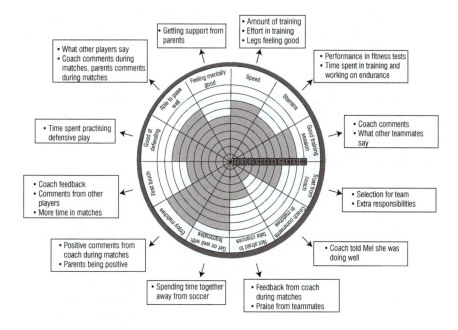

FIGURE 20.1 Confidence performance profile

Feedback

The feedback an athlete receives from his or her coach is important in building the athlete's sport-confidence levels, especially when athletes learn new skills, as they are likely to make mistakes (Feltz et al., 2008). A coach who encourages his or her athlete, by providing positive feedback, may enhance his or her sport-confidence during what can be a difficult time. Jourden et al. (1991) suggested that positive feedback involves the coach focusing on the positive aspects of a skill being performed, but it also involves illustrating any mistakes made by the athlete. It is important that coaches provide information regarding how athletes can reduce the mistakes they typically make. The coach should also inform the athlete that mistakes are a normal part of the learning process. Based on the guidelines proposed by Jourden et al. (1991), Feltz (1994) suggested that coaches should:

1 Acknowledge the athlete's distress (e.g. "I can see that you are very upset and frustrated about the ball not going into the correct service box").

2 Tell the athlete what aspect of the skill he or she performed correctly (e.g. "The acceleration of the racquet head was excellent, as was your follow through. You are generating some excellent power in your serve").

3 Let the athlete know how he or she can correct the mistake (e.g. "You just need to get more consistency in your ball toss, because it is making you hit

the ball from the wrong place, which is why your serve is inconsistent. This is something that many beginners struggle with. Once you get this more consistent your serve will be excellent because all the other parts of your serve are very good").

4 Finish by providing positive feedback to the athlete (e.g. "With more practice you will get the ball toss more consistent and then you will start hitting more powerful and accurate serves!").

Observational learning

Observational learning involves the coach demonstrating a particular skill (e.g. set shot in basketball) or asking an athlete to perform the skill in front of other athletes so others can see how it is performed. Feltz (1980) provided specific recommendations on what coaches can do when they conduct observational learning demonstrations. The coach should verbally explain the skill in the first instance. He or she should give a demonstration and then ask the athlete to repeat the verbal instructions he or she has just heard. Following this procedure, the coach then asks the athlete if he or she is comfortable performing the task unassisted or whether assistance is required. If assistance is required the coach can physically guide the athlete through the movement, but if no assistance is required the athlete performs by themself. Guidance is removed once the athlete can perform the task consistently.

For observational learning to be effective, Bandura (1997) stated that four conditions need to be accomplished: attention, retention, production, and motivation.

- *Attention*: For observational learning to be effective, the coach needs to ensure that the athlete or athletes are paying attention. This may be more difficult when the coach is providing the demonstration to larger groups, so this is something that needs to be considered.
- *Retention*: The athlete must be able to remember the skill that he or she has observed in the demonstration. Therefore, if the skills are very complex, the coach could break the skill into several demonstrations to help the athlete remember what he or she has observed.
- *Production*: It is important that coaches ensure that the athlete has the ability to reproduce the skill that he or she has observed. If athletes do not possess the ability, observational learning will not be effective.
- *Motivation*: Athletes need to be motivated to perform the observed skill. If the athlete is not motivated towards performing a skill, observational learning will be of limited benefit to the athlete. Coaches can enhance motivation by manipulating the sport environment, by rewarding athletes who try hard and make the most improvement, which is referred to as a mastery-oriented climate. Manipulating the motivational climate has resulted in sport being more enjoyable, increased perceived competence, intrinsic motivation,

and improved motor performance (Theeboom et al., 1995). Information regarding how coaches can enhance the motivation of different athletic populations is presented for children (see Chapter 6), adolescents (Chapter 7), and adults (Chapter 8).

Mental imagery

Mental imagery refers to the process of an athlete using his or her imagination to see himself or herself performing a movement (e.g. running) or a certain skill (e.g. catching a high ball in rugby or heading the ball in soccer; Richardson, 1969). A motivational general-mastery intervention in which the athlete imagines themself successfully mastering a skill may help in enhancing confidence (Martin et al., 1999). For more information regarding how coaches can develop an imagery intervention, see Chapter 18.

Manipulating the training environment

Beaumont et al. (2015) suggested coaches should provide a challenging environment within training that tests athletes, but allows them to practise their skills under pressurised situations and helps an athlete build confidence by demonstrating his or her ability to perform under pressure. A consequence of this would be that an athlete would experience challenge as opposed to threat states in training. Information of generating challenge states is provided in Chapter 22 of this book.

Reinforcing ability

Another technique to enhance an athlete's sport-confidence is to reinforce the athlete's ability through regular reminders. Beaumont et al. (2015) suggested that athletes could be regularly reminded of their accomplishments, their strengths, and improvements in either the short or the long term. Indeed, Beaumont and colleagues (2015) advocated laminated reminder cards that are updated each month so athletes can see their accomplishments over the previous four weeks.

Non-verbal behaviour

Furley and Schweizer (2014) found that athletes displayed different non-verbal behaviours depending on whether they were in a winning or losing position, which directly influenced an athlete's confidence in his or her ability to beat an opponent. As such, non-verbal behaviours influence an opponent's confidence in winning. Therefore, coaches could encourage athletes to display confident bodily actions, even if the athlete does not feel confident inside, because acting confident may diminish the confidence levels of opponents.

CASE STUDY 20.1 BUILDING CONFIDENCE

Vicky, a 31-year-old tennis player, was absolutely flying. She obtained a promotion at work and achieved selection for her county team, which was a remarkable achievement, given she had only been playing the sport for three and a half years. She played against a national player in her first match and suffered a heavy defeat (6–2, 6–1). She lost all of her confidence.

Christopher, who was Vicky's county coach, could see a change in Vicky's demeanour, energy levels, and desire to train following her first match. She seemed a shadow of her former previously bubbly and inquisitive self. After the session, Christopher took Vicky to one side and spoke to her about what had happened. Vicky said that she felt horrible, because she had let her team mates down and everything she tried on the court no longer worked. She said that she felt helpless.

Due to time pressures after the coaching session, Christopher asked to speak to Vicky before the next session and they arranged a time for this chat. During this second conversation Christopher explained how confidence is like a fire – it can be burning strong one minute and the next it can disappear. Christopher was keen to listen to Vicky's concerns that included doubts about whether she deserved a place on the county squad, and whether she was good enough to play county tennis. Once he listened to these concerns, Christopher provided reassurance, support, and advice regarding what Vicky could do to improve. He also asked Vicky if she was keen to try an imagery intervention, which she was, so Christopher developed an MG-M imagery training programme, and also encouraged Vicky to think about how she would behave when she was confident, and to display such behaviours at all times on the court. Vicky identified that she would have an extra bounce in her step, would make prolonged eye contact with her opponent, and would display a stronger posture (e.g. shoulders back and chin up).

Christopher knew that it was a delicate time for Vicky, so he ensured his behaviour was always very positive and encouraging around Vicky, to help her get through the sticky patch.

Case study reflection

It is important that coaches consider the needs of the athlete when providing confidence training. In this case study, it is apparent that Vicky is a talented tennis player because she is already playing for her county team. As such, players of a higher ability may require less guidance on their technique, given that it will already be strong, so techniques such as observational learning and instructional strategies that coaches can employ will not be as relevant as they would be for a beginner athlete who is having confidence problems. It is important that coaches encourage athletes to display non-verbal behaviours of being confident.

Summary points

- Sport-confidence refers to an athlete's view about whether he or she has the skill to be able to perform successfully in his or her sport (Vealey and Chase, 2008).
- Sport-confidence is associated with a variety of benefits, including enhanced sports performance.
- Coach behaviours are strong predictors of confidence among teams.
- Research indicates that there are nine sources that athletes derive their confidence from, such as coaches, preparation, and the social support they receive.
- Coaches can assess and monitor an athlete's confidence by using confidence profiling.
- Confidence in athletes can be developed by coaches behaving correctly, using observational learning, mental imagery, and other techniques reported in this chapter.

Practice exam questions

1 Describe Vealey's (2001) model of confidence.
2 Being confident benefits athletes. Discuss.
3 Discuss the extent to which coach behaviour influences sport-confidence.
4 Compare and contrast confidence profiling (Hays et al., 2010a) with performance profiling (Butler, 1989).
5 Confidence is affected by age. Discuss.

Critical thinking questions: applying theory to practice

1 Reflecting on your own practice, how would you try and make observational learning more effective and what would you change in the future?
2 Feltz (1980) stated that a coach could physically help an athlete if he or she cannot perform a skill unassisted. Critically evaluate this instruction.
3 How could you positively impact upon the sources of confidence outlined by Hays (2010a) within your own coaching practice?
4 From the guidelines provided by Feltz et al. (2008), please state which training procedures would benefit elite athletes, and which would be more suitable for beginners.
5 How can you provide feedback to optimise confidence when you coach athletes?

Case study questions

1 Describe non-verbal confidence behaviours that Christopher could teach Vicky to use on the court.

2 Describe some of the key components of the MG–M imagery script that Christopher designed for Vicky.
3 Christopher considered Vicky's ability level when thinking about the best approach to boost her confidence. Discuss the importance of this and how it would influence the content of a confidence-building programme.

21

COPING EFFECTIVENESS TRAINING

The purpose of this chapter is to provide information on coping effectiveness training for athletes and understanding the principles behind this training. More specifically, this chapter contains information on:

- A definition of stress
- Neuroendocrine responses to stress
- A definition of coping
- The coping and sports performance relationship
- The coping functions
- Coping interventions
- A definition of coping effectiveness
- Coping effectiveness training theory
- Developing a CET intervention.

A definition of stress

Defining stress is a very contentious issue, with researchers struggling to agree on a common definition (Lazarus, 1999). Within the sport psychology literature, Lazarus and Folkman's (1984) definition of stress is still widely used. They defined stress as "a particular relationship between the person and the environment that is appraised by the person as taxing or exceeding his or her resources and endangering his or her well-being" (p. 19). This definition is relational, because it assumes that stress is a product of the person who is interacting with his or her environment, who evaluates whether they possess the resources to deal with the environment (Nicholls, 2016). A person experiences stress when he or she evaluates that their resources are insufficient to manage the situation.

Neuroendocrine responses to stress

Experiencing stress can cause parts of the brain to interact with the pituitary and adrenal glands, which produces a variety of hormonal responses (Aldwin, 2007). As such, when an athlete perceives threat (e.g. he or she might lose), the part of the brain known as the hypothalamus is activated, which stimulates the pituitary gland to release hormones that activate the adrenal glands. The activation of the adrenal glands stimulates the sympathetic nervous system (Cannon, 1915). According to Aldwin (2007), the results of the sympathetic nervous system being stimulated include:

- Increased blood pressure, heart rate, respiration rate, and perspiration
- Increased blood sugar levels
- Increased blood clotting
- Dilated pupils
- Piloerections (goosebumps)
- Decreased saliva and mucus
- Gastro-intestinal disturbances
- Blood is diverted from the intestines to the brain and muscles that are being used.

Essentially, these responses to stress prepare athletes to mobilise their efforts to effectively manage the situation they are in, which is known as the fight–flight reaction (Cannon, 1915). The athlete is ready to confront the source of stress (fight) or run away (flight). As such, it is important that coaches understand that stress is not just a figment of an athlete's imagination. When athletes experience stress they will experience an array of physiological symptoms that might not necessarily be conducive to successful performance. Indeed, two meta-analyses (i.e. Craft et al., 2003; Woodman and Hardy, 2003) explored the relationship between pre-competitive anxiety, which is a stress emotion (Lazarus, 1999), and performance. Both meta-analyses reported a negative relationship between these two variables. As such, it is important that coaches help their athletes manage stress. One way athletes attempt to manage stress is through coping.

A definition of coping

Coping refers to "constantly changing cognitive and behavioural efforts to manage specific external and/or internal demands that are appraised as taxing or exceeding the resources of the person" (Lazarus and Folkman, 1984: 141). That is, coping represents the thoughts and behaviours that an athlete engages in, aimed at reducing the stress he or she is experiencing. This definition and conceptualisation of coping was adopted by over 80 per cent of the coping research articles published in the sport psychology literature (Nicholls and Polman, 2007).

The coping and sports performance relationship

A meta-analysis by Nicholls et al. (2016a) examined the relationship between sporting performance and coping from a variety of different sports and among athletes who compete at different levels, ranging from club to professional athletes. The results of this study revealed that coping was associated with performance across 18 sports. In particular, studies classified as mastery coping (i.e. attempts to control and thus eliminate the stressor) were positively associated with sports performance. Goal-withdrawal coping strategies (i.e. ceasing efforts to achieve one's goal) were negatively associated with performance. Internal regulation coping strategies (i.e. managing bodily stress responses) were not associated with performance.

The coping functions

Researchers classify coping in many different ways. For a review of the different ways coping has been classified, please read the chapter by Nicholls and Thelwell (2010). Within the sport psychology literature, researchers have, on the whole, classified all coping strategies within one of the following three dimensions:

- *Problem-focused coping* refers to coping strategies that are aimed directly at the problem which causes the person to experience stress (Lazarus and Folkman, 1984). Coping strategies often classified as problem-focused coping in sport psychology literature include: increased effort (e.g. Reeves et al., 2009), remaining on the task (e.g. Anshel, 2001), time management planning (e.g. Gould et al., 1993), and problem-solving (e.g. Holt and Hogg, 2002).
- *Emotion-focused coping* refers to strategies that regulate the emotional responses to stress. Coping strategies that are classified within the emotion-focused dimension include: seeking support from others (e.g. Poczwardowski and Conroy, 2002), humour (e.g. Crocker and Graham, 1995), prayer (Gould et al., 1993), and thought control (e.g. Holt and Mandigo, 2004).

Based on the recommendations of Kowalski and Crocker (2001), some researchers added a third dimension, called avoidance coping.

- *Avoidance coping* refers to strategies that consist of cognitive and behavioural attempts to disengage from a stressful encounter (Krohne, 1993). Strategies cited as avoidance coping include: blocking (e.g. Nicholls, 2007a), walking away (e.g. Nicholls et al., 2009), and ignoring other people (e.g. Nicholls et al., 2005b).

Coping interventions

Sport psychology researchers developed four types of coping interventions, with the aim of reducing stress, through teaching athletes to cope. These were:

1 *Cognitive-affective stress management training* (SMT; Smith, 1980): The SMT programme consists of the athletes learning behavioural relaxation strategies in addition to cognitive strategies to reduce emotional arousal. Furthermore, the SMT also involves specific phases known as conceptualisation (i.e. the athlete identifying how he or she currently copes), skill acquisition rehearsal (i.e. the athlete being taught new coping strategies), and skill application (i.e. the athlete using the strategies he or she has been taught). However, support for SMT programmes is somewhat mixed. Crocker et al. (1988) found that SMT has a limited affect in reducing the anxiety experienced by athletes, although SMT appears to positively impact upon athletic performance (e.g. Crocker et al., 1988; Smith 1980).

2 *The COPE intervention* (Anshel et al., 1990): In this coping programme athletes are taught to *Control* emotions, *Organise* the most important information to attend to, *Plan* how they will respond to stressful encounters, and *Execute* their responses. This intervention appears to help athletes manage negative feedback, and maintain self-esteem, and self-confidence levels.

3 *Coping skills programme* (Nicholls, 2007b): Based on recommendations from recent coping studies among golfers (e.g. Nicholls, 2007a; Nicholls et al., 2005a, 2005b), Nicholls (2007b) developed a coping skills programme. As such, the golfer was encouraged to use coping strategies that had been deemed effective (e.g. rationalisation and re-appraisal), whilst refraining from using ineffective coping strategies (e.g. speeding up between shots and making routine changes). Results revealed the participant "benefited a lot" from knowing why certain stressors were effective and others were not. This study was limited by the absence of any baseline measurements, so the impact this intervention had on the golfer cannot be deduced.

4 *Future-oriented coping intervention* (Devonport and Lane, 2014): Devonport and Lane (2014) created a coping pack, which high-level netballers completed over a period of 12 months in addition to receiving support from a mentor. The role of the mentors was to encourage the participants to deploy their newly learned coping skills. The pack included information on time management, goal setting, and problem solving, which were intended to help future-oriented coping when athletes were tasked with managing multiple goals (e.g. education goals and sporting goals). The intervention was also designed to enhance communication and emotional intelligence. Results revealed that there were no differences between the group who received the pack and the control group, although the qualitative data identified a number of benefits of engaging in the programme.

Although these four coping interventions yielded some positive results, none of these studies included coping effectiveness. That is because participants in these studies were not specifically taught to assess stress controllability and then direct coping strategies accordingly, depending on whether the athlete felt that he or she could control the stress. Further, these interventions did instruct participants to elicit social support. Therefore, coaches could improve the effectiveness of coping interventions by including elements of coping effectiveness training.

A definition of coping effectiveness

Coping effectiveness is the "degree in which a coping strategy or combination of strategies is or are successful in alleviating stress" (Nicholls, 2010: 264). It is important that athletes cope effectively, especially when they experience immense stress, so that their performance does not deteriorate (e.g. Haney and Long, 1995; Lazarus, 2000a).

Coping effectiveness training theory

Coping Effectiveness Training (CET; Chesney et al., 1996) is underpinned by the transactional theoretical perspective of stress and coping (Lazarus and Folkman, 1984) and in particular the goodness-of-fit model (Folkman, 1984). The goodness-of-fit model states that when an individual can control a stressful situation, problem-focused coping strategies are the most effective strategies (e.g. planning, time management, and information seeking). Conversely, when situations are uncontrollable, emotion-focused and avoidance coping strategies will be more effective (e.g. deep breathing, physical relaxation, and acceptance). CET is different from the four coping interventions developed by Smith (1980), Anshel et al. (1990), Nicholls (2007b), or Devonport and Lane (2014). In addition to being taught how to cope, athletes would also be taught to assess stress controllability and then direct coping strategies accordingly depending on whether the athlete felt that he or she could control the stress. Athletes are also taught how to make the most of social support.

The goal of coping effectiveness training is to reduce stress, enhance emotional well-being, and maximise sporting performance. Furthermore, the literature also indicates that coping is particularly useful in generating both positive and optimal performance states (Hanin, 2004, 2010; Nicholls et al., 2010). As such, coping effectiveness training should help athletes maintain optimal performance states.

Coping effectiveness training was originally designed as a group-based intervention, directed to the needs of the target population, with sessions being based around elements of cognitive and behavioural stress management interventions (e.g. cognitive therapy, relaxation, and problem-solving). However, when Reeves et al. (2011) developed their intervention for F.A. Premier League academy soccer players, each participant received his training individually.

A number of studies from the health and sport psychology literature provided supporting evidence for CET. For instance, Chesney et al. (1996) conducted a randomised control trial among male patients diagnosed with HIV. The recipients of the CET intervention significantly increased coping self-efficacy

(CSE) and significantly decreased perceived stress and burnout. More recently, Chesney et al. (2003) found that CET was also effective in reducing anxiety, perceived stress, and burnout among 128 men diagnosed with HIV. Regression analyses also indicated that higher levels of CSE mediated improvements in perceived stress and burnout, meaning that self-efficacy is an important variable to consider in coping interventions. CSE has been defined as "a person's confidence in his or her ability to cope effectively" (Chesney et al., 2006: 422). Reeves et al. (2011) examined the effects of a Coping Effectiveness Training for Adolescent Soccer Players (CETASP) intervention on coping self-efficacy, coping effectiveness, and subjective performance among five participants. The participants played for an English Premier League Soccer Academy. A single-subject multiple-baseline, across individuals design was employed. The intervention appeared to be successful in enhancing coping effectiveness, coping self-efficacy, and subjective performance among the players.

Developing a CET intervention

To help athletes cope more effectively, coaches can devise a CET programme based on the guidelines proposed in this chapter. As such, information is provided on what coaches should do in each session. The sessions are primarily designed for individual athletes, but can easily be adapted for team settings. The guidelines are based on the study by Reeves et al. (2011), which were developed in accordance with Chesney et al. (2003). A session on stress appraisals has been included in these guidelines. This is because emerging research by Nicholls et al. (2011), who revealed how elite rugby union players appraised stressful environment stimuli (e.g. dropping a ball, opponents scoring a try, being criticised by a coach) shaped emotional reactions. As such, teaching athletes to appraise stress more favourably may generate more positive emotions. More recent research (Nicholls et al., 2012) revealed that appraisals are related to perceived stress and how athletes cope, so shaping appraisals could be very important in helping athletes combat stress. As such, information is provided on how coaches can train athletes in appraisal.

CET training programmes usually contain seven sessions. It is recommended that coaches conduct one session per week, with each session lasting around 60 minutes. If coaches conduct any more than one session per week, athletes may not be able to grasp each concept before moving onto the next. It is important to note that the guidelines presented merely serve as a reference for coaches who may wish to adapt elements of the programme.

Before starting the programme, and after the coach assesses the needs of the athlete, it is important that the coach describes the nature of CET and the level of commitment that will be required from the athlete or the team. This is so the individual or individuals can decide whether they would like to receive CET. It is very important that the athlete is keen to take part in CET.

Session 1: Understanding stress and coping

The aim of the introductory session is to help develop the athlete's self-awareness of stress and coping. First, the coach provides the athlete with a description of what stress is, such as "Stress is when you feel that the situation you are in exceeds your resources and reduces your well-being and is associated with symptoms such as increased heart rate, worrying and muscle tension" (Nicholls et al., 2011: 81). The athlete is then presented with a figure that contains some of the symptoms associated with stress (Figure 21.1), so they are aware that the symptoms they experience are normal.

The coach then asks the athlete to describe and write down several sporting situations in which he or she has experienced stress and the symptoms that were experienced. This is so the coach and the athlete generate an understanding of the stress symptoms the athlete experiences and whether there are any common symptoms or experiences that lead to the athlete experiencing stress. The coach then presents the athlete with a figure that depicts why athletes experience stress. As indicated in Figure 21.2, when the demands of the situation (e.g. taking a

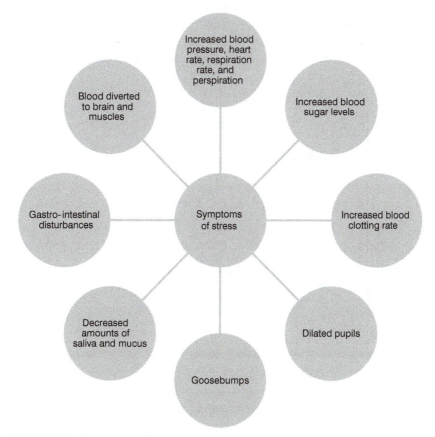

FIGURE 21.1 Symptoms of stress

penalty) are equal to the athlete's resources, stress will not be experienced. When the athlete's resources are high and the demands of the sporting situation are low, boredom will prevail. Only when the demands of the situation are much greater than the person's resources to cope will the athlete experience stress.

The remainder of Session 1 is spent discussing coping. The coach provides a definition of coping such as "Coping refers to the thoughts and behaviours that you make to reduce the stress or the worry that you experience. Coping comes in many forms, and the key is that you purposefully engage in those thoughts or behaviours." The coach then asks the athlete to describe his or her experiences of coping in sport. For example, the coach could say "I would like you to describe some of the strategies you used during instances in which you felt worried or stressed in sport." The coach can also ask the athlete to distinguish between helpful and unhelpful coping strategies. This process helps the athlete's awareness of strategies that might be effective and those that are ineffective. Helping an athlete gain an awareness of effective and ineffective coping strategies is important so that athletes can reduce the number of ineffective coping strategies they use. Some athletes may not realise that what they are doing is ineffective, and require help to reflect upon their experiences. Even though athletes identified ineffective coping strategies they may continue to use them, as did the international golfer in Nicholls (2007b), because they became habitual. After awareness training the golfer knew it was unhelpful to use the ineffective coping strategies and made a concerted effort to stop using them, but that took time.

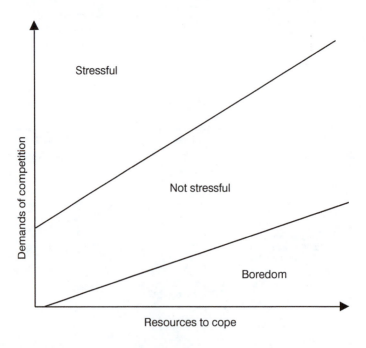

FIGURE 21.2 Demand and coping evaluation

Session 2: Appraisal training

Appraisal refers to an evaluative process in which the athlete evaluates what is his or her environment (i.e. competition or training session) in relation to his or her goals or values (Lazarus, 1999). Appraisal might be a very important construct in shaping emotional well-being given that the emotion a person experiences is shaped by appraisal (Lazarus, 1991, 1999). Lazarus (1991, 1999, 2000a, 2000b) proposed a two-factor schematisation of appraisals, or as he also termed them relational meanings that comprised losses and gains. Loss appraisals comprise (a) anticipated losses and thus the threat of a loss occurring such an opponent scoring a goal, in addition to (b) losses that have already occurred such as a team scoring. Gain appraisals referred to gains that a person anticipates and gains that have already occurred.

A recent study by Nicholls et al. (2011) with a sample of 11 professional rugby players, found that loss evaluations generate predominantly negative emotions (e.g. anxiety, anger, and shame). Gain appraisals generate mainly positive emotions (e.g. happiness, relief, and pride). As such, the coach would ask the athlete to describe instances in which he has experienced stress and then ask the player to "Please describe how you evaluated that stressor. Were you focused on what could be gained or what could be lost?" This will allow the coach to assess the appraisal patterns of the athlete. The coach can then explain the differences between the different types of appraisals and teach the athlete how to appraise stressors as gains, rather than losses. For example, instead of the athlete appraising playing an opponent with a superior ranking as a loss (i.e. anticipating that he or she will lose the match), the athlete could be encouraged to focus on what can be gained from the situation (e.g. ranking points by beating a higher ranked athlete, a chance to monitor progress, a chance to impress coaches with improvements made, etc.) and to view the situation as a challenge.

The coach would also present the athlete with a range of sport scenarios (e.g. "You are about to play a number 1 ranked player, who you possess a losing record against, in the presence of national selectors") and ask how he or she would appraise each situation. Once each scenario has been evaluated, the coach would go through each in turn, especially the negatively appraised events, to ask how they could be appraised differently with an emphasis on what could be gained from a situation. When athletes focus on gains, they will make positive appraisals.

Session 3: Problem-focused coping

The goodness-of-fit approach proposed by Folkman (1984) suggested that athletes should deploy problem-focused coping strategies in relation to stressors or stressful situations that they can control. In this session the coach helps the athlete distinguish between controllable stressors (e.g. lack of fitness) and uncontrollable stressors (e.g. not being selected by a coach). In order for the coach to ensure that the athlete has a good grasp of stressor controllability, the athlete should be tested

TABLE 21.1 Stressor controllability

Stressor	Controllable	Uncontrollable
Making a mental error (e.g. wrong choice)		
Making a physical error (e.g. poor execution of pass)		
Opponents playing well		
Sustaining an injury		
Opponents cheating		
Receiving a poor call from an official		
Weather conditions		
Receiving coach criticism		
Not being selected for the team		
Arguing with team mates		
Being substituted		
Fatigue		
Letting team mates down		

with a range of different stressors before being taught problem-focused coping strategies. That is, the coach will present the athlete with a variety of stressors that are common among athletes in sport literature and ask the athlete to denote whether the stressor is controllable or uncontrollable (Table 21.1).

The coach then explains the concept of problem-focused coping strategies by saying something like "Problem-focused coping strategies involve you using strategies that help you solve the problem that is causing you stress and thus reduce the amount of stress you are experiencing, because the problem is gone." Once the definition has been read out, the coach can teach the athlete a variety of different problem-focused coping strategies such as planning a strategy, increasing concentration, creating a performance routine, and thought stopping. Once the athlete has an understanding of the coping strategies, the coach can ask the athlete to try using them in training sessions, before progressing to matches when the athlete is competent to do so.

Session 4: Emotion-focused coping

When an athlete experiences a stressor that he or she cannot control, it has the potential to be one of the most distressing experiences in sport. This is because the athlete may feel a sense of powerlessness. Folkman (1984), in her goodness-of-fit approach, suggested that in such stressful situations athletes should use emotion-focused coping strategies. The coach explains the concept of emotion-focused coping, by saying something along the lines of "When you experience stress that you can't do anything about, you might feel very distressed, upset, or even angry. When you experience these types of stressors you can use emotion-focused coping strategies. These strategies are aimed at reducing your emotional reactions to the stress you are feeling." As such, the athlete is attempting to take control of his or her emotional reactions to the source of stress. The coach then describes the different emotion-focused coping strategies such as breathing techniques, how to accept mistakes, and positive self-talk. As with the problem-focused coping strategies, the coach should encourage the athlete to practise these strategies in training, before attempting the coping strategies in competitions.

Session 5: Avoidance and ineffective coping

Coaches can also teach athletes to use avoidance coping strategies when they cannot control the stressor. The coach could explain avoidance coping by saying "Avoidance coping is when you try to not think about a stressful situation or you physically remove yourself from the stressor, such as walking away." Avoidance coping comprises cognitive avoidance, such as attempts to mentally withdraw from a stressor, and behavioural avoidance, such as physically removing oneself from a stressor. Following the definition, the coach can teach the athlete to use avoidance coping strategies, such as blocking negative thoughts and walking away from stressful incidents. In Session 1 the coach asked the athlete to identify the coping strategies that he or she found ineffective. The coach can ask the athlete to refrain from using these strategies along with those identified in previous research, such as forcing play, speeding up, focusing on outcome, and not attempting to cope. The coach could emphasise that the athlete might find it difficult to not use the ineffective strategies he or she has previously been using, if any, and that it will take time and practice.

Session 6: Social support

All athletes need a support network, because they might not be able to manage some stressors themselves and thus need to rely on significant others such as the coach, parents, spouse, siblings, or peers. In this session, the coach asks the athlete to identify the people he or she relies on for social support. Following this process the coach asks the athlete to distinguish between the people who are excellent at providing technical support and those who can provide emotional support. The athlete would then be encouraged to speak to those who are good at providing technical support with technical problems, and those who are good at providing emotional support when they worry. The coach then presents the athlete with several stressful situations and asks the athlete to identify who they would speak to when seeking support, with an emphasis on matching the problem with the person he or she speaks to. The athlete is encouraged to speak to members of his support network in the following week and let them know he will be asking them for their advice in the future.

Session 7: Summary

In the seventh and final session, the coach summarises the sessions and answers any questions. This session is very useful to monitor the progress of the athlete, who will be seven weeks into the intervention. The coach could ask the athlete to complete a variety of questionnaires at the start of the intervention relating to constructs such as anxiety, coping, or coping self-efficacy and ask the athlete to complete the same questionnaires during Session 7 to monitor his or her progress. The coach could also monitor the effects of the intervention long after the seven-week process and conduct recap sessions if they are needed.

CASE STUDY 21.1   HELPING A SHOT-PUTTER COPE MORE EFFECTIVELY

Tom, who is a 48-year-old part-time athletics coach, started coaching Karen towards the end of the season. In training, Karen regularly throws over 16 metres, but seems to crumble in competition settings. Tom asked Karen what she felt the reasons for this were and she said that she was just too anxious to perform and did not know how to manage her stress. Tom suggested that a coping effectiveness training programme could be useful and explained what this would involve. She decided to take part in the programme during her close season. Tom conducted seven sessions, which included a session on understanding stress and coping, appraisal training, problem-focused coping, emotion-focused coping, avoidance coping, seeking social support, and a summary. At first, Karen tended to concentrate too much on what she was doing to cope, to the detriment of her technique and her performance deteriorated slightly in training. What she was doing to cope was actually becoming a source of concern to her. Tom asked her to spend more time learning and reviewing the coping strategies and practise these away from training such as when she was driving or working, so that they became second nature to her. After a few weeks, Karen became much more comfortable with using the coping strategies and spent less time thinking about them, which enabled her to perform better. Karen practised using the principles she had used over the close season and felt more than ready to use the strategies when she entered competition again.

Case study reflection

If possible, athletes should undergo psychological training programmes during their off season, so that they get time to work on the different techniques they learn. Sometimes, athletes might struggle to learn new psychological techniques, whereas others will immediately flourish. It is important that coaches are aware of this and allow athletes time to adapt to using their newly acquired psychological strategies.

Summary points

- Defining stress is a very contentious issue, with researchers struggling to agree on a common definition.
- Stress is associated with a variety of symptoms such as increased blood pressure, heart rate, respiration rate, and perspiration.
- Coping refers to the thoughts and behaviours that an athlete engages in to manage stress.
- A meta-analysis revealed that coping is associated with sports performance.
- Coping can be classified as problem-focused, emotion-focused, or avoidance coping.
- CET may improve how an athlete copes with stress, and involves athletes being taught how to use different coping strategies, appraisal training, and seek social support.

Practice exam questions

1. Describe the symptoms associated with stress and the implications for sport performance.
2. Compare and contrast the different coping functions.
3. Discuss how coping effectiveness may influence performance and the emotional well-being of athletes.
4. Outline how coping effectiveness training is different to other coping interventions used with athletes.
5. Critically evaluate the goodness-of-fit approach.

Critical thinking questions: applying theory to practice

1. Reflect on your own coaching experiences and consider whether all athletes will experience the same stressors.
2. With reference to the fight–flight explanation of stress, discuss whether stress is inherently bad for athletes.
3. Think about a player you coached who you believe struggled to cope with stress. How could you help this player?
4. Discuss the practical strengths and limitations of coping effectiveness training.
5. What could a coach do if an athlete continues to use ineffective coping strategies, despite coping effectiveness training?

Case study questions

1. Discuss why Tom started the coping effectiveness training during the close season.
2. What are the advantages and disadvantages of waiting until the close season before commencing coping effectiveness training?
3. What could Tom do differently to help Karen in the first few weeks of receiving the training, when her performance deteriorated?

22

ENHANCING CHALLENGE STATES AND MINIMISING THREAT STATES AMONG ATHLETES

This chapter provides coaches with information regarding how they can help their athletes experience challenge states and minimise the occurrence of threat states in order to enhance performance and well-being in pressurised situations. This chapter contains information on:

- A definition of challenge and threat states
- Challenge states
- Threat states
- Physiological implications of challenge and threat states
- The relationship between challenge and threat states and sporting performance
- The determinants of challenge and threat states and implications for coaches
- Techniques to maximise challenge and minimise threat.

A definition of challenge and threat states

Blascovich's (2008) biopsychosocial model (BPSM) of challenge and threat suggests that prior to a task, such as a sport competition, the athlete will make an evaluation of the demands he or she is likely to encounter and whether he or she possesses the resources to be able to cope effectively with the stress associated with such demands. Such evaluations only occur when an athlete is motivated to perform (Moore et al., 2012). If an athlete perceives that his or her resources are sufficient to cope, a challenge state will occur. Alternatively, if an athlete believes that his or her resources to cope are insufficient, a threat state will occur.

Challenge states

Jones et al. (2009) classified an athlete as being in a challenge state when he or she responds to any stress positively. That is, athletes who focus on what can be gained from a potential stressful situation and believe they possess sufficient resources to cope with the stress are considered as being in a challenge state.

Nicholls et al. (2011) interviewed professional rugby players about times they experienced challenge and threat states in matches. Indeed, the following challenge quote comes from a British and Irish Lions player, who referred to playing in a World Cup quarter-final match (p. 86):

> We were playing good rugby and we approached things differently, we were more confident with one another and accepted our role as underdogs and went out there to enjoy it, so you manage the stress, "If I can be the best I possibly can be, we are in with a good shout, because everybody else seems confident what they are going to be doing." If I am on the ball I can do that, then I will ask another question of myself.

This is typical of a challenge state, as the player mentioned being confident, able to do what will be asked of him, focused on enjoyment, and believed he could manage the stress that would ensue in the World Cup quarter-final match.

Threat states

Moore et al. (2012) suggested that athletes who believe their resources are insufficient to cope with any stressful encounters in sports events will focus on what could potentially go wrong and will experience a threat state.

The following quote is from a Welsh rugby union international who experienced a threat state when he made his debut against South Africa (p. 84):

> When I played for Wales my first cap was against South Africa, which is one of the best second rows you are going to play against. That was really nerve racking as I was sat on the bench thinking "oh crap, oh god, there is 80,000 people watching you, live TV cameras." I was thinking "I am going against these two awesome guys." I was bricking it when I went on. I was worried about letting myself down, I did not want to miss a tackle, drop the ball, I did not want to do something stupid knowing that all my friends and family are watching, it was live on TV and my first cap and I was really nervous.

It is evident from this quotation that the player focused on what could go wrong in terms of him making mistakes and although he did not discuss his perceptions of being able to cope or not, it would appear that the player did not feel he had the resources to cope, as he was going to be playing against opponents who were the best in world at the time.

Physiological implications of challenge and threat states

The way in which a person interprets a stressful situation has physiological implications, given that there are key differences between challenge and threat states (Blascovich, 2008). In particular, there are two key differences between challenge and threat states, which are (a) cardiac, and (b) vascular.

Blascovich (2008) found that challenge responses are associated with an increase in sympathetic-adreno-medullary (SAM), epinephrine (see Figure 22.1), along with less vascular resistance (see Figure 22.2). Conversely, threat responses are associated with increased levels of SAM, but also cortisol, smaller increases in cardiac activity, and increased vascular resistance.

The increased levels of SAM produce an increased heart rate along with stronger contractions from the left ventricle, which produce greater cardiac output. Increased SAM causes widening of blood vessels (vasodilatation) and therefore a decrease in vascular resistance. There is also a release of fatty acids that can be used as fuel by the brain and muscles. These physiological changes help initiate a person's attempts to cope quickly with any stress, because there is increased blood flow to the brain and muscles (Blascovich, 2008).

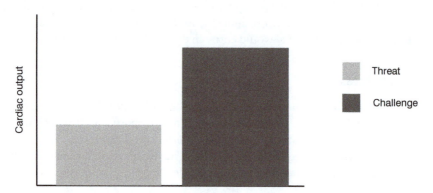

FIGURE 22.1 Cardiac activity associated with challenge and threat states

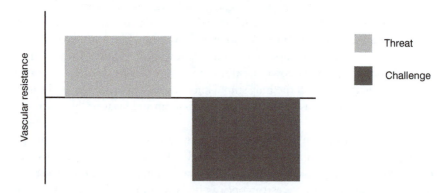

FIGURE 22.2 Vascular resistance associated with challenge and threat states

Although there is an increase in cardiac activity when an athlete is experiencing threat, there is often increased vascular resistance, which means that there is likely to be an increase in blood pressure levels. As such, blood flow to the brain and muscles is not increased and any fatty acids are therefore converted over a longer period of time, which is not conducive to coping with stress (Blascovich, 2008).

The relationship between challenge and threat states and sporting performance

Moore et al. (2012, 2013) examined the relationship between challenge and threat states and performance. Moore et al. (2012) found that golfers who exhibited a challenge state outperformed those who experienced a threat state on a putting task. In another study, Moore et al. (2013) examined challenge and threat states among golfers in an actual competition and on a putting task within a laboratory. They found that the golfers who evaluated their upcoming competitive round as a challenge (i.e. they had the resources to cope with any stress that would ensure) outperformed those golfers who appraised the upcoming round as a threat (i.e. they had insufficient resources to manage the stress). These findings were replicated in the laboratory, as golfers within the challenge group outperformed the golfers in the threat group.

In another study, which contained elite cricketers, Turner et al. (2013) examined the relationship between the cardiovascular reactivity associated with challenge and threat states along with batting performance. Aligned to Moore et al.'s (2013) findings, Turner and colleagues (2013) reported that cricketers with a challenge reactivity outperformed those with a threat reactivity. Interestingly, a small number of cricketers displayed a threat reactivity and performed well, and some cricketers displayed a challenge reactivity, but performed poorly. The additional analyses provided by the authors explained these findings. The cricketers who experienced a threat state but performed well reported higher levels of self-efficacy than those who experienced a threat and performed poorly. The cricketers who experienced a challenge state, but performed poorly used more performance-avoidance goals than those with challenge states who performed well.

The determinants of challenge and threat states and implications for coaching practice

The sport psychology literature indicates that there are three psychological constructs that determine whether athletes will experience a challenge or a threat state: (1) control, (2) self-efficacy, and (3) achievement goal perspective. Other factors that may influence the occurrence of challenge or threat states are perceptions of coach behaviour, the coach–athlete relationship, and dyadic coping. Understanding more about these key determinants is the first step in helping coaches maximise the occurrence of challenge states, whilst minimising threat states.

Control

Moore et al. (2012) found that those who experience challenge states demonstrate greater attentional control, compared with those who experience threat states. That is, athletes are able to maintain their focus on the target better with less flickering of their focus off the particular object. It is imperative that the athletes look at the target long enough to experience quiet eye. As such, a footballer taking a free kick should focus his eyes just on the ball and in particular on a specific part of the ball (e.g. any mark on the ball, the manufacturer's logo, a particular stitch, etc.). As such, coaches could encourage athletes to not take their attentional focus off a specific part of an object (i.e. ball) until after the action has been performed.

Self-efficacy

Self-efficacy refers to a person's belief in his or her ability to be successful (Bandura, 1977). As such, self-efficacy is important because if a person believes that he or she has the ability to be successful in a particular situation, it contributes to whether they believe they will be able to cope with a specific sporting competition (Blascovich, 2008; Jones et al., 2009). In order for coaches to help boost their athletes' self-efficacy, athletes could be encouraged to focus on successful past experiences and think about what helped them achieve that success. They should visualise that performance. They could also think about some of the stressors they are likely to encounter and devise a plan to help them cope with any stress. That is, they should plan what they are going to do with stressors they anticipate occurring.

Achievement goals

Adie et al. (2008) reported that an athlete's goals may determine whether he or she will experience a challenge or a threat state. According to Elliot's (1999) 2 × 2 achievement goal framework, there are four types of goals (see Figure 22.3):

- *Mastery-approach goals*: Athletes with a mastery-approach goal strive to perform better than their previous performance or personal best. As such, achievement is self-referenced and the athlete is focusing on improving.
- *Mastery-avoidance goals*: Striving not to do worse than a previous performance would be an example of a mastery-avoidance goal. The goal is still self-referenced, but has a negative connotation in that there is an emphasis on not performing worse than a desired standard.
- *Performance-approach goals*: If an athlete's main goal is to perform better than his opponents or team mates in training, that goal would be classified as a performance-approach goal. This type of goal is negative, in the sense that the athlete is trying to avoid performing worse than a specific standard.

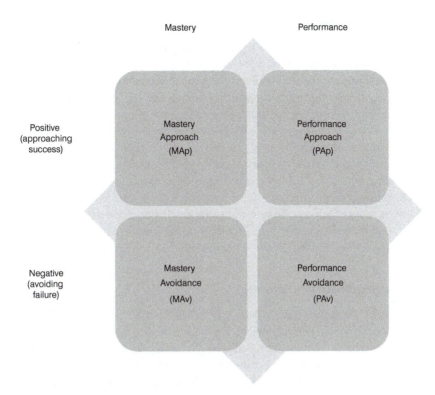

FIGURE 22.3 Achievement goals in sport

- *Performance-avoidance goals*: Striving not to be the worst performer within a competition or on a particular team is an example of an athlete who is motivated by performance-avoidance goals. In some respects, this is an example of a negative goal because the emphasis is on avoiding failure.

Adie et al. (2008) found that mastery-approach goals were positively associated with challenge states, whereas mastery-avoidance goals were predictors of threat states. Further, performance-approach goals were associated with both challenge and threat. As such, coaches could promote mastery-approach goals among their athletes in order to facilitate challenge states. That is, coaches should encourage their athletes to focus on making improvements. This does not necessarily mean that coaches should ask their athletes to always improve their personal best for every single performance, but athletes should be asked to always improve particular aspects of their performance. For example, a golfer might work on his driving in practice, so the goal for particular rounds might be to hit more fairways than his previous round or hit more greens in regulation. Athletes should always strive to improve aspects of their game and the goals they set should reflect this.

Perceptions of coach behaviour

Nicholls et al. (2016a) explored the relationship between perceptions of coach behaviour and whether this was associated with challenge or threat states among a sample of 274 athletes from the United Kingdom, Australia, or Hong Kong. Coach behaviour was classified as supportive (i.e. perceived as helping the athletes) or unsupportive (i.e. perceived as not helping the athletes) after Nicolas et al. (2011) using the Coach Behaviour Scale (Côté et al., 1999).

The results of Nicholls et al. (2016a) revealed that supportive coaching behaviours were positively associated with challenge states, whereas unsupportive coaching behaviours were positively associated with threat states. These findings carry implications for coaches, who should consider how they behave in front of athletes. In order to generate challenge states, coaches should act in a supportive manner (e.g. provide information to athletes on technical skills, goal setting, mental preparation, and build a strong rapport).

The coach–athlete relationship

Research by Nicholls et al. (2016a) and Nicholls and Perry (2016) found an association between perceptions of the coach–athlete relationship and both challenge and threat states among athletes. For example, Nicholls et al. (2016a) reported that closeness was positively associated with challenge states, but negatively associated with threat states. These results were expected by the authors, but they also found that athletes who appraised their coach–athlete relationship as being more committed also experienced higher threat levels.

Having a close relationship may generate challenge and minimise threat levels among athletes. Advice on how coaches can enhance the quality of the coach–athlete relationship is provided in Chapter 11 of this book. However, enhancing commitment levels may enhance threat levels, so coaches could try to alleviate pressures and worries among athletes who are highly committed by informing them that they possess the resources to cope and that they should focus on what they want to achieve. This could stop commitment within the coach–athlete relationship being an inhibiting factor.

Dyadic coping

Dyadic coping refers to the way in which two people, such as a coach and an athlete, interact together in order to alleviate stress. Dyadic coping can be categorised into positive dyadic coping (i.e. dyadic coping that is supportive in nature) and negative dyadic coping (e.g. one member providing insincere support). Nicholls and Perry (2016) reported that positive dyadic coping correlated positively with challenge appraisals, but negatively with threat appraisals. Conversely, negative dyadic coping correlated positively with threat appraisals, but negatively with challenge appraisals.

These findings carry implications for coaches. Coaches should provide supportive dyadic coping by:

- Helping athletes with too much to do.
- Engaging in discussions to resolve problems.
- Refraining from blaming athletes if they do not cope well with stress.
- Sincerely providing support to their athletes.
- Not ignoring athletes when they experience stress.

These dyadic coping behaviours could maximise the occurrence of challenge states and minimise threat states.

Techniques to maximise challenge and minimise threat

Mental imagery

One technique that has been successful in manipulating challenge and threat states is mental imagery. More information on mental imagery is provided in Chapter 18 of this book. For example, Williams et al. (2010) found that their imagery script caused a significant increase in heart rate, stroke volume, and cardiac output. Williams and Cumming (2012) found that an athlete's imagery ability predicted challenge or threat states. For example, athletes who could easily imagine themselves mastering a situation or having a positive effect were more likely to experience a challenge state, but were less likely to experience a threat.

In terms of developing an imagery script, Moore et al. (2013) provided some excellent suggestions for promoting challenge states, which coaches could incorporate within an imagery script. In order to generate a challenge state, Moore and colleagues instructed participants to perceive a putting task as a challenge that could be overcome and that they are capable of meeting the challenge. As such, coaches could create these scenarios within an imagery script.

Re-appraising threat

Although coaches can use a variety of techniques to generate challenge states, such as mental imagery, promoting control, boosting self-efficacy, and encouraging performance-approach goals to generate challenge states among their athletes, threat states might still occur. If threat states do occur, coaches could encourage their athletes to re-appraise or re-evaluate the threat. Indeed, research by Moore et al. (2015) examined the effectiveness of arousal re-appraisal training among 50 participants, who were assigned to the re-appraisal or control group.

The arousal re-appraisal training involved participants being informed that stressful bodily reactions in competition are not harmful. Indeed, participants were told that such stress responses aid performance. Further, participants were instructed to view stress responses associated with threat as being beneficial and thus re-interpret bodily signals as being positive and aiding performance. Following the re-appraisal training the participants were more likely to display responses associated with challenge states and outperformed the control group in a putting task.

Coaches could therefore provide re-appraisal training to their athletes and emphasise that bodily responses are natural consequences of performing in competitive sport, they are not harmful, and are likely to boost performance. As such, coaches could say that such feelings should be welcomed. This should all help athletes manage the stress of competing, particularly among athletes who experience high levels of threat.

CASE STUDY 22.1   ALLEVIATING THREAT

Jenny is a 28-year-old Paralympian, who competed at two Paralympic games in table tennis. She failed to win a medal at both of the games, but is keen to attend one more. She believes that her anxiety and worry in the lead up to and during matches prevented her from achieving her goal of winning a medal, because she regularly beats many of the top players at other competitions around the world. Jenny also views stress negatively, because it detrimentally impacts upon her performance, and generally focuses on what could go wrong.

Jenny goes into matches with the intention of not wanting to perform poorly and embarrass herself. Additionally, she wants to avoid being the worst player on the team so that she can retain her funding and gain a place on the next Olympic team.

Jenny's coach, Eric, is an experienced coach who participated at one Olympic games as a player. He recently started coaching Jenny and is keen to work on her mindset, so that she can get the most out of her potential. After having conversations with Jenny, Eric detected that she lacks belief in her ability to play well at the Paralympics, despite being able to play well at some other smaller competitions. Jenny also gets flustered and is unable to concentrate at the start of matches.

Eric decides that re-appraisal training may help Jenny, along with mental imagery. He devises a script that encourages Jenny to change how she views her stress reactions and see them as essential for optimal performance. The imagery script also asks Jenny to imagine herself overcoming different obstacles.

Eric tells Jenny that he would like her to listen to the script every day for a couple of weeks and also works on some achievement goals with her, after finding out that her main goals are related to not wanting to be the worst on the national team, so she can get selected for the next Olympics. Eric knows that performance-avoidance goals can cause threat states, so encourages Jenny to focus on achieving self-referenced goals and thus concentrate on making improvements.

Case study reflection

Successfully transforming threat states into challenge states is likely to positively impact upon an athlete's performance. There are a number of approaches that a coach can take in order to minimise threat states and increase the likelihood of an athlete experiencing a challenge state, but the key might be to identify some of the underlying reasons why an athlete has been experiencing a threat state. In this case study, Jenny adopted a performance-avoidance type goal, lacked confidence in her ability, and seemed unable to deal with stress responses. Identifying possible causes of threat states and then addressing the causes will help an athlete.

Summary points

- Challenge and threat states can only occur when an athlete is motivated to perform.
- Challenge states are associated with athletes being able to cope with the stress they are likely to encounter.
- Threat states occur when an athlete perceives that his or her resources to cope are insufficient.
- Challenge states are generally associated with superior sporting performance than threat states.
- A number of factors such as achievement goals, coach behaviour, self-efficacy, and the coach–athlete relationship influence challenge and threat states.
- Coaches can manipulate challenge states through their behaviour, statements they make to athletes, and through training in psychological skills such as mental imagery.

Practice exam questions

1   Discuss the psychological differences between challenge and threat states.
2   Discuss the physiological differences between challenge and threat states.
3   Critically evaluate the relationship between challenge and threat states with performance.
4   Discuss the antecedents of challenge and threat states.
5   Discuss how challenge states may lead to superior performance, in comparison with threat states.

Critical thinking questions: applying theory to practice

1   Reflect on your own coaching practice and identify how you generated challenge and threat states among athletes.
2   Consider whether your approach to coaching promotes mastery or avoidance goals and discuss the implications of this.
3   What could you do to enhance self-efficacy in order to promote challenge states? Discuss.
4   What types of coach behaviours are likely to generate challenge appraisals?
5   Discuss the importance of the coach–athlete relationship in determining whether an athlete will experience challenge or threat states.

Case study questions

1   In regard to exploring the possible reasons for Jenny experiencing threat states, discuss the approach Eric adopted.
2   Discuss the impact of enhancing challenges with Jenny.
3   Discuss the symptoms that led Eric to think that Jenny was experiencing threat states.

23

MINDFULNESS-BASED STRESS REDUCTION TRAINING

This chapter provides coaches with information regarding how they can help their athletes become more mindful and thus relax better in pressurised situations. In particular, this chapter provides:

- A definition of mindfulness
- A conceptual model: the 3 axioms of mindfulness
- The benefits of mindfulness training
- Mindfulness techniques.

A definition of mindfulness

Mindfulness, also referred to as mindful awareness, derives from Buddhism traditions (Bränström et al., 2011). According to Bishop et al. (2004), mindfulness involves the self-regulation of awareness in regard to momentary mental states and mental processes. Further, mindfulness also includes non-evaluation, openness, and acceptance of moment-to-moment experiences. One's ability in mindfulness can be enhanced via training, such as mediation (Brown et al., 2007; Gotink et al., 2016).

A conceptual model: the 3 axioms of mindfulness

Shapiro et al. (2006) stated that mindfulness is a state of consciousness, where the person purposefully attends to the moment-to-moment and non-judgemental experience of what is going on. Indeed, these academics refined and re-conceptualised mindfulness as consisting of three component parts, which they referred to as axioms (i.e. attention, attitude, and intention, see Figure 23.1).

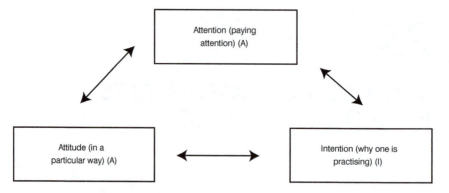

FIGURE 23.1 The axioms of mindfulness

- *Attention* (A): This involves the person observing moment-to-moment experiences as they occur. Crucially, the person is not interpreting the situation and therefore not thinking about any future consequences, he or she is just noticing what is happening.
- *Attitude* (A): This refers to the way in which the person attends to moment-to-moment experiences. That is, Shapiro et al. (2006) suggested that attention can be a cold or critical quality, or it can represent a friendly or compassionate quality and an acceptance of what is occurring.
- *Intention* (I): This relates to the goal of the person and why he or she decided to engage in mindfulness training.

It is important to note that these axioms are not separate processes. Indeed, attention, attitude, and intention occur simultaneously when the person achieves a mindfulness state.

A + I + A = reperceiving

Shapiro et al. (2006) stated that attending (A) intentionally (I) with a non-judgemental attitude (A) results in a shift in the way a person perceives his or her situation, which they termed reperceiving. Essentially, this represents a large shift in an individual's perception and involves him, or her being able to stand back and witness what is occurring rather than being immersed in it. Indeed, Shapiro and colleagues (2006) attributed reperceiving to the positive outcomes associated with mindfulness, as it leads to better psychological outcomes (e.g. enhanced well-being, reduced stress, or enhanced optimism).

The benefits of mindfulness training

Mindfulness training can produce many biological and psychological benefits (see Figure 23.2). In particular, scholars such as Manzaneque et al. (2010)

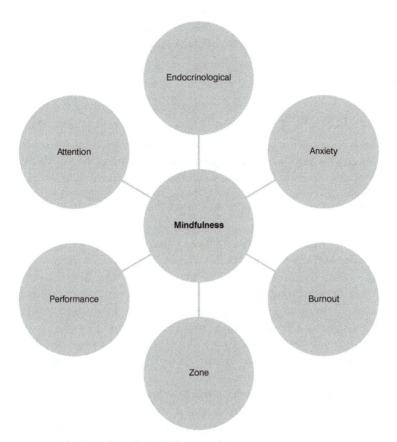

FIGURE 23.2   The benefits of mindfulness training

found that a mindfulness meditation programme had a significant effect on the endocrine system, which is involved in the pathophysiology of both anxiety and depression. As such, mindfulness enhances well-being by influencing hormones.

Gotink et al. (2016) published a systematic review of 30 studies, which used Magnetic Resonance Imagining (MRI) or functional Magnetic Resonance Imagining (fMRI), to examine the effects of 8-week mindfulness training programmes on brain structure and function. They reported changes in structure and function in areas of the brain such as the prefrontal cortex, insula, hippocampus, and amygdala. Mindfulness training may help athletes regulate emotions more effectively, such as anxiety, due to these functional and structural changes in the brain.

Within sport, Moen et al. (2015) reported that a mindfulness training intervention positively impacted on burnout, anxiety, and performance. Additionally, Cathcart et al. (2014) found that mindfulness training helped athletes get into the zone much more frequently, and thus boosted performance. Mindfulness training also enhanced attention and performance among national level swimmers (Mardon et al., 2016). There are numerous benefits of mindfulness training, so this could be a vital tool for coaches to use.

Mindfulness techniques

The meditation body scan

A crucial aspect of mindfulness training is awareness or attention on moment-to-moment observations. One technique advocated by Wilde McCormick (2012) is the mediation body scan. This involves the athlete attending to feelings in his or her body. As a coach, you can provide the following adapted instructions to your athlete:

1   Either sit or lie down on the floor in a comfortable position where you will be warm and not be disturbed. When you feel ready, close your eyes.
2   Now take a few breaths and allow time to get in tune with the movement of your breath, along with any sensations. Once you are ready, observe the physical sensations in your body. As you exhale, let yourself to let go and sink deeper into the chair or floor with each exhalation.
3   Now think about your intention – this is not to feel relaxed or calm, but to be aware of any sensations or feelings that you detect as your attention is directed to different parts of your body.
4   Bring your awareness to the physical sensations in your lower stomach, becoming aware of any changing sensations in your lower stomach, as you exhale. Take a couple of minutes to feel these sensations as you inhale and exhale.
5   Having directed your awareness to your lower stomach, now bring your awareness down to your right leg, into the right foot, and now to the toes of your right foot, focusing on each of the toes of your right foot in turn.
6   After doing this for a few moments, when you inhale, imagine all of the air entering your lungs, passing down the stomach, right leg, right foot, and to the toes of the right foot. As you exhale, imagine all of the air coming up through your right foot, right leg, stomach, chest, and through your nose as the air leaves your body. Practise doing this for a few breaths.
7   Now bring your awareness to the left side of your body. As you inhale, feel the air go down to your stomach, left leg, left foot, and left toes, then feel it come back up through your toes, left foot, left leg, stomach, chest, and then out through your nose as you exhale. Continue for a few more breaths.
8   Now bring your awareness to other parts of your body, such as your chest, shoulders, arms, wrists, hands, and fingers. As you become aware of the sensations in each body part breathe in, and then exhale when your awareness shifts to another part of your body.
9   If you feel any tension in any part of your body, you can dispel this tension by taking a deep breath in and releasing the tension with a deep exhalation.

If the tension is still there, take another deep inhalation and then exhale to let the tension go.

10 After scanning your whole body and relieving any tension, spend several minutes being aware of your body as a whole and how the air flows in and out.

Tips for more effective meditation

- It is only natural for the athlete's mind to wonder when he or she is performing the body scan. Inform the athlete of this and let him or her know that when their attention wanders away from the breath or body, they should acknowledge this by noticing where the mind has gone to, and then return the focus to the part of the body that was being focused on before the mind wandered.
- If the athlete finds themself falling asleep whilst meditating, they could try propping themself up on a pillow or meditating whilst sitting up.
- How much time the athlete dedicates to this meditation is up to them, and this time can vary depending on how much free time he or she has available.

Sending caring thoughts for self and team mates

Another facet of mindfulness training relates to increasing feelings of warmth, kindness, and caring towards oneself and others (Baltzell et al., 2014). This involves coaches encouraging athletes to be kind to themselves and other team mates if mistakes are made (e.g. a defender misses a tackle and opponents score). As such, coaches could instruct athletes not to shout or degrade their ability, but tell them to accept mistakes as things that happen. Further, Baltzell and colleague's (2014) intervention involved athletes being taught to wish warmth and kindness to their team mates. As such, coaches could ask players to think about other players on their team and imaging being kind to them if they make a mistake or them being kind to themselves. Coaches can monitor this in training and matches.

The technique of being caring towards oneself was used by the British tennis player, Andy Murray (*The Guardian*, 2015). Murray wrote down a list of notes that he took on court, which included a list of psychological cues (e.g. 1. Be good to yourself; 2. Try your best; 3. Be intense with your legs; 4. Be proactive during points; and 5. Focus on each point and the process) and technical instructions (e.g. 1. Try to be the one dictating; 2. Try to keep him at the base line, make him move; 3. Keep going for your serve; 4. Stick to the baseline as much as possible; and 5. Stay low on passes and use your legs).

Of relevance to the present chapter is the first instruction about Andy Murray being good to himself. In the past, Andy was known for losing his temper and berating himself on court, but this was a conscious attempt to refrain from that form of behaviour.

Breathing ladders for enhanced concentration

Another mindfulness technique that can aid concentration is a breathing ladder. This technique formed part of a mindfulness training intervention with Division 1 soccer players in the United States (Baltzell et al., 2014).

After each exhalation the athlete is instructed to silently say a number to themself. After the first exhalation the athlete should say "one" silently. Following the next exhalation he or she says "two" silently. After the third exhalation they say "three", and carry on until 10 is reached. After the athlete has reached 10, he or she starts descending after each breath to 9, then 8, and then all the way to 1. At this point the athlete repeats the initial cycle, but only ascends to 9 and then back down to 1. Once he or she gets back down from 9, they repeat up to 8 and back down, and then up to 7, and back down. This process is continued until the athlete reaches 1. Once the athlete gets back down to 1, he or she can even start the cycle again, going all the way up to 10 again.

There is a catch: if the athlete loses his or her place at any point, they start back at the beginning and ascend up to 10.

Practising acceptance of negative mindsets

Unfortunately, we've all made mistakes whilst playing sport, and if we continue playing sport we will make more mistakes. Therefore, our reaction to mistakes is important. Rather than being angry or berating ourselves, researchers such as Baltzell et al. (2014) advocated that athletes should be encouraged to accept mistakes.

In order to do this, coaches could encourage their athletes to consider a time when they played sport with a negative mindset, such as feeling anger due to a wrong call from an official, shame from making a mistake, and/or letting their team mates down. The coach should then ask the athlete to focus on the experience with as much detail as possible, so that the experience is as vivid as it can be, and the athlete is able to really relive those emotions. In particular, the athlete should be instructed to notice how that made them feel. The coach should instruct the athlete to accept those feelings (e.g. anger, shame, or anxiety) as emotions that everyone has experienced at one point or another. Performing this exercise will help athletes become more accepting of negative emotions.

Summary points

- The three main components of mindfulness are attention, intention, and attitude.
- If successful, the application of attending intentionally with a non-judgemental attitude can lead to reperceiving.
- There are numerous physiological and psychological benefits of mindfulness.
- There are many different techniques associated with mindfulness (e.g. meditation body scan, caring thoughts, breathing ladder, and acceptance).

CASE STUDY 23.1   HELPING A HOCKEY PLAYER WITH PRE-COMPETITIVE ANXIETY

Danielle, a national under-19 hockey coach, noticed that one of her players is extremely uptight and anxious before matches, to the extent that the player (Georgie) is considering quitting playing hockey, because it is affecting her too much. In particular, Georgie has always struggled with sleeping the night before a match, but in recent weeks she noticed that her sleep was also affected from three nights before a hockey match. Georgie is also very anxious on the morning of a match. As soon as she wakes up she starts thinking about mistakes that she could make and what could go wrong. As such, she struggles to eat because she is so nervous and feels so nauseous.

In order to help Georgie, Danielle spent some time chatting to her about how she is afflicted by anxiety in the lead up to matches, so she could gather a thorough understanding of what was happening.

Danielle believed that Georgie would benefit from mindfulness training, because there was evidence that it can relieve anxiety and enhance psychological well-being. As such, Danielle recorded some mindfulness techniques on Georgie's phone, and asked Georgie to regularly practise mindfulness training techniques.

Interestingly, through trial and error, Georgie preferred different techniques depending on the situation. For example, if Georgie was having problems getting to sleep or if she woke up in the middle of the night, she liked the breathing ladders exercise, and felt this helped her get to sleep better. On the morning of a match she found the meditation body scan and practising accepting previous mistakes really helpful, because they calmed her down. Over time, these different mindfulness techniques became a crucial part of Georgie's pre-match routine and she also used the techniques when contending with other stressful events in her life that were not related to hockey. The more Georgie practised mindfulness training, the less anxious she became.

Case study reflection

Some athletes may really struggle with anxiety in the lead up to matches. For many, the anxiety will be worst just before the match starts, but some may get nervous a few days before a match. Mindfulness training can really help athletes who struggle with anxiety, but it is important to note that the full benefits of such training may occur after several weeks of practice. Also, some athletes may prefer different techniques to others, and as a coach it is important that athletes are encouraged to find out what works best for them by a process of trial and error.

Practice exam questions

1 Describe the benefits of mindfulness training.
2 Critically evaluate Shapiro et al.'s (2006) conceptual model of mindfulness.
3 Discuss the benefits of mindfulness training.
4 Compare and contrast mindfulness training with traditional forms of progressive muscular relaxation.
5 Discuss the relationship between mindfulness and sports performance.

Critical thinking questions: applying theory to practice

1 Discuss the potential difficulties of providing mindfulness training to athletes.
2 With reference to the meditation body scan, plan a training schedule for an athlete who is struggling with anxiety.
3 Discuss how a coach could monitor the effectiveness of mindfulness training for his or her athletes.
4 How would a coach know whether an athlete was reperceiving or not? Discuss.
5 What could a coach do if an athlete is sceptical about the benefits of mindfulness training? Discuss.

Case study questions

1 How could Danielle assess Georgie's anxiety?
2 Would Danielle need to monitor how often Georgie was engaging in mindfulness training? Discuss your answer.
3 If the mindfulness training proved to be ineffective after a number of weeks, and Georgie's anxiety gets worse, what should Danielle do?

24

PREVENTING CHOKING UNDER PRESSURE IN SPORT

The purpose of this chapter is to provide coaches with information on choking under pressure in sport, so they can help their athletes to prevent this from occurring in pressurised situations. As such, information is provided on:

- A definition of choking under pressure in sport
- Physical and psychological feelings associated with choking
- Theoretical explanations of why athletes choke
- How to prevent choking under pressure.

A definition of choking under pressure in sport

Beilock et al. (2004: 584) defined choking as "performing more poorly than expected given one's skill level ... thought to occur across diverse task domains where incentives for optimal performance are at a maximum". An athlete's desire to perform at, or very close to his or her best, in a competition or match that is deemed to be very important, creates performance pressure (Baumeister, 1984). Athletes who compete in individual sports are more likely to choke than team sport athletes (Iwatsuki and Wright, 2016).

Beilock and Gray (2007) suggested that instances of choking contain a clear beginning and end, so a coach would be able to distinguish the period in which an athlete is choking and the climax of this episode. This is because an athlete's performance will dip below his or her normal level during choking, but will return to the expected level after the choking episode has concluded. Furthermore, Beilock and Gray argued that choking normally occurs across short periods of time, from a soccer player hitting a very poor penalty to a hockey player performing poorly for an 80-minute match.

Physical and psychological feelings associated with choking

When athletes choke, they experience a variety of physical and psychological symptoms. Nideffer (1992) outlined some of the physical symptoms, which are presented in Figure 24.1. The psychological symptoms are presented in Figure 24.2.

Theoretical explanations of why athletes choke

Two main explanations attempt to explain why athletes' skills can sometimes fail under pressurised conditions. These are the self-focus or the explicit monitoring hypothesis and the distraction hypothesis.

The self-focus or explicit monitoring hypothesis

The self-focus or explicit monitoring hypothesis, proposed by Baumeister (1984) and expanded upon by Masters (1992), suggests that performance pressure increases (a) the amount of anxiety an athlete will experience, and (b) his or her self-consciousness of the skill being performed. The desire to perform at a high level and the athlete being more self-conscious of performing certain movements (e.g. a putt in golf or a serve in tennis) results in the athlete focusing on the sequence of movements that make the entire skill. As the pressure to perform increases, the athlete tries even harder to control the sequence of movements that make up an entire skill in the hope that the performance of the skill will be more accurate through being more controlled. When athletes attempt to consciously monitor or control movements, the automated processes that they usually engage in are disrupted, which is why performance suffers (Beilock et al., 2004).

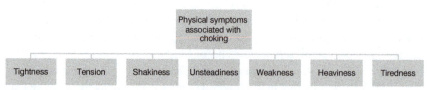

FIGURE 24.1   The physical symptoms associated with choking

FIGURE 24.2   The psychological symptoms associated with choking

Distraction hypothesis

The distraction hypothesis, proposed by Nideffer (1992), was extended by Hardy et al. (2001) and Mullen et al. (2005). Nideffer (1992) suggested that as anxiety increases in highly pressurised situations, athletes' attention shifts from task-relevant thoughts (e.g. about how to execute specific tactics) to task-irrelevant thoughts (e.g. worries about team selection in future matches). As such, the athlete whose attention is diverted towards task-irrelevant cues no longer attends to the relevant cues that he or she would normally attend to, which are conducive to higher levels of sport performance. Therefore, anxiety acts as a distraction for the athlete, which reduces the working memory and the task-focused attention.

Hardy et al. (2001) and Mullen et al. (2005) supplemented the distraction hypothesis theory by arguing that increased anxiety and task-irrelevant thoughts do not result automatically in choking. They cause choking when they simultaneously compete with the attention an athlete usually allocates to performing the task. That is, an athlete chokes when his or her attentional threshold to maintain performance is exceeded. According to Mesagno and Mullane-Grant (2010) the distraction hypothesis is the most widely supported model, but these two models may co-exist.

How to prevent choking under pressure

Researchers in sport psychology conducted studies that provide some useful guidelines for how coaches can help their athletes avoid choking.

Reducing the stigma associated with choking

Coaches can reduce the stigma associated with choking by informing their athletes that this is something that happens to many athletes and will happen to lots more athletes in the future.

Pre-performance routine

A pre-performance routine, according to Moran (1996), is a sequence of task-relevant thoughts and behaviours that an athlete engages in before performing in a sports skill. A pre-performance routine may be more suitable in sports that are self-paced, such as golf, tennis, or for regular free-kick takers in soccer. A pre-performance routine can reduce the likelihood of choking, because it helps focus an athlete's attention on task-related cues as opposed to task-irrelevant cues (Mesagno and Mullane-Grant, 2010). Researchers found that a pre-performance routine can improve performance, within high-pressure situations, by as much as 29 per cent compared with when athletes were not provided with a pre-performance routine (Mesagno et al., 2008). The pre-performance routine described by Mesagno et al. involved deep breathing, using task-relevant cue words, in addition to the participants spending a consistent amount of time on each pre-performance routine.

Mesagno and Mullane-Grant (2010) extended the findings of Mesagno et al. (2008) and found that a pre-performance routine that included all the elements (e.g. timing consistency training, deep breathing, and cue words) enabled athletes to perform the most successfully under pressurised situations.

Coaches can help their athletes perform in pressurised sporting events by providing training on pre-performance routines. This training should involve:

- *Cue words*: The coach could ask the athlete to consider some task-relevant cue words, which he or she thinks are important for performing in their sport. For example, a rugby union goal kicker may chose the words "coil" and "follow through". Once the athlete has identified two or three keywords he or she can say these key words prior to performing, as a part of a pre-performance routine.
- *Deep breathing*: An athlete can be taught to take two deep breaths prior to performing, whereby the athlete is instructed to inhale deeply to a count of 5 through the nose and exhale through the mouth to a count of 9 or 10.
- *Timing*: The coach could time the athlete and let him or her know how consistently the pre-performance routine has been performed to maximise consistency.

A pre-performance routine should be individualised (Mesagno and Mullane-Grant, 2010). That is, the keywords should be chosen by the athlete. Some athletes might prefer to say their keywords whilst they are taking their deep breaths, others might want to say their keywords before taking the breaths, whereas other athletes might want to say their keywords after taking their breaths. There is no wrong or right approach, but it is important that once the athletes try different pre-performance routines, they establish their own routine, which they consistently perform. This is because athletes perform better when they stick to their established pre-performance routine compared with when they deviate away from it (Lonsdale and Tam, 2008).

Pressure acclimatisation training

Oudejans and Pijpers (2010) found evidence to suggest that training with anxiety present may reduce choking. Further, Hodge and Smith (2014) suggested that athletes should also be encouraged to make decisions and solve problems when under pressure in training situations. When athletes train whilst feeling anxious they learn to perform their skill in conditions that promote self-conscious behaviour (Jordet, 2010). Coaches can create situations that promote anxiety in training among athletes by:

- *Stating the importance of training*: Prior to the training session starting, the coach can tell his or her players that he or she is going to rate the performance of each player in terms of the effort exerted, skills executed, and impact on other players (if in a team sport). The coach could then inform the players that this information will help him or her decide team selection.

- *Encouraging athletes to set their own performance targets*: Nicholls and Callard (2012) suggested that players should set themselves targets in training sessions and play competitive games among themselves. For instance, a player might set themself the target of catching 50 high balls in a row. Once the player drops a ball, he or she starts again from the beginning so by the time the player gets to around 40 they might start feeling anxious.
- *Mimicing anxiety symptoms*: Coaches can develop drills that mimic the symptoms of stress and anxiety and ask athletes to perform drills whilst experiencing similar symptoms (Nicholls and Callard, 2012). For example, stress is associated with symptoms such as an increased heart-rate, breathing rate, and perspiration rate, so a coach could ask athletes to do some sprints before conducting penalty practice in soccer. As such, the athlete would be taking a penalty whilst experiencing some of the same symptoms as when they take a penalty in competitions.
- *Facilitating problem solving and decision making*: In their study of choking among All Blacks rugby union players, Hodge and Smith (2014) advocated that coaches identify the decision-making skills that are required in their sport and then create training drills which require athletes to make decisions and solve problems when in pressurised situations that are realistic of matches.

Although inducing anxiety among athletes has the potential to help them become accustomed to playing in high-pressured situations (e.g. Oudejans and Pijpers, 2010), coaches need to be careful regarding how they create this anxiety and ensure that it does not detrimentally affect athletes.

Movement acclimatisation training

Another technique that Beilock and Carr (2001) advocated involved athletes being encouraged by the coach to focus on their movements whilst performing. Athletes will become used to performing whilst feeling self-conscious. As such, when athletes perform in important competitions and start becoming self-conscious about their movements, they will be acclimatised to this level of consciousness. Therefore, sporting performance should remain unaffected.

Compassion

Jordet (2010) stated that athletes can be very hard on themselves, especially after making a mistake. As such, coaches can provide support to athletes and tell them that they are not perfect and that mistakes will occur when they try to win matches or competitions.

Reframing pressure

Hodge and Smith (2014) advocated that athletes reframe pressure as a privilege. For example, they suggested that coaches should identify the sources of pressure in an athlete's sport and (a) encourage athletes to re-appraise the situations as a privilege (e.g. it is an honour to play for my international team, it is exciting to play in front of a large crowd, etc.), and (b) teach athletes to view pressurised situations as a challenge (see Chapter 22).

Secondary task strategies

Coaches working with high-level athletes could use secondary task strategies to help distract their athletes and facilitate performance. Land and Tennenbaum (2012) asked high-level and novice golfers to say the word "hit" when putting a ball. This improved performance among the high-level golfers, but not for the novices. As such, coaches could devise task-relevant words and encourage their high-level athletes to say them out loud or quietly to themselves.

Coping

Hill and Hemmings (2015) interviewed six elite golfers regarding instances where they choked or excelled under pressure and found that different coping strategies were associated with choking or clutch experiences. For example, avoidance coping strategies were associated with athletes choking, whereas approach or task-focused strategies were associated with athletes performing well under pressure. As such, coaches could provide coping training to their athletes (see Chapter 21).

Summary points

- Choking is when an athlete performs worse than would be expected in an important competition.
- Choking may be more prevalent among individual sport athletes than team sport athletes.
- Choking is associated with a variety of physical and psychological symptoms.
- Two theoretical models attempted to explain why athletes choke in sport – the self-focus, or explicit monitoring hypothesis theory, and the distraction hypothesis theory.
- Coaches can help athletes not to choke by providing choking prevention training, which may include developing a pre-performance routine, pressure acclimatisation training, movement acclimatisation training, encouraging an athlete to be more compassionate towards themself, reframing pressure, and engaging in secondary task strategies.

CASE STUDY 24.1 CHOKING UNDER PRESSURE IN PROFESSIONAL RUGBY UNION

James is a 54-year-old professional rugby union coach, who coaches attacking play and has recently taken an interest in coaching the kickers in his team. His team's leading kicker, Dave, is a 19-year-old player who is playing his first season as a professional player. Dave made his first team debut as an 18-year-old and made a good start playing the last four games of the previous season. Dave played the first two games of the present season, but had a poor game in which he missed four goal kicks and was dropped from the team.

As the kicking coach, James was keen to speak to Dave to try to help establish what went wrong and develop a plan regarding what they could work on. First, James spoke to Dave about the match prior to him being dropped, to try to explain Dave's performance. In particular, James asked Dave how he felt during the match. Dave said that he started the match feeling fine, successfully kicking his first kick, but after missing his next kick he felt more worried. This worry increased with each kick that was missed, especially when he had a kick within four minutes from the end of the match to lead by a point, which he missed. James also watched Dave's performance on video and timed his pre-performance kicking routine. As the match went on Dave's routine became much quicker, until the last kick where he spent much longer stood over the ball. James also noticed that the behaviours in James' pre-performance routine were inconsistent. He would look at the posts three times prior to some kicks, but would only look at the posts once prior to taking other kicks.

James suggested to Dave that he should develop a more consistent pre-performance routine to use before every kick, regardless of how easy or difficult the kick is. Dave agreed with this, and they developed an ideal pre-performance kicking routine which involved secondary task strategies (e.g. keywords that James would say to himself), and behaviours (e.g. looking at posts), by writing this down. They then took the piece of paper with them onto the training pitch and experimented with the routine and made some minor tweaks to the routine.

Dave was asked to engage in his pre-performance routine before every kick that he took, whether that was in training, warming up for matches, or in the match.

Case study reflection

There are a number of things a coach can do to help athletes who are prone to choking. It is important that the coach is supportive of the athlete, because choking can be a very distressing experience. Athletes are likely to respond differently to forms of training to prevent choking, so coaches might need to try a number of techniques before finding what works best for an athlete.

Practice exam questions

1   Why do athletes choke? Discuss.
2   Describe the physical and psychological symptoms associated with choking.
3   Describe the explicit hypothesis theory of choking and research that has supported this theory.
4   Critically evaluate the distraction hypothesis theory of choking.
5   Compare and contrast the explicit hypothesis theory of choking and the distraction hypothesis theory of choking.

Critical thinking questions: applying theory to practice

1   Describe the circumstances that may contribute to athletes feeling performance pressure.
2   Discuss the advantages and disadvantages of performance pressure.
3   What key characteristics should be included in a pre-performance routine? Discuss.
4   Critically evaluate the process of increasing anxiety within training sessions.
5   Discuss the potential positive and negative implications of teaching athletes to be more compassionate towards themselves.

Case study questions

1   What are the advantages and limitations of James' approach to assessing why Dave choked under pressure?
2   Describe how James could provide training in the use of task-relevant strategies.
3   Develop a pre-performance routine for Dave.

REFERENCES

Adams, C., Coffee, P., and Lavallee, D. (2015) 'Athletes' perceptions about the availability of social support during within-career transitions', *Sport & Exercise Psychology Review*, 11, 37–48.

Adie, J.W., Duda, J.L., and Ntoumanis, N. (2008) 'Achievement goals, competition appraisals, and the psychological and emotional welfare of sport participants', *Journal of Sport & Exercise Psychology*, 30, 302–322.

Adie, J.W., Duda, J.L., and Ntoumanis, N. (2012) 'Perceived coach-autonomy support, basic need satisfaction and the well- and ill-being of elite youth soccer players: A longitudinal investigation', *Psychology of Sport and Exercise*, 13, 51–59.

Ahlberg, M., Mallett, C., and Tinning, R. (2008) 'Developing autonomy supportive coaching behaviours: An action research approach to coach development', *International Journal of Coaching Science*, 2, 1–20.

Ahsen A. (1984) 'ISM: The Triple Code Model for imagery and psychophysiology', *Journal of Mental Imagery*, 8, 15–42.

Aldwin, C.M. (2007) *Stress, coping and development: An integrative perspective*, New York: Guilford Press, 2nd edn.

American Psychiatric Association (2000) *Diagnostic and statistical manual of mental disorders – IV-TR*, Washington, DC: APA, 4th edn.

Ames, C. (1992) 'Achievement goals, motivational climate, and motivational processes', in G.C. Roberts (ed.), *Advances in motivation in sport and exercise*, Champaign, IL: Human Kinetics, pp. 161–176.

Amorose, A.J. (2007) 'Coaching effectiveness,' in M.S. Hagger and N.L.D. Chatzisarantis (eds), *Intrinsic motivation and self-determination in exercise and sport*, Champaign, IL: Human Kinetics, pp. 209–228.

Amorose, A.J., and Anderson-Butcher, D. (2007) 'Autonomy-supportive coaching and self-determined motivation in high school and colleague athletes: A test of self-determination theory', *Psychology of Sport and Exercise*, 8, 657–670.

Amorose, A.J., and Anderson-Butcher, D. (2015) 'Exploring the independent and interactive effects of autonomy-supportive and controlling coaching behaviors on adolescent athletes' motivation for sport', *Sport, Exercise, and Performance Psychology,* 4, 206–218.

Amorose, A.J., and Horn, T.S. (2000) 'Intrinsic motivation: Relationships with collegiate athletes' gender, scholarship status, and perceptions of their coaches' behavior', *Journal of Sport and Exercise Psychology,* 22, 63–84.

Amorose, A.J., and Horn, T.S. (2001) 'Pre- and post-season changes in intrinsic motivation of first year college athletes: Relationships with coaching behavior and scholarship status', *Journal of Applied Sport Psychology,* 13, 355–373.

Amorose, A.J., Anderson-Butcher, D., Newman, T.J., Fraina, M., and Iachini, A. (2016) 'High school athletes' self-determined motivation: The independent and interactive effects of coach, father, and mother autonomy support', *Psychology of Sport and Exercise,* 26, 1–8.

Andersen, M.B. (2000) 'Beginnings: Intakes and the initiation of relationships', in M.B. Andersen (ed.), *Doing sport psychology,* Champaign, IL: Human Kinetics, pp. 3–16.

Andersen, M.B. (2011) 'Who's mental, who's tough and who's both? Mutton constructs dressed up as lamb', in D. Gucciardi and S. Gordon (eds), *Mental toughness in sport: Developments in Research and Theory,* London: Routledge, pp. 69–88.

Andersen, M.B., and Van Raalte, J.L. (2005) 'Over one's head: Referral processes', in M.B. Andersen (ed.), *Sport Psychology in Practice,* Champaign, IL: Human Kinetics, pp. 159–170.

Anhalt, K., McNeil, C.B., and Bahl, A.B. (1998) 'The ADHD classroom kit: A whole-classroom approach for managing disruptive behaviour', *Psychology in the Schools,* 35, 67–79.

Anshel, M.H. (2001) 'Qualitative validation of a model for coping with acute stress in sport', *Journal of Sport Behaviour,* 24, 223–246.

Anshel, M.H., Gregory, W.L., and Kaczmarek, M. (1990) 'The effectiveness of a stress training program in coping with criticism in sport: A test of the COPE model', *Journal of Sport Behaviour,* 13, 194–217.

Appleton, P.R., Ntoumanis, N., Quested, E., Viladrich, C., and Duda, J.L. (2016) 'Initial validation of the coach-created Empowering and Disempowering Motivational Climate Questionnaire (EDMCQ-C)', *Psychology of Sport and Exercise,* 22, 53–65.

Arden, C.L., Österberg, A., Tagesson, S., Gauffin, H., Webster, K.E., and Kvist, J. (2014) 'The impact of psychological readiness to return to sport and recreational activities after anterior cruciate ligament reconstruction', *British Journal of Sports Medicine,* 48, 1613–1619.

Arvinen-Barrow, M., Clement, D., Hamson-Utley, J.J., Zakrajsek, R.A., Lee, S.-M., Kamphoff, C., Lintuenen, T., Hemmings, B., and Martin, S.B. (2015) 'Athletes' use of mental skills during sport injury rehabilitation', *Journal of Sport Rehabilitation,* 24, 189–197.

Arvinen-Barrow, M., Massey, W.V., and Hemmings, B. (2014) 'Role of sport medicine professionals in addressing psychosocial aspects of sport-injury rehabilitation: Professional athletes' views', *Journal of Athletic Training,* 49, 764–772.

Atkins, M.R., Johnson, D.M., Force, E.C., and Petrie, T.A. (2015) 'Peers, parents, and coaches, oh my! The relation of the motivational climate to boys' intention to continue in sport', *Psychology of Sport and Exercise,* 16, 170–181.

Auld, F., Hyman, M., and Rudzinski, D. (2005) *Resolution of inner conflict: An introduction to psychoanalytic therapy,* 2nd edn. Washington, DC: American Psychological Association,

Backhouse, S.H., Whitaker, L., and Petróczi, A. (2013) 'Gateway to doping? Supplement use in the context of preferred competitive situations, doping attitude, beliefs, and norms', *Scandinavian Journal of Medicine and Science in Sports,* 23, 244–252.

Badami, R., Vaez Mousavi, M., Wulf, G., and Namazizadeh, M. (2011) 'Feedback after good versus poor trials after intrinsic motivation', *Research Quarterly for Exercise and Sport*, 82, 360–364.

Badan, M., Hauert, C.A., and Moumoud, P. (2000) 'Sequential pointing in children and adults', *Journal of Experimental Child Psychology*, 75, 43–69.

Baltzell, A., Caraballo, N., Chipman, K., and Hayden, L. (2014) 'A qualitative study of the mindfulness meditation training for sport: Division I female soccer players' experience', *Journal of Clinical Sport Psychology*, 8, 221–244.

Bandura, A. (1977) 'Self-efficacy: Toward a unifying theory of behavioral change', *Psychological Review*, 84, 191–215.

Bandura, A. (1997) *Self-efficacy: The exercise of control*, New York: Freeman.

Baron-Thiene, A., and Alfermann, D. (2015) 'Personal characteristics as predictors for dual career dropout versus continuation: A prospective study of adolescent athletes from German elite sport schools', *Psychology of Sport and Exercise*, 21, 42–49.

Bartholomew, K.J., Ntoumanis, N., and Thogersen-Ntoumani, C. (2010) 'The controlling interpersonal style in a coaching context: Development and initial validation of a psychometric scale', *Journal of Sport & Exercise Psychology*, 32, 193–216.

Baumeister, R.F. (1984) 'Choking under pressure: Self-consciousness and paradoxical effects of incentives on skilful performance', *Journal of Personality and Social Psychology*, 46, 610–620.

Beauchamp, P.H., Halliwell, W.R., Fournier, J.F., and Koestner, R. (1996) 'Effects of cognitive-behavioural psychological skills training on motivation, preparation, and putting performance of novice golfers', *The Sport Psychologist*, 10, 157–170.

Beaumont, C., Maynard, I.W., and Butt, J. (2015) 'Effective ways to develop and maintain robust sport-confidence: Strategies advocated by sport psychology consultants', *Journal of Applied Sport Psychology*, 27, 301–318.

Beilock, S.L., and Carr, T.H. (2001) 'On the fragility of skilled performance: What governs choking under pressure?', *Journal of Experimental Psychology: General*, 130, 701–725.

Beilock, S.L., and Gray, R. (2007) 'Why do athletes choke under pressure?', in G. Tenenbaum, and R.C. Eklund (eds), *Handbook of sport psychology*, Hoboken, NJ: John Wiley and Sons, 3rd edn, pp. 425–444.

Beilock, S.L., Kulp, C.A., Holt, L.E., and Carr, T.H. (2004) 'More on the fragility of performance: Choking under pressure in mathematical problem solving', *Journal of Experimental Psychology: General*, 133, 584–600.

Bell, J.J., Hardy, L., and Beattie, S. (2013) 'Enhancing mental toughness and performance under pressure in elite young cricketers: A 2-year longitudinal intervention', *Sport, Exercise, and Performance Psychology*, 2, 281–297.

Bengoechea, E.G., and Strean, W.B. (2007) 'On the interpersonal context of adolescents' sport motivation', *Psychology of Sport and Exercise*, 8, 195–217.

Bennett, J., and Lindsay, P. (2016) 'Case study 3: An acceptance commitment and mindfulness based intervention for a female hockey player experiencing post injury performance anxiety', *Sport & Exercise Psychology Review*, 12, 36–45.

Benson, A.J., Siska, P., Eys, M., Priklerova, S., and Slepicka, P. (2016) 'A prospective multilevel examination of the relationship between cohesion and team performance in elite youth sport', *Psychology of Sport and Exercise*, 27, 39–46.

Bernstein, D.A., and Nietzel, M.T. (1980) 'Introduction to clinical psychology', New York: McGraw-Hill.

Beyer, R., Flores, M.M., and Vargas-Tonsing, T.M. (2008) 'Coaches' attitudes towards youth sport participants with attention deficit hyperactivity disorder', *International Journal of Sport Science & Coaching*, 3, 555–563.

Beyer, R., Flores, M.M., and Vargas-Tonsing, T.M. (2009) 'Strategies and methods for coaching athletes with invisible disabilities in youth sport activities', *The Journal of Youth Sports,* 4, 10–15.

Bianco, T. (2001) 'Social support and recovery from sport injury: Elite skiers share their experiences', *Research Quarterly for Exercise and Sport,* 72, 376–388.

Bird, S.R., Goebel, C., Burke, L.M., and Greaves, R.F. (2016) 'Doping in sport and exercise: anabolic, ergogenic, health, and clinical issues', *Annals of Clinical Biochemistry,* 53, 196–221.

Bishop, S.R., Lau, M., Shapiro, S., Carlson, L., Anderson, N.D., Carmody, J. et al. (2004) 'Mindfulness: A proposed operational definition', *Clinical Psychology: Science and Practice,* 11, 230–241.

Black, S.J., and Weiss, M.R. (1992) 'The relationship among perceived coaching behaviours, perceptions of ability, and motivation in competitive age-group swimmers', *Journal of Sport and Exercise Psychology,* 14, 309–325.

Blakeslee, T.R. (1980). *The right brain,* New York: Anchor Press.

Blascovich, J. (2008) 'Challenge and threat', in A.J. Elliot (ed.), *Handbook of approach and avoidance motivation,* New York: Psychology Press, pp. 431–445.

Blegen, M.D., Stenson, M.R., Micek, D.M., and Matthews, T.D. (2012) 'Motivational differences for participation among championship and non-championship caliber NCAA Division III football teams', *Journal of Strength and Conditioning Research,* 26, 2924–2928.

Bloom, G., Stevens, D.E., and Wickwire, T.L. (2003) 'Expert coaches' perceptions of team building', *Journal of Applied Sport Psychology,* 15, 129–143.

Boekaerts, M. (1996) 'Coping with stress in childhood and adolescence', in M. Zeidner and N.S. Endler (eds), *Handbook of coping: Theory research and applications,* New York: Wiley, pp. 452–484.

Bränström, R., Duncan, L.G., and Moskowitz, J.T. (2011) 'The association between dispositional mindfulness, psychological well-being, and perceived health in a Swedish population-based sample', *British Journal of Health Psychology,* 16, 300–316.

Brawley, L.R., and Paskevich, D.M. (1997) 'Conducting team building research in context of sport and exercise', *Journal of Applied Sport Psychology,* 9, 11–40.

Bray, C.D., and Whaley, D.E. (2001) 'Team cohesion, effort and objective individual performance of high school basketball players', *The Sport Psychologist,* 15, 260–275.

Brewer, B.W. (2000) 'Doing sport psychology in the coaching role', in M.B. Andersen (ed.), *Doing sport psychology,* Champaign, IL: Human Kinetics, pp. 237–248.

Bronfenbrenner, U. (ed.) (2005). *Making human beings human: Bioecological perspectives on human development,* Thousand Oaks, CA: Sage.

Brown, K.W., Ryan, R.M., and Creswell, J.D. (2007) 'Mindfulness: Theoretical foundations and evidence for its salutary effects', *Psychological Inquiry,* 18, 211–237.

Buceta, J.M. (1993) 'The sport psychologist/athletic dual role: Advantages, difficulties, and ethical considerations', *Journal of Applied Sport Psychology,* 5, 64–77.

Bull, S.J., Shambrook, C.J., James, W., and Brooks, J.E. (2005) 'Towards an understanding of mental toughness in elite English cricketers', *Journal of Applied Sport Psychology,* 17, 209–227.

Buning, M.M., and Thompson, M.A. (2015) 'Coaching behaviors and athlete motivation: Female softball athletes' perspectives', *Sport Science Review,* 24, 345–370.

Burton, D. (1989) 'Winning isn't everything: Examining the impact of performance goals on collegiate swimmers' cognitions and performance', *The Sport Psychologist,* 3, 105–132.

Burton, D., and Naylor, S. (2002) 'The Jekyll/Hyde nature of goals: Revisiting and updating goal setting in sport', in T. Horn (ed.), *Advances in sport psychology,* Champaign, IL: Human Kinetics, pp. 459–499.

Burton, D., Naylor, S., and Holliday, B. (2001) 'Goal setting in sport: Investigating the goal effectiveness paradigm', in R. Singer, H. Hausenblaus, and C. Janelle (eds), *Handbook of sport psychology,* New York: Wiley, pp. 497–528.

Butler, R.J. (1989) *'The performance profile: Developing elite performance',* London: British Olympic Association Publishers.

Butler, R.J. (1996a) *Performance profiling,* Leeds: National Coaching Foundation.

Butler, R.J. (1996b) 'Performance profiling' in R.J. Butler (ed.), *Sports psychology in action,* Oxford: Butterworth-Heinmann, pp. 9–19.

Butler, R.J., and Hardy, L. (1992) 'The performance profile: Theory and application', *The Sport Psychologist,* 6, 253–264.

Butler, R.J., Smith, M., and Irwin, I. (1993) 'The performance profile in practice', *Journal of Applied Sport Psychology,* 5, 48–63.

Callow, N., and Hardy, L. (2001) 'Types of imagery associated with sport confidence in netball players of varying skill levels', *Journal of Applied Sport Psychology,* 13, 1–17.

Callow, N., and Walters, A. (2005) 'The effect of kinaesthetic imagery on the sport confidence of flat-race horse jockeys', *Psychology of Sport and Exercise,* 6, 443–459.

Callow, N., Smith, M.J., Hardy, L., Arthur, C.A., and Hardy, J. (2009) 'Measurement of transformational leadership and its relationship with team cohesion and performance level', *Journal of Applied Sport Psychology,* 21, 395–412.

Calmels, C., Berthoumieux, C., and d'Arrie-Longueville, F. (2004) 'Effects of an imagery training programme on selective attention of national softball players', *The Sport Psychologist,* 18, 272–296.

Cannon, W.B. (1915) *Bodily chances in pain, hunger, fear, and rage: An account of recent researches into the functions of emotional excitement,* New York: Appleton.

Capio, C.M., Poolton, J.M., Sit, C.H.P., Holmstrom, M., and Masters, R.S.W. (2013) 'Reducing errors benefits the field-based learning of a fundamental movement skill in children', *Scandinavian Journal of Medicine and Science in Sports,* 23, 181–188.

Carpenter, W.B. (1894) *Principles of mental physiology,* New York: Appleton.

Carron, A., and Hausenblas, H.A. (1998) *Group dynamics in sport,* second edition. West Virginia, WV: Fitness Information Technology (FIT).

Carron, A.V., Brawley, L.R., and Widmeyer, W.N. (1998) 'The measurement of cohesiveness in sport groups', in J. Duda (ed.), *Advances in sport and exercise psychology measurement,* Morgantown, WV: Fitness Information Technology, pp. 213–226.

Carron, A.V., Colman, M.M., Wheeler, J., and Stevens, D. (2002) 'Cohesion and performance in sport: A meta-analysis', *Journal of Sport & Exercise Psychology,* 24, 168–188.

Carron, A.V., Eys, M.A., and Burke, S.M. (2007) 'Team cohesion: Nature, correlates, and development', in S. Jowett and D. Lavallee (eds), *Social Psychology in sport,* Champaign, IL: Human Kinetics, pp. 91–101.

Carron, A.V., Widmeyer, W.N., and Brawley, L.R. (1985) 'The development of an instrument to assess cohesion in sport teams: The group environment questionnaire', *Journal of Sport Psychology,* 7, 244–266.

Carson, F., and Polman, R.C.J. (2010) 'The facilitative nature of avoidance coping within sports injury rehabilitation', *Scandinavian Journal of Medicine and Science in Sports,* 20, 235–240.

Cary, P. (2004) 'Fixing kids' sport', *U.S. News and World Report,* 136, 44–53.

Cathcart, S., McGregor, M., and Groundwater, E. (2014) 'Mindfulness and flow in elite athletes', *Journal of Clinical Sport Psychology*, 8, 119–141.

Chambers, D. (2009) *Race against me: My story*, Valencia: Libros International.

Chesney, M.A., Chambers, D.B., Taylor, J.M., Johnson, L.M., and Folkman, S. (2003) 'Coping effectiveness training for men living with HIV: Results from a randomized clinical trial testing a group-based intervention', *Psychosomatic Medicine*, 65, 1038–1046.

Chesney, M.A., Folkman, S., and Chambers, D.B. (1996) 'Coping effectiveness training for men living with HIV: preliminary findings', *International Journal of STD & AIDS*, 7, 75–82.

Chesney, M.A., Neilands, T.B., Chambers, D.B., Taylor, J.M., and Folkman, S. (2006) 'A validity and reliability study of the coping self-efficacy scale', *British Journal of Health Psychology*, 11, 421–437.

Chesterfield, G., Potrac, P., and Jones, R. (2010) 'Studentship and impression management in advanced soccer coach education award', *Sport, Education, and Society*, 15, 299–314.

Chiviacowsky, S., and Wulf, G. (2002) 'Self-controlled feedback: Does it enhance learning because performers get feedback when they need it?', *Research Quarterly for Exercise and Sport*, 73, 408–415.

Chiviacowsky, S., Wulf, G., Laroque de Medeiros, F., and Kaefer, A. (2008a) 'Self-controlled feedback in 10-year-old children: Higher feedback frequencies enhance learning', *Research Quarterly for Exercise and Sport*, 79, 122–127.

Chiviacowsky, S., Wulf, G., Laroque de Medeiros, F., Kaefer, A., and Tani, G. (2008b) 'Learning benefits of self-controlled knowledge of results in 10-year-old children', *Research Quarterly for Exercise and Sport*, 79, 405–410.

Chiviacowsky, S., Wulf, G., Wally, R., and Borges, T. (2009) 'Knowledge of results after good trials enhances learning in older adults', *Research Quarterly for Exercise and Sport*, 80, 663–668.

Chow, G.M., Murray, K.E., and Feltz, D.L. (2009) 'Individual, team, and coach predictors of players' likelihood to aggress in youth soccer', *Journal of Sport & Exercise Psychology*, 31, 425–443.

Clancy, R.B., Herring, M.P., MacIntyre, T.E., and Campbell, M.J. (2016) 'A review of competitive sport motivation research', *Psychology of Sport and Exercise*, 27, 232–242.

Clough, P., and Strycharczyk, D. (2012) *Developing mental toughness: Improving performance, wellbeing and positive behavior in others*, London: Kogan Page.

Clough, P.J., Earle, K., Perry, J.L., and Crust, L. (2012) 'Comment on "Progressing measurement in mental toughness: A case example of the Mental Toughness Questionnaire 48" Gucciardi, Hanton, and Mallett', *Sport, Exercise, and Performance Psychology*, 1, 283–287.

Clough, P., Earle, K., and Sewell, D. (2002) 'Mental toughness: The concept and its measurement', in I. Cockerill (ed.), *Solutions in Sport Psychology*, London: Thomson, pp. 32–45.

Coatsworth, J.D., and Conroy, D.E. (2006) 'Enhancing the self-esteem of youth swimmers through coach training: Gender and age effects', *Psychology of Sport and Exercise*, 7, 173–192.

Compas, B.E., Connor-Smith, J.K., Saltzman, H., Harding Thomsen, A., and Wadsworth, M.E. (2001) 'Coping with stress during childhood and adolescence: Problems, progress, and potential in theory and research', *Psychological Bulletin*, 12, 87–127.

Connaughton, D., Hanton, S., and Jones, G. (2010) 'The development and maintenance of mental toughness in the world's best performers', *The Sport Psychologist,* 24, 168–193.

Connaughton, D., Hanton, S., Jones, G., and Wadey, R. (2008a) 'Mental toughness research: Key issues in this area', *International Journal of Sport Psychology*, 39, 192–204.

Connaughton, D., Wadey, R., Hanton, S., and Jones, G. (2008b) 'The development and maintenance of mental toughness: Perceptions of elite performers', *Journal of Sports Sciences*, 26, 83–95.

Connolly, K. (1970) *Mechanisms of motor skill development,* London: Academic Press.

Conroy, D.E., Elliot, A.J., and Coatsworth, J.D. (2007) 'Competence motivation in sport and exercise', in M.S. Hagger and N.L.D. Chatzisarantis (eds), *Intrinsic motivation and self-determination in exercise and sport,* Champaign, IL: Human Kinetics, pp. 181–192.

Conroy, D.E., Elliot, A.J., and Hofer, S. (2003) 'A 2 × 2 achievement goals questionnaire for sport: Evidence for the factorial invariance, temporal stability, and external validity', *Journal of Sport & Exercise Psychology,* 25, 456–476.

Cormier, M.L., Bloom, G.A., and Harvey, W.J. (2015) 'Elite coach perceptions of cohesion on coaching teams', *International Journal of Sports Science & Coaching,* 10, 1039–1053.

Côté, J. (1999) 'The influence of the family in the development of talent in sport', *The Sport Psychologist,* 13, 395–417.

Côté, J., and Gilbert, W.D. (2009) 'An integrative definition of coaching effectiveness and expertise', *International Journal of Sports Science & Coaching,* 4, 307–323.

Côté, J., Bruner, M., Erickson, K., Strachan, L., and Fraser-Thomas, J. (2010) 'Athlete development and coaching', in J. Lyle and C. Cushion (eds), *Sports coaching: Professionalisation and practice*, Edinburgh: Churchill Livingston, pp. 63–84.

Côté, J., Yardley, J., Hay, J., Sedgwick, W., and Baker, J. (1999) 'An Exploratory Examination of the Coaching Behavior Scale for Sport', *Avante,* 5, 82–92.

Cotterill, S., Sanders, R., and Collins, D. (2010) 'Developing effective pre-performance routines in golf: Why don't we ask the golfer', *Journal of Applied Sport Psychology,* 22, 51–64.

Craft, L.L., Magyar, M., Becker, B.J., and Feltz, D.L. (2003) 'The relationship between the Competitive State Anxiety Inventory – 2 and sport performance: A meta-analysis', *Journal of Sport & Exercise Psychology,* 25, 44–65.

Crocker, P.R.E., and Graham, T.R. (1995) 'Coping with competitive athletes with performance stress: Gender differences and relationships with affect', *The Sport Psychologist,* 9, 325–338.

Crocker, P.R.E., Alderman, R.B., and Smith, F.M. (1988) 'Cognitive-Affective Stress Management Training with high performance youth volleyball players: Effects on affect, cognition, and performance', *Journal of Sport & Exercise Psychology,* 10, 448–460.

Crocker, P.R.E., Hoar, S., McDonough, M., Kowalski, K., and Niefer, C. (2004) 'Emotional experience in youth sport', in M. Weiss (ed.), *Development sport and exercise psychology: A lifespan perspective,* Morgantown, WV: Fitness Information Technology, pp. 197–222.

Curran, T., Hill, A.P., Hall, H.K., and Jowett, G.E. (2015) 'Relationships between the coach-created motivational climate and athlete engagement in youth sport', *Journal of Sport & Exercise Psychology*, 37, 193–198.

Cushion, C.J. (2007a) 'Modelling the complexity of the coaching process', *International Journal of Sports Science & Coaching,* 2, 395–401.

Cushion, C.J. (2007b) 'Modelling the complexity of the coaching process: A response to commentaries', *International Journal of Sports Science & Coaching,* 2, 427–433.

Dale, G.A., and Wrisberg, C.A. (1996) 'The use of a performance profiling technique in a team setting: Getting the athletes and the coach on the "same page"', *The Sport Psychologist*, 10, 261–277.

De Backer, M., Boen, F., Ceux, T., De Cuyper, B., Høigaard, R., Callens, F., Fransen, K., and Vande Broek, G. (2011) 'Do perceived justice and need support of the coach predict team identification and cohesion? Testing their relative importance among top volleyball and handball players in Belgium and Norway', *Psychology of Sport and Exercise*, 12, 192–201.

Deci, E.L., and Ryan, R.M. (1985) *Intrinsic motivation and self-determination in human behavior*, New York: Plenum Press.

Deci, E.L., and Ryan, R.M. (2000) 'The "what" and "why" of goal pursuits: Human needs and the self-determination of behaviour', *Psychological Inquiry*, 11, 227–268.

de Franco Tobar, L., Meurer, S.T., and Benedetti, T.B. (2013) 'Motivational factors of senior athletes to participate in the Ironman', *Science and Sports*, 28, e63–e65.

Defreese, J.D., and Smith, A.L. (2014) 'Athlete social support, negative social interactions, and psychological health across a competitive sport season', *Journal of Sport & Exercise Psychology*, 36, 619–630.

DePauw, K.P., and Gavron, S.J. (1991) 'Coaches of athletes with disabilities', *Physical Educator*, 48, 33–40.

Devonport, T.J., and Lane, A.M. (2014) 'Evaluation of a 12-month coping intervention intended to enhance future-oriented coping in goal-oriented domains', *Journal of Clinical Sport Psychology*, 8, 38–56.

Donovan, R.J., Eggar, G., Kapernick, V., and Mendoza, J. (2002) 'A conceptual framework for achieving performance enhancing drug compliance in sport', *Sports Medicine*, 32, 269–284.

Driskell, J.E., Copper, C., and Moran, A. (1994) 'Does mental practice enhance performance?', *Journal of Applied Psychology*, 79, 481–492.

Dubois, P. (1990) 'The youth sport coach as an agent of socialisation: An exploratory study', *Journal of Sport Behavior*, 4, 95–107.

Duda, J.L. (2013) 'The conceptual and empirical foundations of Empowering Coaching™: Setting the stage for the PAPA project', *International Journal of Sport and Exercise Psychology*, 11, 311–318.

D'Urso, V., Petrosso, A., and Robazza, C. (2002) 'Emotions, perceived qualities, and performance of rugby players', *The Sport Psychologist*, 16, 173–199.

Durso-Cupal, D.D. (1996) 'The efficacy of guided imagery for recovery from anterior cruciate ligament (ACL) replacement', *Journal of Applied Sport Psychology*, 8(Suppl.), S56.

Dweck, C.S. (1986) 'Motivational process affecting learning', *American Psychologist*, 41, 1040–1048.

Ebert, B.W. (1997) 'Dual-relationship prohibitions: A concept whose time never should have come', *Applied and Preventive Psychology*, 6, 137–156.

Ellickson, K.A., and Brown, D.R. (1990) 'Ethical considerations in dual relationships: The sport psychologist-coach', *Journal of Applied Sport Psychology*, 2, 186–190.

Elliot, A.J. (1999) 'Approach and avoidance motivation and achievement goals', *Educational Psychologist*, 34, 169–189.

Ellis, M.C. (1992) 'Tempo perception and performance of elementary students, grades 3–6', *Journal of Research in Music and Education*, 40, 329–341.

Erickson, K., McKenna, J., and Backhouse, S.H. (2015) 'A qualitative analysis of the factors that protect athletes against doping in sport', *Psychology of Sport and Exercise*, 16, 149–155.

ESPAD (2011) *The 2011 ESPAD Report: Substance Use Among Students in 36 European*

Countries. Retrieved from: www.espad.org/uploads/espad_reports/2011/the_2011_espad_report_full_2012_10_29.pdf

European Commistion (2007) White Paper on Sport. Retrieved from http://eur-lex.europa.eu/legal-content/EN/TXT/?uri=CELEX:52007DC0391

Eys, M.A., Loughead, T.M., Bray, S.R., and Carron, A.V. (2009) 'Perceptions of cohesion by youth sport participants', *The Sport Psychologist*, 23, 330–345.

Feldman, G.C., Hayes, A.M., Kumar, S.M., Greerson, J.M., and Laurenceau, J.P. (2007) 'Mindfulness and emotion regulation: The development and initial validation of the Cognitive and Affective Mindfulness Scale – Revised (CAMS-R)', *Journal of Psychopathology and Behavioral Assessment*, 29, 177–190.

Feltz, D.L. (1980) 'Teaching a high-avoidance motor task to a retarded child through participant modelling', *Education and Training of the Mentally Retarded*, 15, 152–155.

Feltz, D.L. (1994) 'Self-confidence and performance', in D. Druckman and R.A. Bjork (eds), *Learning, remembering, believing: Enhancing human performance*, Washington, DC: National Academy Press, pp. 173–206.

Feltz, D.L., Short, S.E., and Sullivan, P.J. (2008) *Self-efficacy in sport: Research and strategies for working with athletes, teams, and coaches*, Champaign, IL: Human Kinetics.

Filho, E., Tenenbaum, G., and Yang, Y. (2015) 'Cohesion, team mental models, and collective efficacy: towards an integrated framework of team dynamics in sport', *Journal of Sports Sciences*, 33, 641–653.

Fiore, T.A., Becker, E.A., and Nero, R.C. (1993) 'Educational interventions for students with Attention Deficit Disorder', *Exceptional Children*, 60, 163–173.

Flores, F.S., Francisco, J., and Chiviacowsky, S. (2015) 'Benefits of external focus instructions on the learning of a balance task in children of different ages', *International Journal of Sport Psychology*, 46, 311–321.

Folkman, S. (1984) 'Personal control and stress and coping processes: A theoretical analysis', *Journal of Personality and Social Psychology*, 46, 839–852.

Ford, P.R., Yates, I., and Williams, A.M. (2010) 'An analysis of practice activities and instructional behaviours used by youth soccer coaches during practice: Exploring the link between science and application', *Journal of Sports Sciences*, 28, 483–495.

Forsman, H., Blomqvist, M., Davids, K., Konttinen, N., and Liukkonen, J. (2016) 'The role of sport-specific play and practice during childhood in the development of adolescent Finnish team sport athletes', *International Journal of Sports Science & Coaching*, 11, 69–77.

Francisco Guzmán, J., and Kingston, K. (2012) 'Prospective study of sport dropout: A motivational analysis as a function of age and gender', *European Journal of Sport Science*, 12, 431–442.

Fransen, K., Vanbeselaere, N., De Cuyper, B., Vande Broek, G., and Boen, F. (2015) 'Perceived sources of team confidence in soccer and basketball', *Medicine and Science in Sports and Exercise*, 47, 1470–1484.

Fraser-Thomas, J., Côté, J., and Deakin, J. (2008) 'Examining adolescent sport dropout and prolonged engagement from a developmental perspective', *Journal of Applied Sport Psychology*, 20, 318–333.

Freeman, P., Coffee, P., Moll, T., Rees, T., and Sammy, N. (2014) 'The ARSQ: The Athletes' Received Support Questionnaire', *Journal of Sport & Exercise Psychology*, 36, 189–202.

Friend, M., and Bursuck, W.D. (2009) *Including students with special needs: A practical guide for classroom teachers*, Boston, MA: Allyn and Bacon.

Frühauf, S., Figlioli, P., Oehler, D., and Caspar, F. (2015) 'What to expect in the intake interview? Impression management tactics of psychotherapy patients', *Journal of Social and Clinical Psychology*, 34, 28–49.

Fry, M.D., and Gano-Overway, L.A. (2010) 'Exploring the contribution of the caring climate to the youth sport experience', *Journal of Applied Sport Psychology*, 22, 294–304.

Furley, P., and Schweizer, G. (2014) '"I'm pretty sure that we will win!": The influence of score-related nonverbal behavioural changes on the confidence in winning a basketball game', *Journal of Sport & Exercise Psychology*, 36, 316–320.

Gardner, L.A., Magee, C.A., and Vella, S.A. (2016a) 'Social climate profiles in adolescent sports: Associations with enjoyment and intention to continue', *Journal of Adolescence*, 52, 112–123.

Gardner, L.A., Vella, S.A., and Magee, C.A. (2016b) 'A motivational model to understand youth sport dropout and enjoyment', *International Journal of Sport Psychology*, 47, 203–224.

Gardner, L.A., Vella, S.A., and Magee, C.A. (2017) 'Continued participation in youth sports: The role of achievement motivation', *Journal of Applied Sport Psychology*, 17, 31.

Gaudreau, P., and Blondin, J.-P. (2002) 'Development of a questionnaire for the assessment of coping strategies employed by athletes in competitive sport settings', *Psychology of Sport and Exercise*, 3, 1–34.

Gaudreau, P., Morinville, A., Gareau, A., Verner-Filion, J., Green-Demers, I., and Franche, V. (2016) 'Autonomy support from parents and coaches: Synergistic or compensatory effects on sport-related outcomes of adolescent athletes?', *Psychology of Sport and Exercise*, 25, 89–99.

Giges, B. (2000) 'Removing psychological barriers: Clearing the way', in M.B. Andersen (ed.), *Doing sport psychology*, Champaign, IL: Human Kinetics, pp. 17–32.

Gillet, N., Berjot, S., Vallerand, R.J., and Amoura, S. (2012) 'The role of autonomy support and motivation in the prediction of interest and dropout intentions in sport and education settings', *Basic and Applied Social Psychology*, 34, 278–286.

Gillet, N., Vallerand, R.J., Amoura, S., and Baldes, B. (2010) 'Influence of coaches' autonomy support on athletes' motivation and sport performance: A test of the hierarchical model of intrinsic and extrinsic motivation', *Psychology of Sport and Exercise*, 11, 155–161.

Gonzalez, S.P., Metzler, J.N., and Newton, M. (2011) 'The influence of a simulated "pep talk" on athlete inspiration, situational motivation, and emotion', *International Journal of Sports Science & Coaching*, 3, 445–459.

Gotink, R.A., Meijboom, R., Vernooij, M.W., Smits, M., and Myriam Hunink, M.G. (2016) '8-week Mindfulness Based Stress Reduction induces brain changes similar to traditional long-term meditation practice – A systematic review', *Brain and Cognition,* 108, 32–41.

Gould, D., Eklund, R.C., and Jackson, S.A. (1993) 'Coping strategies used by US Olympic wrestlers', *Research Quarterly for Exercise and Sport*, 64, 83–93.

Gould, D., Udry, E., Bridges, D., and Beck, L. (1997) 'Coping with season-ending injuries', *The Sport Psychologist*, 11, 379–399.

Gray, J.A., and McNaughton, N. (2000) *The neuropsychology of anxiety: An enquiry into the functions of the septo-hippocampal system*, Oxford: Oxford University Press.

Gucciardi, D.F., Gordon, S., and Dimmock, J.A. (2008) 'Towards an understanding of mental toughness in Australian football', *Journal of Applied Sport Psychology*, 20, 261–281.

Gucciardi, D.F., Gordon, S., and Dimmock, J.A. (2009a) 'Evaluation of a mental toughness training program for youth aged Australian footballers: I. A quantitative analysis', *Journal of Applied Sport Psychology*, 21, 307–323.

Gucciardi, D.F., Gordon, S., Dimmock, J.A., and Mallett, C.J. (2009b) 'Understanding the coach's role in the development of mental toughness: Perspective of elite Australian football coaches', *Journal of Sports Sciences,* 27, 1483–1496.

Gucciardi, D.F., Hanton, S., Gordon, S., Mallett, C.J., and Temby, P. (2015) 'The concept of mental toughness: Tests of dimensionality, nomological network, and traitness', *Journal of Personality,* 83, 26–44.

Gucciardi, D.F., Hanton, S., and Mallett, C.F. (2012) 'Current issues for measuring mental toughness: A case example of the Mental Toughness Questionnaire-48', *Sport, Exercise and Performance Psychology,* 1, 194–214.

Gucciardi, D.F., Hanton, S., and Mallett, C.F. (2013) 'Progressing measurement in mental toughness: A response to Clough, Earle, Perry, and Crust', *Sport, Exercise, and Performance Psychology,* 2, 157–172.

Gucciardi, D., Jalleh, G., and Donovan, R.J. (2011a) 'An examination of the sport drug control model with elite Australian athletes', *Journal of Science & Medicine in Sport,* 14, 469–476.

Gucciardi, D.F., Mallett, C.J., Hanrahan, S.J., and Gordon, S. (2011b) 'Measuring mental toughness', in D.F. Gucciardi and S. Gordon (eds), *Mental toughness in sport: Developments in research and theory,* London, England: Routledge, pp. 108–132.

Gucciardi, D.F., Peeling, P., Ducker, K.J., and Dawson, B. (2016) 'When the going gets tough: Mental toughness and its relationship with behavioural perseverance', *Journal of Science and Medicine in Sport,* 19, 81–86.

Gudjonsson, G.H., and Sigurdsson, J.F. (2010) 'The relationship of compliance with inattention and hyperactivity/impulsivity', *Personality and Individual Differences,* 49, 651–654.

Haibach, P.S., Reid, G., and Collier, D.H. (2011) *Motor learning and development,* Champaign, IL: Human Kinetics.

Hampson, R., and Harwood, C. (2016) 'Case Study 2: Employing a group goal setting intervention within an elite sport setting', *Sport & Exercise Psychology Review,* 12, 22–31.

Hampson, R., and Jowett, S. (2014) 'Effects of coach leadership and coach–athlete relationship on collective efficacy', *Scandinavian Journal of Medicine and Science in Sports,* 24, 454–460.

Haney, C.J., and Long, B.C. (1995) 'Coping effectiveness: A path analysis of self-efficacy, control, coping and performance in sport competitions', *Journal of Applied Social Psychology,* 25, 1726–1746.

Hanin, Y.L. (2004) 'Emotions in Sport: An Individualized Approach', in C.D. Spielberger (ed.), *Encyclopaedia of Applied Psychology,* Oxford: Elsevier Academic Press, Vol. 1, pp. 739–750.

Hanin, Y.L. (2010) 'Coping with anxiety in sport', in A.R. Nicholls (ed.), *Coping in Sport: Theory, Methods, and Related Constructs,* New York: Nova Science, pp. 159–176.

Hardy, J., Hall, C.R., and Hardy, L. (2005) 'Quantifying athlete self-talk', *Journal of Sports Sciences,* 23, 905–917.

Hardy, L., Bell, J., and Beattie, S. (2014) 'Preliminary evidence for a neuropsychological model of mentally tough behavior', *Journal of Personality,* 82, 69–81.

Hardy, L., Mullen, R., and Martin, N. (2001) 'Effect of task-relevant cues and state anxiety on motor performance', *Perceptual and Motor Skills,* 92, 942–946.

Harter, S. (1999) *The construction of the self: A developmental perspective,* New York: Guilford Press.

Harwood, C., and Swain, A. (2002) 'The development and activation of achievement goals within tennis: II. A player, parent, and coach intervention', *The Sport Psychologist*, 16, 111–137.

Harwood, C., Spray, C.M., and Keegan, R. (2008) 'Achievement goal theories in sport', in T.S. Horn (ed.), *Advances in sport psychology*, Champaign, IL: Human Kinetics, 3rd edn, pp. 157–185.

Hassan, M.F.H., and Morgan, K. (2015) 'Effects of a mastery intervention programme on the motivational climate and achievement goals in sport coaching: A pilot study', *International Journal of Sports Science & Coaching*, 10, 487–503.

Hays, K., Maynard, I., Thomas, O., and Bawden, M. (2007) 'Sources and types of confidence identified by world class sport performers', *Journal of Applied Sport Psychology*, 19, 434–456.

Hays, K., Thomas, O., Maynard, I., and Bawden, M. (2009) 'The role of confidence in world class sport performance', *Journal of Sports Sciences*, 27, 1185–1199.

Hays, K., Thomas, O., Maynard, I., and Butt, J. (2010a) 'The development of confidence profiling for sport', *The Sport Psychologist*, 18, 373–392.

Hays, K., Thomas, O., Maynard, I., and Butt, J. (2010b) 'The role of confidence profiling in cognitive-behavioural interventions in sport', *The Sport Psychologist*, 18, 393–414.

Healy, L.C., Ntoumanis, N., Veldhuijzen van Zanten, J.J.C.S., and Paine, N. (2014) 'Goal striving and well-being in sport: The role of contextual and personal motivation', *Journal of Sport & Exercise Psychology*, 36, 436–449.

Heil, J. (1993) *Psychology of sport injury*, Champaign, IL: Human Kinetics.

Helsen, W.F., Starkes, J.L., and Winckel, J.V. (1998) 'The influence of relative age on success and dropout in male soccer players', *American Journal of Human Biology*, 10, 791–798.

Heppner, P.P., and Claiborn, C.D. (1989) 'Social influence research in counselling: A review and critique', *Journal of Counseling Psychology*, 36, 365–387.

Hill, D.M., and Hemmings, B. (2015) 'A phenomenological exploration of coping responses associated with choking in sport', *Qualitative Research in Sport, Exercise, and Health*, 7, 521–538.

Hill, G.M. (1988) 'Celebrate diversity (not specialisation) in school sports', *The Executive Educator*, 10, 24.

Hodge, K., and Gucciardi, D.F. (2015) 'Antisocial and prosocial behavior in sport: the role of motivational climate, basic psychological needs, and moral disengagement', *Journal of Sport & Exercise Psychology*, 37, 257–273.

Hodge, K., and Smith, W. (2014) 'Public expectation, pressure, and avoiding the choke: A case study from elite sport', *The Sport Psychologist*, 28, 375–389.

Hogue, C.M., Fry, M.D., Fry, A.C., and Pressman, S.D. (2013) 'The influence of a motivational climate intervention on participants' salivary cortisol and psychological responses', *Journal of Sport & Exercise Psychology*, 35, 85–97.

Høigaard, R., Jones, G.W., and Peters, D.M. (2008) 'Preferred coach leadership behaviour in elite soccer in relation to success and failure', *International Journal of Sport Sciences & Coaching*, 2, 241–250.

Holmes, P., and Collins, D. (2001) 'The PETTLEP approach to motor imagery: A functional equivalence model for sport psychologists', *Journal of Applied Sport Psychology*, 13, 60–83.

Holt, N.L., and Hogg, J.M. (2002) 'Perceptions of stress and coping during preparations for the 1999 women's soccer world cup finals', *The Sport Psychologist*, 16, 251–271.

Holt, N.L., and Mandigo, J.L. (2004) 'Coping with performance worries among male youth cricket players', *Journal of Sport Behaviour*, 27, 39–57.

Horn, T.S., Bloom, P., Berglund, K.M., and Packard, S. (2011) 'Relationship between collegiate athletes' psychological characteristics and their preferences for different types of coaching behaviour', *The Sport Psychologist*, 25, 190–211.

Horn, T.S., Glenn, S.D., and Wentzell, A.B. (1993) 'Sources of information underlying personal ability judgements in high school athletes', *Paediatric Exercise Science*, 5, 263–274.

Horn, T.S., Lox, C.L., and Labrador, F. (2006) 'The self-fulfilling prophecy theory: When coaches' expectations become reality', in J. Williams (ed.), *Applied sport psychology: Personal growth to peak performance*, Boston, MA: McGraw Hill, 5th edn, pp. 82–108.

Houston, M., and Newton, M. (2011) 'Building confidence', in T. Morris and P. Terry (eds), *The new sport and exercise psychology companion*, Morgantown, WV: Fitness Information Technology, pp. 257–274.

Hurst, J.F., Thompson, A., Visek, A.J., Fisher, B., and Gaudreau, P. (2011) 'Towards a dispositional version of the Coping Inventory for Competitive Sport', *International Journal of Sport Psychology*, 42, 167–185.

Hutchinson, J.C., Sherman, T., Martinovic, N., and Tenenbaum, G. (2008) 'The effect of manipulated self-efficacy on perceived and sustained effort', *Journal of Applied Sport Psychology*, 20, 457–472.

Ievleva, L., and Orlick, T. (1991) 'Mental links to enhanced healing', *The Sport Psychologist*, 5, 25–40.

Isoard-Gautheur, S., Guillet-Decas, E., and Gustafsson, H. (2016a) 'Athlete burnout and the risk of dropout among young elite handball players', *The Sport Psychologist*, 30, 123–130.

Isoard-Gautheur, S., Guillet-Descas, E., and Lemyre, P.-N. (2012) 'A prospective study of the influence of perceived coaching style on burnout propensity in high level young athletes: Using a self-determination theory perspective', *The Sport Psychologist*, 26, 282–298.

Isoard-Gautheur, S., Trouilloud, D., and Gustafsson, H. (2016b) 'Associations between the perceived quality of the coach–athlete relationship and athlete burnout: An examination of the mediating role of achievement goals', *Psychology of Sport and Exercise*, 22, 210–217.

Ivarsson, A., Johnson, U., Andersen, M.B., Fallby, J., and Altemyr, M. (2015) 'It pays to pay attention: A mindfulness-based program for injury prevention with soccer players', *Journal of Applied Sport Psychology*, 27, 319–334.

Ivarsson, A., Johnson, U., and Podlog, L. (2013) 'Psychological predictors of injury occurrence: A prospective investigation of professional Swedish soccer players', *Journal of Sport Rehabilitation*, 22, 19–26.

Iwatsuki, T., and Wright, P. (2016) 'Relationships among movement reinvestment, decision-making reinvestment, and perceived choking', *International Journal of Coaching Science*, 10, 25–35.

Jaakkola, T., Ntoumanis, N., and Liukkonen, J. (2016) 'Motivational climate, goal orientation, perceived sport ability, and enjoyment within Finnish junior ice hockey players', *Scandinavian Journal of Medicine and Science in Sports*, 26, 109–115.

Jackson, B., Dimmock, J.A., Gucciardi, D.F., and Grove, J.R. (2011) 'Personality traits and relationship perceptions in coach–athlete dyads: Do opposites really attract?', *Psychology of Sport and Exercise*, 12, 222–230.

Jalleh, G., Donovan, R.J., and Jobling, I. (2014) 'Predicting attitudes towards performance enhancing substance use: A comprehensive test of the Sport Drug Control Model with elite Australian athletes', *Journal of Science and Medicine in Sport*, 17, 574–579.

Janelle, C.M., Kim, J., and Singer, R.N. (1995) 'Subject-controlled performance feedback and learning of a closed motor skill', *Perceptual and Motor Skills*, 81, 627–634.

Johnson, D.W., and Johnson, F.P. (1987) *Joining together: Group therapy and group skills,* Englewood Cliffs, NJ: Prentice Hall.

Johnson, M.B. (2012) 'A systemic social-cognitive perspective on doping', *Psychology of Sport and Exercise,* 13, 317–323.

Johnston, L.H., and Carroll, D. (1998) 'The provision of social support to injured athletes: A qualitative analysis', *Journal of Sport Rehabilitation,* 7, 267–284.

Jones, D.F., Housner, L.D., and Kornspan, A.S. (1995) 'A comparative analysis of expert and novice basketball coaches' practice planning', *Applied Research in Coaching and Athletics Annual,* 10, 201–226.

Jones, G. (1993) 'The role of performance profiling in cognitive behavioral interventions in sport', *The Sport Psychologist,* 7, 160–172.

Jones, G., Hanton, S., and Connaughton, D. (2002) 'What is this thing called mental toughness? An investigation of elite performers', *Journal of Applied Sport Psychology,* 14, 205–218.

Jones, G., Hanton, S., and Connaughton, D. (2007) 'A framework of mental toughness in the world's best performers', *The Sport Psychologist,* 21, 243–264.

Jones, M., Meijen, C., McCarthy, P.J., and Sheffield, D. (2009) 'A theory of challenge and threat states in athletes', *International Review of Sport and Exercise Psychology,* 2, 161–180.

Jones, M.V., Lane, A.M., Bray, S.R., Uphill, M., and Catlin, J. (2005) 'Development and Validation of the Sport Emotion Questionnaire', *Journal of Sport & Exercise Psychology,* 27, 407–431.

Jordet, G. (2010) 'Choking under pressure as self-destructive behavior', in A.R. Nicholls (ed.). *Coping in Sport: Theory, Methods, and Related Constructs,* New York: Nova Science, pp. 239–259.

Jourden, F.J., Bandura, A., and Banfield, J.T. (1991) 'The impact of conceptions of ability on self-regulatory factors and motor skill acquisition', *Journal of Sport and Exercise Psychology,* 8, 213–226.

Jowett, S. (2005) 'On enhancing and repairing the coach-athlete relationship', in S. Jowett and M. Jones (eds), *The psychology of coaching.* Leicester: British Psychological Society, pp. 14–26.

Jowett, S., and Chaundry, V. (2004) 'An investigation into the impact of the coach leadership and coach–athlete relationship on group cohesion', *Group Dynamics: Theory, Research, and Practice,* 8, 302–311.

Jowett, S., and Cockerill, I.M. (2003) 'Olympic Medallists' perspective of the athlete–coach relationship', *Psychology of Sport and Exercise,* 4, 313–331.

Jowett, S., and Meek, G.A. (2000) 'Coach–athlete relationships in married couples: An exploratory content analysis', *The Sport Psychologist,* 14, 157–175.

Jowett, S., and Ntoumanis, N. (2004) 'The coach–athlete relationship questionnaire (CART-Q): development and initial validation', *Scandinavian Journal of Medicine & Science in Sports,* 14, 245–257.

Jowett, S., and Poczwardowski, A. (2007) 'Understanding the coach–athlete relationship', in S. Jowett and D. Lavallee (eds), *Social Psychology in Sport,* Champaign, IL: Human Kinetics, pp. 3–14.

Jowett, S., Paull, G., and Pensgaard, A.M. (2005) 'Coach–athlete relationship', in J. Taylor and G.S. Wilson, *Applying sport psychology: Four perspectives,* Champaign, IL: Human Kinetics, pp. 153–170.

Kamphoff, C.S., Gill, D.L., and Huddleston, S. (2005) 'Jealousy in sport: Exploring jealousy's relationship to cohesion', *Journal of Applied Sport Psychology,* 17, 290–305.

Kapalka, G.M. (2004) 'Longer eye contact improves ADHD children's compliance with parents' commands', *Journal of Attention Disorders,* 8, 17–23.

Keegan, R.J., Harwood, C.G., Spray, C.M., and Lavallee, D.E. (2009) 'A qualitative investigation exploring the motivational climate in early career sports participants: Coach, parent and peer influences on sport motivation', *Psychology of Sport and Exercise,* 10, 361–372.

Keetch, K.M., and Lee, T.D. (2007) 'The effect of self-regulated and experimenter-imposed practice schedules on motor learning for tasks of varying difficulty', *Research Quarterly for Exercise and Sport,* 78, 476–486.

Kelly, G.A. (1991) *The psychology of personal constructs: A theory of personality,* London: Routledge (original work published 1955), Vol. 1.

Kerr, H.A., Curtis, C., Micheli, L.J., Kocher, M.S., Zurakowski, D., Kemp, S.P.T., and Brooks, J.H.M. (2008) 'Collegiate rugby union injury patterns in New England: A prospective cohort study', *British Journal of Sports Medicine,* 42, 595–603.

Kiluk, B.D., Weden, S., and Culotta, V.P. (2009) 'Sport participant and anxiety in children with ADHD', *Journal of Attention Disorders,* 12, 499–506.

Kindermann, W. (1988) 'Metabolic and hormonal reactions in overtraining', *Seminars in Orthopaedics,* 3, 207–216.

Kingston, K.M., and Hardy, L. (1997) 'Effects of different types of goals on processes that support performance', *The Sport Psychologist,* 11, 277–293.

Knowles, M.S. (1995) *Designs for adult learning,* Alexandria, VA: American Society for Training and Development.

Knowles, M.S., Holton, E.F., and Swanson, R.A. (2011) *The adult learner: The definitive classic in adult education and human resource development,* Oxford: Butterworth-Heinemann.

Kobasa, S.C. (1979) 'Stressful life events, personality, and health: An enquiry into hardiness', *Journal of Personality and Social Psychology,* 37, 1–11.

Koedijker, J.M., Oudejans, R.R.D., and Beck, P.J. (2007) 'Explicit rules and directions of attention in learning and performing the table tennis forehand', *International Journal of Sport Psychology,* 38, 227–244.

Koehn, S., Pearce, A.J., and Morris, T. (2013) 'The integrated model of sport confidence: A canonical correlation and mediational analysis', *Journal of Sport & Exercise Psychology,* 35, 644–654.

Koocher, G.P., and Keith-Spiegel, P. (1998) *Ethics in psychology: Professional standards and cases,* New York: Oxford University Press, 2nd edn.

Kowalski, K.C., and Crocker, P.R. (2001) 'Development and validation of the Coping Function Questionnaire for adolescents in sport', *Journal of Sport and Exercise Psychology,* 23, 136–155.

Krohne, H.W. (1993) 'Vigilance and cognitive avoidance as concepts in coping research', in H.W. Krohne (ed.), *Attention and Avoidance: Strategies in Coping with Aversiveness,* Seattle, WA: Hogrefe & Huber, pp. 19–50.

Kühn, A.A., Brücke, C., Hübl, J., Schneider, G.H., Kupsch, A., Eusebio, A., Ashkan, K., Holland, P., Aziz, T., Vandenberghe, W., Nuttin, B., and Brown, P. (2008) 'Motivation modulates motor-related feedback activity in the human basal ganglia', *Current Biology,* 18, R648–R650.

Kvist, J., Ek, A., Sporrstedt, K., and Good, L. (2005) 'Fear of re-injury: a hindrance for returning to sports after anterior cruciate ligament reconstruction', *Knee Surgery, Sports Traumatology, Arthroscopy,* 13, 393–397.

Lafrenière, M.-A.K., Jowett, S., Vallerand, R.J., and Carbonneau, N. (2011) 'Passion for coaching and the quality of the coach–athlete relationship: The mediating role of coaching behaviours', *Psychology of Sport and Exercise,* 12, 144–152.

Lam, W.K., Maxwell, J.P., and Masters, R. (2009) 'Analogy learning and the performance of motor skills under pressure', *Journal of Sport & Exercise Psychology,* 31, 337–357.

Lambert, J., and Bard, C. (2005) 'Acquisition of visuomanual skills and improvement of information processing capacities in 6- to 10-year-old children performing a 2D pointing task', *Neuroscience Letters,* 377, 1–6.

Land, W., and Tennenbaum, G. (2012) 'An outcome- and process-oriented examination of a golf-specific secondary task strategy to prevent choking under pressure', *Journal of Applied Sport Psychology,* 24, 303–322.

Lang, P.J. (1977) 'Imagery in therapy: An information-processing analysis of fear', *Behaviour Therapy,* 8, 862–886.

Langan, E., Blake, C., Toner, J., and Lonsdale, C. (2015) 'Testing the effects of a self-determination theory-based intervention with youth Gaelic football coaches on athlete motivation and burnout', *The Sport Psychologist,* 29, 293–301.

LaVoi, N.M. (2007) 'Expanding the interpersonal dimension: Closeness in the coach–athlete relationship', *International Journal of Sport Science and Coaching,* 4, 497–512.

Law, J., Masters, R., Bray, S.R., Eves, F., and Bardswell, I. (2003) 'Motor performances as a function of audience affability and metaknowledge', *Journal of Sport & Exercise Psychology,* 25, 484–500.

Law, M., Côté, J., and Ericsson, K.A. (2007) 'Characteristics of expert development in rhythmic gymnastics: A retrospective study', *International Journal of Sport and Exercise Psychology,* 5, 82–103.

Lazarus, R.S. (1991) *Emotion and adaptation,* New York: Oxford University Press.

Lazarus, R.S. (1999) *Stress and Emotion: A New Synthesis,* New York: Springer.

Lazarus, R.S. (2000a) 'How emotions influence performance in competitive sports', *The Sport Psychologist,* 14, 229–252.

Lazarus, R.S. (2000b) 'Cognitive-motivational-relational theory of emotion', in Y.L. Hanin (ed.), *Emotions in sport,* Champaign, IL: Human Kinetics, pp. 39–63.

Lazarus, R.S., and Folkman, S. (1984) *Stress, appraisal and coping,* New York: Springer.

Lemez, S., Baker, J., Horton, S., Wattie, N., and Weir, P. (2014) 'Examining the relationship between relative age, competition level, and dropout rates in male youth ice-hockey players', *Scandinavian Journal of Medicine and Science in Sports,* 24, 935–942.

Leo, F.M., González-Ponce, I., Sánchez-Miguel, P.A., Ivarsson, A., and Garcia-Calvo, T. (2015) 'Role ambiguity, role conflict, team conflict, cohesion and collective efficacy in sport teams: A multilevel analysis', *Psychology of Sport and Exercise,* 20, 60–66.

Lepper, M.R., and Hodell, M. (1989) 'Intrinsic motivation in the classroom', in C. Ames and R. Ames (eds), *Research on motivation in education,* New York: Academic Press, pp. 73–105.

Lewthwaite, R., and Wulf, G. (2010) 'Social-comparative feedback affects motor skill learning', *Quarterly Journal of Experimental Psychology,* 63, 738–749.

Liao, C.M., and Masters, R.S.W. (2001) 'Analogy learning: A means to implicit motor learning', *Journal of Sports Sciences,* 19, 307–319.

Lindeman, E.C. (1926) 'Andragogik: The method of teaching adults', *Workers' Education,* 4, 38–45.

Lindqvist, A.S., Moberg, T., Ehrnborg, C., Eriksson, B.O., Fahlke, C, and Rosen, T. (2014) 'Increased mortality rate and suicide in Swedish former elite male athletes in power sports', *Scandinavian Journal of Medicine and Science in Sports,* 24, 1000–1005.

Liu, T., and Jensen, J.L. (2011) 'Effects of strategy use on children's motor performance in continuous timing task', *Research Quarterly for Exercise and Sport,* 82, 198–209.

Locke, E.A., and Latham, G.P. (1990) *A theory of goal setting and task performance,* Englewood Cliffs, NJ: Prentice Hall.

Locke, E.A., and Latham, G.P. (2002) 'Building a practically useful theory of goal setting and task motivation: A 35-year odyssey', *American Psychologist*, 57, 705–717.

Lonsdale, C., and Tam, J.T. (2008) 'On the temporal and behavioural consistency of pre-performance routines: an intra-individual analysis of elite basketball players' free throw shooting accuracy', *Journal of Sports Sciences*, 26, 259–266.

Lonsdale, C., Hodge, K., and Rose, E.A. (2008) 'The Behavioral Regulation in Sport Questionnaire (BRSQ): instrument development and initial validity', *Journal of Sport & Exercise Psychology*, 30, 323–355.

Lorimer, R., and Jowett, S. (2009) 'Empathic accuracy, meta perspective, and satisfaction in the coach–athlete relationship', *Journal of Applied Sport Psychology*, 21, 201–212.

Lumia, A.R., and McGinnis, M.Y. (2010) 'Impact of anabolic androgenic steroids on adolescent males', *Physiology & Behaviour*, 100, 199–204.

Lyle, J. (2007) 'Modelling the complexity of the coaching process: A commentary', *International Journal of Sports Science & Coaching*, 2, 407–409.

Lyle, J. (2011) 'What is a coach and what is coaching?', in I. Stanford (ed.), *Coaching children in sport*, London: Routledge, pp. 5–16.

MacPhail, A., Gorely, T., Kirk, D., and Kinchin, G. (2008) 'Children's experiences of fun and enjoyment during a season of sport education', *Research Quarterly in Exercise and Sport*, 79, 344–355.

Madan, C.R., and Singhal, A. (2013) 'Introducing TAMI: An objective test of ability in movement imagery', *Journal of Motor Behavior*, 45, 153–166.

Madan, C.R., and Singhal, A. (2014) 'Improving the TAMI for use with athletes', *Journal of Sports Sciences*, 32, 1351–1356.

Madrigal, L., and Gill, D.L. (2014) 'Psychological responses of division I female athletes throughout injury recovery: A case study approach', *Journal of Clinical Sport Psychology*, 8, 276–298.

Mageau, G.A., and Vallerand, R.J. (2003) 'The coach–athlete relationship: A motivational model', *Journal of Sports Sciences*, 21, 883–904.

Mahoney, J.W., Gucciardi, D.F., Mallett, C.J., and Ntoumanis, N. (2014) 'Adolescent performers' perspectives on mental toughness and its development: The utility of the bioecological model', *The Sport Psychologist*, 28, 233–244.

Manzaneque, J.M., Vera, F.M., Ramos, N.S., Godoy, Y.A., Rodriguez, F.M., Blanca, M.J., Fernandez, A., and Enguix, A. (2010) 'Psychobiological modulation in anxious and depressed patients after a mindfulness meditation programme: A pilot study', *Stress and Health*, 27, 216–222.

Marcos, F.M.L., Miguel, P.A.S., Olivia, D.S., and Calvo, T.G. (2010) 'Interactive effects of team cohesion on perceived efficacy in semi-professional sport', *Journal of Sport Science and Medicine*, 9, 320–325.

Mardon, N., Richards, H., and Martindale, A. (2016) 'The effect of mindfulness training on attention and performance in national-level swimmers: An exploratory investigation', *Journal of Clinical Sport Psychology*, 9, 263–281.

Marsh, H.W., and Kleitman, S. (2003) 'School athletic participation: Mostly gain with little pain', *Journal of Sport & Exercise Psychology*, 25, 205–228.

Marshall, H.H., and Weinstein, R.S. (1984) 'Classroom factors affecting students' self evaluations: An interactional model', *Review of Educational Research*, 54, 301–325.

Martin, K.A., Moritz, S.E., and Hall, C.R. (1999) 'Imagery use in sport: A literature review and applied model', *The Sport Psychologist*, 13, 245–268.

Martin, L.J., Carron, A.V., and Burke, S.M. (2009) 'Team building interventions in sport: A meta-analysis', *Sport and Exercise Psychology Review*, 5, 3–18.

Martin, S.B., Dale, G.A., and Jackson, A.W. (2003) 'Youth coaching preferences of adolescent athletes and their parents', *Journal of Sport Behavior,* 24, 197–212.

Masters, R.S.W. (1992) 'Knowledge, nerves and know-how', *British Journal of Psychology,* 83, 343–358.

Masters, R.S.W. (2000) 'Theoretical aspects of implicit learning in sport', *International Journal of Sport Psychology,* 31, 530–541.

McLaren, C.D., Eys, M.A., and Murray, R.A. (2015) 'A coach-initiated motivational climate intervention and athletes' perceptions of group cohesion in youth sport', *Sport, Exercise, and Performance Psychology,* 4, 113–126.

Meichenbaum, D. (1977) *Cognitive-behaviour modification: An integrative approach*, New York: Plenum Press.

Merriam, S., and Brockett, R.G. (1997) *The profession and practice of adult education: An introduction,* San Francisco, CA: Jossey-Bass.

Mesagno, C., and Mullane-Grant, T. (2010) 'A comparison of different pre-performance routines as possible choking interventions', *Journal of Applied Sport Psychology,* 22, 343–360.

Mesagno, C., Marchant, D., and Morris, T. (2008) 'A pre-performance routine to alleviate choking in "choking-susceptible" athletes', *The Sport Psychologist,* 22, 439–457.

Millar, S.-K., Oldham, A.R.H., and Donovan, M. (2011) 'Coaches' self-awareness of timing, nature and intent of verbal instructions to athletes', *International Journal of Sports Science and Coaching,* 6, 503–513.

Miller, A., and Donohue, B. (2003) 'The development and controlled evaluation of athletic mental preparation strategies in high school distance runners', *Journal of Applied Sport Psychology,* 15, 321–334.

Miller, S., and Weinberg, R. (1991) 'Perceptions of psychological momentum and their relationship to performance', *The Sport Psychologist,* 5, 211–222.

Mitchell, I., Evans, L., Rees, T., and Hardy, L. (2014) 'Stressors, social support, and tests of the buffering hypothesis: Effects on psychological responses of injured athletes', *British Journal of Health Psychology,* 19, 486–508.

Moen, F., Federici, R.A., and Abrahamsen, F. (2015) 'Examining possible relationships between mindfulness, stress, school- and sport performances and athlete burnout', *International Journal of Coaching Science,* 9, 3–19.

Møller, M. (2014) 'The analyst's anxieties in the first interview: Barriers against analytic presence', *International Journal of Psychoanalysis,* 95, 485–503.

Møllerløkken, N.E., Lorås, H., and Vorland Pedersen, A. (2015) 'A systematic review and meta-analysis of dropout rates in youth soccer', *Perceptual and Motor Skills,* 121, 913–922.

Moore, L.J., Vine, S.J., Wilson, M.R., and Freeman, P. (2012) 'The effect of challenge and threat states on performance: An examination of potential mechanisms', *Psychophysiology,* 49, 1417–1425.

Moore, L.J., Vine, S.J., Wilson, M.R., and Freeman, P. (2015) 'Reappraising threat: How to optimize performance under pressure', *Journal of Sport & Exercise Psychology,* 37, 339–343.

Moore, L.J., Wilson, M.R., Vine, S.J., Coussens, A.H., and Freeman, P. (2013) 'Champ or chump?: Challenge and threat states during pressurized competition', *Journal of Sport & Exercise Psychology,* 35, 551–562.

Moran, A.P. (1996) *The psychology of concentration in sport performers: A cognitive analysis,* London: Taylor & Francis.

Morente-Sánchez, J., and Zabala, M. (2015) 'Knowledge, attitudes, and beliefs of technical staff towards doping in Spanish football', *Journal of Sports Sciences,* 33, 1267–1275.

Morgan, T.K., and Giacobbi, P.R. (2006) 'Toward two grounded theories of the talent development and social support process of highly successful collegiate athletes', *The Sport Psychologist*, 20, 295–313.

Morozova, L.V., Zvyagina, N.V., and Terebova, N.N. (2008) 'Characteristics of visual perception in seven-year-old children differing in functional maturity of brain structures', *Human Physiology*, 34, 14–21.

Mullen, R., Hardy, L., and Tattersall, A. (2005) 'The effects of anxiety on motor performance: A test of the Conscious Processing Hypothesis', *Journal of Sport & Exercise Psychology*, 27, 212–225.

Munroe, K., Giacobbi, P., Hall, C., and Weinberg, R. (2000) 'The 4W's of imagery use: Where, when, why, and what', *The Sport Psychologist*, 14, 119–137.

Munroe, K., Terry, P.C., and Carron, A. (2002) 'Cohesion and teamwork', in B. Hale and D. Collins (eds), *Rugby Tough,* Champaign, IL: Human Kinetics, pp. 137–154.

Muris, P., Meesters, C., van den Hout, A., Wessels, S., Franken, I., and Rassin, E. (2007) 'Personality and temperament correlates of pain catastrophizing in young adolescents', *Child Psychiatry and Human Development*, 38, 171–181.

Murphy, S. (1996) *The achievement zone,* New York: Putnam's.

Murphy, S., Nordin, S., and Cumming, J. (2008) 'Imagery in sport, exercise, and dance', in T.S. Horn (ed.), *Advances in sport psychology,* Champaign, IL: Human Kinetics, pp. 297–324.

Murphy, S.M. (1990) 'Models of imagery in sport psychology: A review', *Journal of Mental Imagery*, 14, 153–172.

Nicholls, A.R. (2007a) 'A longitudinal phenomenological analysis of coping effectiveness among Scottish international adolescent golfers', *European Journal of Sport Science*, 7, 169–178.

Nicholls, A.R. (2007b) 'Can an athlete be taught to cope more effectively? The experiences of an international level adolescent golfer during a training program for coping', *Perceptual and Motor Skills*, 104, 494–500.

Nicholls, A.R. (2010) 'Effective versus ineffective coping', in A.R. Nicholls (ed.). *Coping in Sport: Theory, Methods, and Related Constructs,* New York: Nova Science, pp. 263–276.

Nicholls, A.R. (2016) 'Adaptation, stress, and coping', in R. Schinke, K. McGannon, and B. Smith (eds), *The Routledge International Handbook of Sport Psychology,* London: Routledge, pp. 119–127.

Nicholls, A.R., and Callard, J. (2012) *Focused for Rugby,* Champaign, IL: Human Kinetics.

Nicholls, A.R., and Perry, J.L. (2016) 'Perceptions of the coach–athlete relationship are more important to coaches than athletes in predicting dyadic coping and stress appraisals: An actor-partner independence mediation model', *Frontiers in Psychology*, 7, 447.

Nicholls, A.R., and Polman, R.C.J. (2007) 'Coping in sport: A systematic review', *Journal of Sports Sciences*, 25, 11–31.

Nicholls, A.R., and Thelwell, R. (2010) 'Coping conceptualized and unraveled', in A.R. Nicholls (ed.), *Coping in Sport: Theory, Methods, and Related Constructs*, New York: Nova Science, pp. 3–14.

Nicholls, A.R., Hemmings, B., and Clough, P.J. (2010) 'Stressors, coping, and emotion among international adolescent golfers', *Scandinavian Journal of Medicine & Science in Sports,* 20, 346–355.

Nicholls, A.R., Holt, N.L., and Polman, R.C.J. (2005a) 'A phenomenological analysis of coping effectiveness in golf', *The Sport Psychologist*, 19, 111–130.

Nicholls, A.R., Holt, N.L., Polman, R.C.J., and James, D.W.G. (2005b) 'Stress and coping among international adolescent golfers', *Journal of Applied Sport Psychology*, 17, 333–340.

Nicholls, A.R., Jones, C.R., Polman, R.C.J., and Borkoles, E. (2009) 'Stressors, coping, and emotion among professional rugby union players during training and matches', *Scandinavian Journal of Medicine and Science in Sports*, 19, 113–120.

Nicholls, A.R., Levy, A.R., Jones, L., Meir, R., Radcliffe, J.N., and Perry, J.L. (2016a) 'Committed relationships and enhanced threat levels: Perceptions of coach behavior, the coach–athlete relationship, stress appraisals, and coping among athletes', *International Journal of Sport Science and Coaching*, 11, 16–26.

Nicholls, A.R., Levy, A.R., Jones, L., Rengamani, M., and Polman, R.C.J. (2011) 'An exploration of the two-factor schematization of relational meaning and emotions among professional rugby union players', *International Journal of Sport and Exercise Psychology*, 9, 78–91.

Nicholls, A.R., Levy, A.R., and Polman, R.C.J. (2012) 'A path analysis of stress appraisals, emotions, coping, and performance satisfaction among athletes', *Psychology of Sport and Exercise*, 13, 263–270.

Nicholls, A.R., Morley, D., and Perry, J.L. (2016c) 'Mentally tough athletes are more aware of unsupportive coaching behaviours: Perceptions of coach behaviour, motivational climate, and mental toughness in sport', *International Journal of Sport Science and Coaching*, 11, 172–181.

Nicholls, A.R., Perry, J.L., Levy, A.R., Meir, R., Jones, L., Baghurst, T., Sanctuary, C., and Thompson, M.A. (2015) 'Coach perceptions of performance enhancement in adolescence: The Sport Drug Control Model for Adolescent Athletes', *Performance Enhancement & Health*, 3, 93–101.

Nicholls, A.R., Polman, R.C.J., Levy, A.R., and Backhouse, S.H. (2008) 'Mental toughness, optimism, pessimism, and coping among athletes', *Personality and Individual Differences*, 44, 1182–1192.

Nicholls, A.R., Polman, R.C.J., Levy, A.R., Taylor, J.A., and Cobley, S.P. (2007) 'Stressors, coping, and coping effectiveness: Gender, sport type, and skill differences', *Journal of Sports Sciences*, 25, 1521–1530.

Nicholls, A.R., Taylor, N.J., Carroll, S., and Perry, J.L. (2016b) 'The development of a new sport-specific classification of coping and a meta-analysis of the relationship between different coping strategies and moderators on sporting outcomes', *Frontiers in Psychology*, 7, 1674.

Nicholls, J.G. (1989) *The competitive ethos and democratic education*, Cambridge, MA: Harvard University Press.

Nicolas, M., Gadureau, P., and Franche, V. (2011) 'Perception of coaching behaviors, coping, and achievement in a sport competition', *Journal of Sport & Exercise Psychology*, 33, 460–468.

Nideffer, R.M. (1992) *Psyched to win*, Champaign, IL: Leisure Press.

Nikbin, D., Hyun, S.S., Iranmanesh, M., and Foroughi, B. (2014) 'Effects of perceived justice for coaches on athletes' trust, commitment, and perceived performance: A study of futsal and volleyball players', *International Journal of Sport Science and Coaching*, 9, 561–578.

Nippert, A.H., and Smith, A.M. (2008) 'Psychological stress related to injury and impact on sport performance' *Physical Medicine and Rehabilitation Clinics of North America*, 19, 399–418.

Nordin, S., and Cumming, J. (2005) 'More than meets the eye: Investigating imagery type, direction, and outcome', *The Sport Psychologist*, 19, 1–17.

Occhino, J.L., Mallett, C.J., Rynne, S.B., and Carlisle, K.N. (2014) 'Autonomy-supportive pedagogical approach to sports coaching: Research challenges and opportunities', *International Journal of Sports Science & Coaching*, 9, 401–415.

Paige Pope, J., and Wilson, P.M. (2012) 'Understanding motivational processes in university rugby players: A preliminary test of the hierarchical model of intrinsic and extrinsic motivation at the contextual level', *International Journal of Sports Science & Coaching*, 7, 89–107.

Pain, M.A., Harwood, C., and Anderson, R. (2011) 'Pre-competition imagery and music: The impact on flow and performance in competitive soccer', *The Sport Psychologist*, 25, 212–232.

Park, C.L., Cohen, L.H., and Murch, R.L. (1996) 'Assessment and prediction of stress-related growth', *Journal of Personality*, 64, 71–105.

Perreault, M.E., and French, K.E. (2015) 'External-focus feedback benefits free-throw learning in children', *Research Quarterly for Exercise and Sport*, 86, 422–427.

Podlog, L., and Dionigi, R. (2010) 'Coach strategies for addressing psychosocial challenges during the return to sport from injury', *Journal of Sports Sciences*, 28, 1197–1208.

Prapavessis, H., and Carron, A.V. (1996) 'The effect of group cohesion on competitive state anxiety', *Journal of Sport & Exercise Psychology*, 18, 64–74.

Oudejans, R.R.D., and Pijpers, J.R. (2010) 'Training with mild anxiety may prevent choking under high levels of anxiety', *Psychology of Sport & Exercise*, 11, 44–50.

Owusu-Sekyere, F., and Gervis, M. (2016) 'In the pursuit of mental toughness: Is creating mentally tough players a disguise for emotional abuse?', *International Journal of Coaching Science*, 10, 3–23.

Peacock, E.J., and Wong, P.T.P. (1990) 'The Stress Appraisal Measure (SAM): A multidimensional approach to cognitive appraisal', *Stress Medicine*, 6, 227–236.

Pelletier, L.G., Rocchi, M.A., Vallerand, R.J., Deci, E.L., and Ryan, R.M. (2013) 'Validation of the revised sport motivation scale (SMS-II)', *Psychology of Sport and Exercise*, 14, 329–341.

Perkins, A.M., and Corr, P.J. (2006) 'Reactions to threat and personality: Psychometric differentiation of intensity and direction dimensions of human defensive behaviour', *Behavioural Brain Research*, 169, 21–28.

Perkins, A.M., Kemp, S.E., and Corr, P.J. (2007) 'Fear and anxiety as separable emotions: An investigation of the revised reinforcement sensitivity theory of personality', *Emotion*, 7, 252–261.

Petitpas, A.J. (2000) 'Managing stress on and off the field: The littlefoot approach to learned resourcefulness', in M.B. Andersen (ed.), *Doing sport psychology*, Champaign, IL: Human Kinetics, pp. 33–44.

Petróczi, A., and Aidman, E. (2009) 'Measuring explicit attitude toward doping: Review of the psychometric properties of the performance enhancement attitude scale', *Psychology of Sport and Exercise*, 10, 390–396.

Philippe, R.A., Sagar, S.S., Gerber, M., and Hauw, D. (2016) 'Players' perceptions of coaches' contributions to their mental toughness,' *International Journal of Coaching Science*, 10, 37–51.

Poczwardowski, A. (1997) 'Athletes and coaches: An exploration of their relationship and its meaning', Unpublished doctoral dissertation, University of Utah, Salt Lake City.

Poczwardowski, A., and Conroy, D.E. (2002) 'Coping responses to failure and success among elite athletes and performing artists', *Journal of Applied Sport Psychology*, 14, 313–329.

Post, P.G., Fairbrother, J.T., and Barros, J.A.C. (2011) 'Self-controlled amount of practice benefits learning of a motor skill', *Research Quarterly for Exercise and Sport*, 82, 474–481.

Prevatt, F., and Levrini, A. (2015) *ADHD coaching: A guide for mental health professionals*, Washington, DC: American Psychological Association.

Proteau, L., Marteniuk, R.G., and Lé Vesque, L. (1992) 'A sensorimotor basis for motor learning: Evidence indicating specificity of practice', *Quarterly Journal of Experimental Psychology*, 44A, 557–575.

Raedeke, T.D., and Smith, A.L. (2009). *The athlete burnout questionnaire manual*. Morgantown, WV: West Virginia University, Fitness Information Technology.

Rahim, M. (2002) 'Toward a theory of managing organizational conflict,' *International Journal of Conflict Management*, 13, 206–235.

Rees, T. (2007) 'Influence of social support on athletes', in S. Jowett and D. Lavallee (eds), *Social Psychology in Sport*, Champaign, IL: Human Kinetics, pp. 223–232.

Rees, T., and Freeman, P. (2009) 'Social support moderates the relationship between stressors and task performance through self-efficacy', *Journal of Social and Clinical Psychology*, 28, 245–264.

Rees, T., and Freeman, P. (2010) 'Social support and performance in a golf-putting experiment', *The Sport Psychologist*, 18, 333–348.

Rees, T., Hardy, L., and Freeman, P. (2007) 'Stressors, social support and effects upon performance in golf', *Journal of Sports Sciences*, 25, 33–42.

Reeve, J. (1998) 'Autonomy support as an interpersonal motivating style: Is it teachable?', *Contemporary Educational Psychology*, 23, 312–330.

Reeve, J.M. (2009) 'Why teachers adopt a controlling motivating style toward students and how they can become more autonomy supportive', *Educational Psychologist*, 44, 159–175.

Reeves, C., Nicholls, A.R., and McKenna, J. (2009) 'Stress and coping among academy footballers: Age-related differences', *Journal of Applied Sport Psychology*, 21, 31–48.

Reeves, C.W., Nicholls, A.R., and McKenna, J. (2011) 'The effects of a coping intervention on coping self-efficacy, coping effectiveness, and subjective performance among adolescent soccer players', *International Journal of Sport and Exercise Psychology*, 9, 126–142.

Reid, G. (2009) *Dyslexia: A practitioner's handbook*, Chichester: Wiley-Blackwell.

Reischmann, H., and Jost, N. (2004) 'Andragogy: History, meaning, context, function'. Retrieved from www.andragogy.net, on 9 September 2004.

Rhind, D.J.A., and Jowett, S. (2010) 'Relationship maintenance strategies in the coach–athlete relationship: The development of the COMPASS model', *Journal of Applied Sport Psychology*, 22, 106–121.

Richardson, A. (1969) *Mental Imagery*, New York: Springer.

Rief, S.F. (2008) *The ADD/ADHD checklist: A practical reference for parents and teachers*, San Francisco, CA: Jossey-Bass.

Rieke, M., Hammermeister, J., and Chase, M. (2008) 'Servant leadership in sport: A new paradigm for effective coach behaviour', *International Journal of Sports Science & Coaching*, 2, 227–239.

Rizzo, T.L., Bishop, P., and Tobar, D. (1997) 'Attitudes of soccer coaches toward youth players with mild mental retardation: A pilot study', *Adapted Physical Activity Quarterly*, 14, 238.

Robin, N., Domonique, L., Tousasaint, L., Blandin, Y., Guillot, A., and LeHer, M. (2007) 'Effects of motor imagery training on service returns accuracy in tennis: The role of image ability', *International Journal of Sport and Exercise Psychology*, 2, 175–186.

Rodgers, W., Hall, C.R., and Buckholtz, E. (1991) 'The effect of an imagery training programme on imagery ability, imagery, use, and figure skating performance', *Journal of Applied Sport Psychology*, 3, 109–125.

Roiger, T., Weidauer, L., and Kern, B. (2015) 'A longitudinal pilot study of depressive symptoms in concussed and injured/nonconcussed national collegiate athletic association Division I student-athletes', *Journal of Athletic Training*, 50, 256–261.

Rosenberg, M. (1979) *Conceiving the self*, New York: Basic Books.

Rosenfeld, L.B., and Richman, J.M. (1997) 'Developing effective social support: Team building and the social support process', *Journal of Applied Sport Psychology*, 9, 133–153.

Rosenfeld, L.B., Richman, J.M., and Hardy, C.J. (1989) 'Examining social support networks among athletes: Description and relationship to stress', *The Sport Psychologist*, 3, 23–33.

Ruddock-Hudson, M., O'Halloran, P., and Murphy, G. (2014) 'The psychological impact of long-term injury on Australian football league players', *Journal of Applied Sport Psychology*, 26, 377–394.

Ryan, R.M., and Deci, E.L. (2000) 'Self-determination theory and the facilitation of intrinsic motivation, social development, and well-being', *American Psychologist*, 55, 68–78.

Ryan, R.M., and Deci, E.L. (2007) 'Active human nature: Self-determination theory and the promotion and maintenance of sport, exercise, and health', in M.S. Hagger and N.L.D. Chatzisarantis (eds), *Intrinsic motivation and self-determination in exercise and sport*, Champaign, IL: Human Kinetics, pp. 1–20.

Ryska, T.A., Yin, Z., Cooley, D., and Ginn, R. (1999) 'Developing team cohesion: A comparison of cognitive-behavioural strategies of U.S. and Australian Sport Coaches', *The Journal of Psychology*, 133, 523–539.

Sachse, R. (2001). 'Persönlichkeitsstörung als Interaktionsstörung: Der Beitrag der Gesprächspsychotherapie zur Modellbildung und Intervention'. *Psychotherapie*, 5, 282–292.

Sackett, R.S. (1934). 'Influence of symbolic rehearsal upon retention of maze habit', *Journal of General Psychology*, 10, 376–396.

Sagar, S.S., and Jowett, S. (2015) 'Fear of failure and self-control in the context of the coach–athlete relationship quality', *International Journal of Coaching Science*, 9, 3–21.

Sandström, E., Linnér, L., and Stambulova, N. (2016) 'Career profiles of athlete–coach relationships: Descriptions and interpretations', *International Journal of Sports Science & Coaching*, 11, 395–409.

Scanlan, T.K., and Lewthwaite, R. (1986) 'Social psychological aspects of competition for male youth sport participants: IV. Predictors of enjoyment', *Journal of Sport Psychology*, 8, 25–35.

Scanlan, T.K., Carpenter, P.J., Lobel, M., and Simons, J.P. (1993) 'Sources of enjoyment for youth sport athletes', *Pediatric Exercise Science*, 5, 275–285.

Schack, T., Whitmarsh, B., Pike, R., and Redden, C. (2005) 'Coach–athlete relationship', in J. Taylor and G.S. Wilson, *Applying sport psychology: Four perspectives*, Champaign, IL: Human Kinetics, pp. 137–150.

Schmidt, R.A., and Bjork, R.A. (1992) 'New conceptualisations of practice: Common principles in thee paradigms suggest new concepts for training', *Psychological Science*, 3, 207–217.

Schmidt, R.A., and Lee, T.D. (2005) *Motor control and learning*, Champaign, IL: Human Kinetics, 4th edn.

Schneider, W.F., Gruman, J.A., and Coutts, L.M. (2005) *Applied social psychology. Understanding and addressing social and practical problems*, London: Sage.

Seligman, M.E.P. (1991) *Learned optimism*, New York: A.A. Knopf.

Seligman, M.E.P. (2006) *Learned optimism: How to change your mind and your life*, New York: Vintage Books.

Shapiro, S.L., Carlson, L.E., Astin, J.A., and Freedman, B. (2006) 'Mechanisms of mindfulness', *Journal of Clinical Psychology,* 62, 373–386.

Sheard, M., and Golby, J. (2006) 'Effect of a psychological skills training program on swimming performance and positive psychological development', *International Journal of Sport and Exercise Psychology,* 4, 149–169.

Sheldon, K.A., and Watson, A. (2011) 'Coach's autonomy support is especially important for varsity compared to club and recreational athletes', *International Journal of Sports Science and Coaching,* 6, 109–123.

Sheridan, D., Coffee, P., and Lavallee, D. (2014) 'A systematic review of social support in youth sport', *International Review of Sport and Exercise Psychology,* 7, 198–228.

Shilts, M.K., Horowitz, M., and Townsend, M.S. (2004) 'An innovative approach to goal setting for adolescents: Guided goal setting', *Journal of Nutritional Education and Behaviour,* 36, 155–156.

Shumaker, S.A., and Brownell, A. (1984) 'Toward a theory of social support: Closing conceptual gaps', *Journal of Social Issues,* 40, 11–36.

Siegenthaler, K.L., and Gonzalez, G.L. (1997) 'Youth sports as serious leisure: A critique'. *Journal of Sport and Social Issues,* 21, 298–314.

Singer, R.N., and Janelle, C.M. (1999) 'Determining sport expertise: From genes to supremes', *International Journal of Sport Psychology,* 30, 117–150.

Smith, C., and Strick, L. (2010) *Learning disabilities: A to Z,* New York: Free Press.

Smith, D. (1992) 'The coach as sport psychologist: An alternative view', *Journal of Applied Sport Psychology,* 2, 56–62.

Smith, H.W. (1994) *The 10 natural laws of successful time and life management: Proven strategies for increased productivity and inner peace,* New York: Warner.

Smith, M. and Cushion, C.J. (2006). 'An investigation of the in-game behaviours of professional, top-level youth soccer coaches', *Journal of Sport Sciences* 24, 355–366.

Smith, R.E. (1980) 'A cognitive-affective approach to stress management training for athletes', in C.H. Nadeau, W.R. Halliwell, K.M. Newell, and G.C. Roberts (eds), *Psychology of motor behaviour in sport – 1979,* Champaign, IL: Human Kinetics, pp. 54–72.

Smith, R.E., and Smoll, F.L. (1997) 'Coaching the coaches: Youth sports as a scientific and applied behavioural setting', *Current Directions in Psychological Science,* 6, 16–21.

Smith, R.E., Smoll, F.L., and Cumming, S.P. (2007) 'Effects of a motivational climate intervention for coaches on young athletes' sport performance anxiety', *Journal of Sport & Exercise Psychology,* 29, 39–59.

Smith, R.E., Zane, N.W.S., Smoll, F.L., and Coppel, D.B. (1983) 'Behavioral assessment in youth sports: Coaching behaviors and children's attitudes', *Medicine and Science in Sport and Exercise,* 15, 208–214.

Smith, D., Wright, C., Allsopp, A., and Westhead, H. (2007) 'It's All in the Mind: PETTLEP-Based Imagery and Sports Performance', *Journal of Applied Sport Psychology,* 19, 80–92.

Smoll, F.L., and Smith, R.E. (2006) 'Enhancing coach–athlete relationships: Cognitive behavioural principles and procedures', in J. Dosil (ed.), *The sport psychologist's handbook: A guide for sport-specific performance enhancement,* Chichester: John Wiley & Sons, pp. 19–38.

Smoll, F.L., and Smith, R.E. (2008) *Coaches who never lose: Making sure athletes win, no matter what the score,* Palo Alto, CA: Warde, 3rd edn.

Smoll, F.L., Smith, R.E., Barnett, N.P., and Everett, J.J. (1993) 'Enhancement of children's self-esteem through social support training for youth sport coaches', *Journal of Applied Psychology,* 4, 602–610.

Sommers-Flanagan, J. (2016) 'Clinical interview', in J.C. Norcross, G.R. VandenBos, and D.K. Freeheim (eds), *APA handbook of clinical psychology: Vol. 3. Applications and methods*. Washington, DC: American Psychological Association.

Spaniol, J., Voss, A., Bowen, H.J., and Grady, C.L. (2011) 'Motivational incentives modulate age differences in visual perception', *Psychology and Aging*, 26, 932–939.

Staufenbiel, K., Lobinger, B., and Strauss, B. (2015) 'Home advantage in soccer – a matter of expectations, goal setting, and tactical decisions of coaches?', *Journal of Sports Sciences*, 33, 1932–1941.

Stebbings, J., Taylor, I.M., and Spray, C. (2011) 'Antecedents of perceived coach autonomy supportive and controlling behaviours: Coach psychological need satisfaction and well-being', *Journal of Sport & Exercise Psychology*, 33, 255–272.

Stein, J.F., Richardson, A.J., and Fowler, M.S. (2000) 'Monocular occlusion can improve binocular control and reading in dyslexics', *Brain*, 123, 164–170.

Stowe, C.M. (2000) *How to reach and teach children and teens with dyslexia*, San Francisco, CA: Jossey-Bass.

Strong, S.R. (1968) 'Counselling: An interpersonal influence process', *Journal of Counselling Psychology*, 15, 215–224.

Tamminen, K.A., and Holt, N.L. (2012) 'Adolescent athletes' learning about coping and the roles of parents and coaches', *Psychology of Sport and Exercise*, 13, 69–79.

Taylor, S.E., and Brown, J.D. (1988) 'Illusion and well-being: A social psychological perspective on mental health,' *Psychological Bulletin*, 103, 193–210.

Taylor, J., and Schneider, B.A. (1992) 'The sport-clinical intake protocol: A comprehensive interviewing instrument for applied sport psychology', *Professional Psychology: Research and Practice*, 23, 318–325.

Taylor, J., and Taylor, S. (1997) *Psychological approaches to sports injury rehabilitation*, Gaithersburg, MD: Aspen Publications.

Taylor, K.E., and Walter, J. (2003) 'Occupation choices of adults with and without symptoms of dyslexia', *Dyslexia*, 9, 177–185.

Taylor, S.E., and Brown, J.D. (1988) 'Illusion and well-being: A social psychological perspective on mental health', *Psychological Bulletin*, 103, 193–210.

te Wierike, S.C.M., van der Sluis, A., van den Akker-Scheek, I., Elferink-Gemser, M.T., and Visscher, C. (2013) 'Psychosocial factors influencing the recovery of athletes with anterior cruciate ligament injury: A systematic review', *Scandinavian Journal of Medicine and Science in Sports*, 23, 527–540.

Tennen, H., and Affleck, G. (1993) 'The puzzles of self-esteem: A clinical perspective', in R. F. Baumeister, (ed.), *Plenum series in social/clinical psychology*. New York: Plenum Press, pp. 241–262.

The Guardian (2015) 'Be good to yourself: Andy Murray's motivational on-court notes revealed'. 17 February Retrieved from: www.theguardian.com/ sport/2015/feb/17/andy-murray-motivational-court-notes

Theeboom, M., De Knop, P., and Weiss, M.R. (1995) 'Motivational climate, psychological responses, and motor skill development in children's sport: a field-based intervention study', *Journal of Sport & Exercise Psychology*, 17, 294–311.

Thelwell, R.C., Such, B.A., Weston, N.J.V., Such, J.D., and Greenlees, I.A. (2010) 'Developing mental toughness: Perceptions of elite female gymnasts', *International Journal of Sport and Exercise Psychology*, 8, 170–188.

Treasure, D. (1993) 'A social-cognitive approach to understanding children's achievement behaviour, cognitions, and affect in competitive sport', unpublished doctoral dissertation, University of Illinois.

Treasure, D. (2001) 'Enhancing young people's motivation in youth sport: An achievement goal approach', in G.C. Roberts (ed.), *Advances in motivation in sport and exercise,* Champaign, IL: Human Kinetics, pp. 79–100.

Turner, M.J., Jones, M.V., Sheffield, D., Slater, M.J., Barker, J.B., and Bell, J.J. (2013) 'Who thrives under pressure? Predicting the performance of elite academy cricketers using the cardiovascular indicators of challenge and threat states', *Journal of Sport & Exercise Psychology,* 35, 387–397.

Udry, E., Gould, D., Bridges, D., and Tuffey, S. (1997) 'People helping people? Examining the social ties of athletes coping with burnout and injury stress', *Journal of Sport & Exercise Psychology,* 19, 368–395.

U.S. Department of Education (2007) Digest of education statistics, retrieved on 19 October 2016 from https://nces.ed.gov/programs/digest/d07/tables/dt07_047.asp.

Ungerleider, S. (2013) *Faust's gold: Insider the East German doping machine.* Luxembourg: CreateSpace Independent Publishing Platform, 2nd edn.

Vallerand, R.J. (1997) 'Toward a hierarchical model of intrinsic and extrinsic motivation', in M. Zanna (ed.), *Advances in experimental social psychology,* New York: Academic Press, pp. 271–360.

Vallerand, R.J. (2001) 'A hierarchical model of intrinsic and extrinsic motivation for sport and exercise', in G.C. Roberts (ed.) *Advances in motivation in sport and exercise,* Champaign, IL: Human Kinetics, pp. 263–320.

Vallerand, R.J. (2007) 'A hierarchical model of intrinsic and extrinsic motivation for sport and physical activity', in M.S. Hagger and N.L.D. Chatzisarantis (eds), *Intrinsic motivation and self-determination in exercise and sport,* Champaign, IL: Human Kinetics, pp. 255–279.

Vallerand, R.J., and Ratelle, C.F. (2002) 'Intrinsic and extrinsic motivation: a hierarchical model', in E.L. Deci and R.M. Ryan (eds), *Handbook of self-determination research,* Rochester, NY: University of Rochester Press, pp. 37–64.

Vallerand, R.J., and Rousseau, F.L. (2001) 'Intrinsic and extrinsic motivation in sport and exercise: a review using the Hierarchical Model of Intrinsic and Extrinsic Motivation', in R.N. Singer, H.A. Hausenblas, and C.M. Janelle (eds), *Handbook of Sport Psychology,* New York: Wiley, 2nd edn, pp. 389–416.

Vallerand, R.J., Colavecchio, P.G., and Pelletier, L.G. (1988) 'Psychological momentum and performance inferences: A preliminary test of the antecedents–consequences psychological momentum model', *Journal of Sport & Exercise Psychology,* 10, 92–108.

Vargas-Tonsing, T.M., and Guan, J. (2007) 'Athletes' preferences for informational and emotional pre-game speech content', *International Journal of Sports Science & Coaching,* 2, 171–180.

Vargas-Tonsing, T.M., Myers, N.D., and Feltz, D.L. (2004) 'Coaches' and athletes' perceptions of efficacy enhancing techniques', *The Sport Psychologist,* 18, 397–414.

Vealey, R. (1986) 'Conceptualization of sport-confidence and competitive orientation: Preliminary investigation and instrument development', *Journal of Sport Psychology,* 8, 221–246.

Vealey, R.S. (2001) 'Understanding and enhancing self-confidence in athletes', in R. Singer, H. Hausenblas, and C. Janelle (eds), *Handbook of sport psychology,* New York: Wiley, pp. 550–565.

Vealey, R.S., and Chase, M.A. (2008) 'Self-confidence in sport', in T.S. Horn (ed.), *Advances in sport psychology,* Champaign, IL: Human Kinetics, 3rd edn, pp. 66–97.

Vealey, R.S., Hayashi, S.W., Garner-Holman, M., and Giacobbi, P. (1998) 'Sources of sport-confidence: Conceptualization and instrument development', *Journal of Sport & Exercise Psychology,* 20, 54–80.

Vieira, J.L.L., Ferreira, L., Cheuczuk, F., Flores, P.P., Vissoci, J.R.N., da Rocha, F.F., et al. (2015) 'Impact of coach–athlete relationship on the collective efficacy of young volleyball players', *Brazilian Journal of Kinanthropometry & Human Performance,* 17, 650–660.

WADA (2015) *World Anti-Doping Code.* Quebec, Canada: World Anti-Doping Agency.

Wadey, R., Podlog, L., Galli, N., and Mellalieu, S.D. (2016) 'Stress-related growth following sport injury: Examining the applicability of the organismic valuing theory', *Scandinavian Journal of Medicine and Science in Sports,* 26, 1132–1139.

Walters, S.R., Schluter, P.J., Oldham, A., Thomson, R.W., and Payne, D. (2012) 'The sideline behaviour of coaches at children's team sports games', *Psychology of Sport & Exercise,* 13, 208–215.

Wandzilak, T., Ansorge, C.J., and Potter, G. (1988) 'Comparison between selected practice and game behaviors of youth sport soccer coaches', *Journal of Sport Behavior,* 11, 78–88.

Weinberg, R., and Butt, J. (2011) 'Building mental toughness', in D. Gucciardi and S. Gordon (eds), *Mental toughness in sport: Developments in Research and Theory,* London: Routledge, pp. 212–229.

Weinberg, R., Freysinger, V., Mellano, K., and Brookhouse, E. (2016) 'Building mental toughness: Perceptions of sport psychologists', *The Sport Psychologist,* 30, 231–241.

Weinberg, R., Yukelson, D., and Jackson, A. (1980) 'Effect of public versus private efficacy expectations on competitive performance', *Journal of Sport Psychology,* 2, 340–349.

Weiss, M.R. (1995) 'Children in sport: An educational model', in S.M. Murphy (ed.), *Sport psychology interventions,* Champaign, IL: Human Kinetics, pp. 39–69.

Weiss, M.R., and Amorose, A.J. (2008) 'Motivational orientations and sport behaviour', in T.S. Horn (ed.), *Advances in sport psychology,* Champaign, IL: Human Kinetics, pp. 115–155.

Weiss, M.R., and Williams, L. (2004) 'The why of youth sport involvement: A developmental perspective on motivational processes: A lifespan perspective', in M.R. Weiss (ed.), *Developmental sport and exercise psychology: A lifespan perspective.* Morgantown, WV: Fitness Information Technology, pp. 223–268.

Weiss, M.R., Amorose, A.J., and Wilko, A.M. (2009) 'Coaching behaviours, motivational climate, and psychosocial outcomes among female adolescent athletes', *Paediatric Exercise Science,* 21, 475–492.

Weston, N.J.V., Greenlees, I.A., and Thelwell, R.C. (2011a) 'The impact of a performance profiling intervention on athletes' intrinsic motivation', *Research Quarterly for Exercise and Sport,* 82, 151–155.

Weston, N.J.V., Greenlees, I.A., and Thelwell, R.C. (2011b) 'Athlete perceptions of the impacts of performance profiling', *International Journal of Sport and Exercise Psychology,* 9, 173–188.

Westre, K.R., and Weiss, M.R. (1991) 'The relationship between perceived coaching behaviours and group cohesion in high school football teams', *The Sport Psychologist,* 5, 41–54.

Widmeyer, W.N., and Ducharme, K. (1997) 'Team building through team goal setting', *Journal of Applied Sport Psychology,* 9, 97–113.

Wilde McCormick, E. (2012) *Change for the Better,* London: Sage, 4th edn.

Wilkman, J.M., Stelter, R., Melzer, M., Hauge, M.-L.T., and Elbe, A.-M. (2014) 'Effects of goal setting on fear of failure in young elite athletes', *International Journal of Sport and Exercise Psychology,* 12, 185–205.

Williams, A.M., and Hodges, N.J. (2005) 'Practice, instruction and skill acquisition: Challenging tradition', *Journal of Sports Sciences*, 23, 637–650.

Williams, S.E., and Cumming, J. (2012) 'Sport imagery ability predicts trait confidence, and challenge and threat appraisal tendencies', *European Journal of Sport Science*, 12, 499–508.

Williams, S.E., Cumming, J., and Balanos, G.M. (2010) 'The use of imagery to manipulate challenge and threat appraisal states in athletes', *Journal of Sport & Exercise Psychology*, 32, 339–358.

Wilson, R.C., Sullivan, P.J., Myers, N.D., and Felt, D.L. (2004) 'Sources of sport confidence of master athletes', *Journal of Sport & Exercise Psychology*, 26, 369–384.

Woodman, T., and Hardy, L. (2003) 'The relative impact of cognitive anxiety and self confidence upon sport performance: A meta-analysis', *Journal of Sports Sciences*, 21, 443–457.

Wrisberg, C.A., and Pein, R.L. (2002) 'Note on learners' control of the frequency of model presentation during skill acquisition', *Perceptual and Motor Skills*, 94, 738–794.

Wu, W.F.W., and Magill, R.A. (2011) 'Allowing learners to choose: Self-controlled practice schedules for learning multiple movement patterns', *Research Quarterly for Exercise and Sport*, 82, 449–457.

Wulf, G., and Shea, C.H. (2004) 'Understanding the role of augmented feedback: The good, the bad, and the ugly', in A.M. Williams and N.J. Hodges, (eds), *Skill Acquisition in Sport: Research, theory and practice*, London: Routledge, pp. 121–144.

Wulf, G., and Toole, T. (1999) 'Physical assistance devices in complex motor skill learning: Benefits of a self-controlled practice schedule', *Research Quarterly for Exercise and Sport*, 70, 265–272.

Wulf, G., Chiviacowsky, S., and Lewthwaite, R. (2010) 'Normative feedback effects on learning a timing task', *Research Quarterly for Exercise and Sport*, 81, 425–431.

Zourbanos, N., Harzigeorgiadis, A., Goudas, M., Papaioannou, A., Chroni, S., and Theodorakis, Y. (2011) 'The social side of self-talk: Relationships between perceptions of support received from the coach and athletes' self-talk', *Psychology of Sport and Exercise*, 12, 407–414.

Zourbanos, N., Harzigeorgiadis, A., and Theodorakis, Y. (2007) 'A preliminary investigation of the relationship between athletes' self-talk and coaches' behaviour and statements', *International Journal of Sports Science & Coaching*, 1, 57–66.

Zourbanos, N., Harzigeorgiadis, A., Tsiakaras, S.C., Chroni, S., and Theodorakis, Y. (2010) 'A multimethod examination of the relationship between coaching behaviour and athletes inherent self-talk', *Journal of Sport & Exercise Psychology*, 32, 764–785.

INDEX

Italic page numbers indicate figures and tables.

3+1 Cs: coach–athlete relationship 107–8
3 axioms of mindfulness 231–2
3 Ps 190–1
4 Cs model of mental toughness 184, 192
4 Ws of mental imagery 172, 182
8 principles to help adults learn more effectively 71–2, 78

ABCDE: learned optimism 19.
Abdominal breathing 97
acceptance 67, 87, 117, 211, 231–2, 236
achievement goals 27, 64, 66, 69, 223–5, 228–9
adolescents instruction 62–3; dropout 64; enjoyment 61, 66–7, 74; motivation 61–2, 64–5; RESISTANCE 135–8; self–esteem 61, 66–7, 69; well-being 61, 66–9
Adams, C. 123
Adie, J. W. 67, 224–5
adults: andragogy 70, 78; antecedents of coach behaviour 70, 77; control 72–3, 76–8; effects of coach behaviour 70, 76; enhancing learning 72–5; principles to help adults learn more effectively 71–2, 78
Affleck, G. 66
Ahlberg, M. 154

Ahsen, A. 174
Aidman, E. 26
Aldwin, C. M. 208
American Psychiatric Association 81
Ames, C. 132, 134, 139, 142–3
Amorose, A. J. 132, 135, 139–40, 149–53, 189
analogy learning 75–76
Andersen, M. B. 10, 18, 183
andragogy 70, 78
Anhalt, K. 86–7
Anshel, M. H. 209–11
anxiety 3, 16, 23, 25, 27, 34, 41, 75, 82, 91, 100–1, 121, 126–27, 135, 140–2, 149, 181, 195, 208, 210, 212, 215, 218, 228, 233, 236–43, 246
Appleton, P. R. 27
appraisal 26, 106, 159, 161, 185, 210, 212, 215, 218–19, 226, 230
appraisal training 190, 215, 218–19, 227–8
Arden, C. L. 98
Arvinen-Barrow, M. 93, 96
Atkins, M. R. 58, 140
attention deficit hyperactive disorder (ADHD) 79, 81–2, 84–7, 89–90
Auld, F. 16, 19
autonomy 26, 65, 68, 98, 149–54, 156

Backhouse, S. H. 162

Badami, R. 74, 132
Badan, M. 55
Baltzell, A. 235–6
Bandura, A. 194, 202, 224
Baron-Thiene, A. 64
Bartholomew, K. J. 26, 153, 250
basic psychological needs 24, 65, 98, 148–54, 156
Baumeister, R. F. 239–40
Beaumont, C. 203
Beilock, S. L. 239–40, 243
Bell, J. J. 64, 188–89
Bengoechea, E. G. 62, 133–5
Bennett, J. 100
Benson, A. J. 116
Bernstein, D. A. 15
Beyer, R. 79–80, 82, 84, 86
Bianco, T. 92
bioinformational theory 173–4
Bird, S. R. 157–58
Bishop, S.R. 231
Bjork, R. A. 73
Black, S. J. 132–33
Blascovich, J. 220, 222–4
Blegen, M. D. 131
Blondin, J.-P. 28
Bloom, G. 117
Boekaerts, M. 61
Bränström, R. 231
Brawley, L.R. 119
Bray, C.D. 116
breathing ladders 236–7
Brewer, B. W. 9–11
British Association of Sport and Exercise Sciences (BASES) 11
Bronfenbrenner, U. 187
Brown, D. R. 10
Brown, J. D. 66
Brown, K. W. 231
Brownell, A. 122
Buceta, J. M. 10
Bull, S. J. 185–6
Buning, M. M. 132
Bursuck, W. D. 80
Burton, D. 34–5, 39
Butler, R. J. 43–4, 46–7, 197, 199, 205
Butt, J. 184, 189

Callard, J. 3, 9, 243
Calmels, C. 173
Cannon, W. B. 208
Capio, C. M. 57
Carroll, D. 93
Carron, A. V. 113–15, 118–19, 121

Carson, F. 96–7
Cary, P. 58
Cathcart, S. 233
challenge 6, 24–5, 27, 63, 68, 76, 125, 139–40, 152, 155, 179, 183, 184, 189–90, 193
challenge and threat states: achievement goals 224–5, 228–9; coach–athlete relationship 223, 226, 229; coach behaviour 223, 226, 229; control 223–4, 227–8; dyadic coping 223, 226–7; mental imagery 227–9; physiological implications 222; performance 223–5 227–9; re-appraising threat 227; self-efficacy 223–4, 227, 230; sympathetic-adreno-medullary (SAM) 222
Chambers, D. 159, 161
Chesney, M. A. 211–12
Chesterfield, G. 162
children coach behaviour 57–8; enhancing learning 55; enjoyment 57–8; extrinsic achievement 58; extrinsic non achievement 58; feedback 55–60; fun 58–60; intrinsic achievement 58; intrinsic non-achievement 58; timing based skills 56
Chiviacowsky, S. 55–6, 73–4, 132,189
choking under pressure coping 244; definition 239; distraction hypothesis 241; movement acclimatisation training 243; physical symptoms 240; pre-performance routines 241–2, 244; pressure acclimatisation training 242, 244; preventing choking under pressure 241; psychological symptoms 240; reframing pressure 244; secondary task strategies 244; the self-focus or explicit monitoring hypothesis 240
Chow, G. M. 61–2
Clancy, R. B. 131
Clough, P. 24, 27, 183–4, 190–1, 193
coach–athlete relationship: closeness 107, 112; commitment 106–8; 112; COMPASS 109–10, 112; complementarity 107–8, 112; conflict management 109–10; co-orientation 107–8, 112; definition 105; improving 109
coach behaviour 26, 49, 60–3, 66–8, 70, 76–8, 116–17, 121, 126, 132–3, 140–2, 150–1, 185, 188, 195, 205, 223, 226, 229–30
Coach Effectiveness Training 66, 124
coach performance profiling 49–51

Coatsworth, J. D. 66
cognitive–affective stress management
   training (SMT) 210
Collins, D. 175, 177, 182
Compas, B. E.
commitment 10, 24–5, 27, 40, 67, 106–8,
   112, 164, 184, 197, 212, 226,
competence 11, 58–9, 65, 68, 83, 98, 132,
   134, 140–1, 147, 149–52, 154, 156, 202
concentration 21, 45–6, 173, 179–80, 185,
   187–8, 191–2, 216, 236
confidence profiling 197–9, 205
confidence *see* sport confidence
conflict management 109–10, 112
Connaughton, D. 184, 186
Connolly, K. 55
Conroy, D. E. 27, 66, 130, 209
COPE intervention 210
coping avoidance 96–7, 209, 211, 217–19,
   244; coping effectiveness training
   (CET) 24, 189–90, 192, 211–20;
   definition 208; emotion-focused
   coping 209, 216–18; goodness-of-
   fit 211, 215, 219; problem-focused
   coping 209, 211, 215–16, 218; sports
   performance 209
coping self–efficacy 211–12, 218
Cormier, M. L 118
Côté, J. 2, 55, 226
Cotterill, S. 191
Craft, L. L. 208
Crocker, P. R. E. 58, 209–10
Cumming, J. 173, 227
Curran, T. 140
Cushion, C. J. 2, 62

Dale, G. A. 44, 47, 49
De Backer, M. 117
de Franco Tobar, L. 132
Deci, E. L. 130–1, 137, 148–50
Defreese, J. D. 123
DePauw, K.P. 84
Devonport, T. J. 210–11
Dionigi, R. 94
dissociation 97
distraction hypothesis 240–1, 244, 246
Donovan, R.J. 158–9, 162, 167
doping advice for coaches 164–5;
   Anabolic Androgenic Steroids (AAS)
   158; attitudes: definition 157; health
   158; mental health 159; role of coaches
   162; Sport Drug Control Model
   158–62; Sport Drug Control Model
   for Adolescent Athletes *163*

Driskell, J. E. 172
dropout 5, 58, 61, 64–6, 68–9, 106, 132,
   137
Dubois, P. 57
Duda, J. L. 149–50
D'Urso, V. 44
Durso-Cupal, D. D. 96
Dweck, C. S. 134
dyadic coping 223, 226–7

Ebert, B. W. 9
enjoyment 4, 12, 55, 57–8, 61, 66–7, 74,
   116, 124, 126, 128, 132, 137, 141–2,
   147, 149, 173, 187, 197, 221
explicit monitoring hypothesis 240, 244
extrinsic motivation 130–1, 137, 149,
   156

Feltz, D. L. 199–202, 205
Filho, E. 116
fine motor skill disabilities 79
Fiore, T. A. 86
Flores, F. S 57
flow 151, 173, 195
Folkman, S. 207–9, 211, 215–16
Ford, P. R. 62–3
Forsman, H. 63
Francisco Guzmán, J. 64–5
Fransen, K. 195
Fraser-Thomas, J. 64–6
Freeman, P. 26, 123
French, K. E. 57
Friend, M. 80
Frühauf, S. 20
Fry, M. D. 67
Furley, P. 203

Gano-Overway, L. A. 67
Gardner, L. A. 64, 106
Gaudreau, P. 28, 151, 153
Gervis, M. 187
Giges, B. 19
Gillet, N. 132
goal-setting: benefits 33; definition
   33; individual 37; problems 39;
   SMARTS 36, styles 38; team 38;
   types of goals 34
Golby, J. 187–8
Gonzalez, G. L. 58
Gonzalez, S. P. 74
Gotink, R. A. 231, 233
Gould, D. 92, 209
Gray, J. A. 185
Gray, R. 239

Gucciardi, D. F. 28, 63, 140, 161, 183–6, 188–9, 191–3
Gudjonsson, G. H. 85
Guan, J. 75

Haibach, P. S. 83
Hampson, R. 39–40, 106
Haney, C. J. 211
Hanin, Y.L. 177, 211
Hardy, J. 28, 34, 43–4,
Hardy, L. 116, 123–4, 178, 184–5, 192–3, 196, 208, 241
Harter, S. 66
Harwood, C. 39–40, 132, 135–6
Hassan, M. F. H. 140–1
Hays, K. 11, 195–200, 205
Health Care and Professions Council (HCPC) 11
Healy, L. C. 26
Heil, J. 99
Helsen, W. F. 65
Heppner, P. P. 19
hierarchical model of intrinsic and extrinsic motivation 131
Hill, D. M. 244
Hill, G. M. 65
Hodge, K. 140, 242, 244
Hodges, N. J. 63
Hogg, J. M. 209
Hogue, C. M. 140, 142
Høigaard, R. 126
Holmes, P. 175, 177, 182
Holt, N. L. 64, 209
Horn, T. S. 58, 126, 132, 134
Houston, M. 195
Hurst, J. F. 28
Hutchinson, J. C. 74, 132

Ievleva, L. 173
imagery *see* mental imagery
implicit learning 75
impression management 19–20
injury: basic psychological needs 98; coach, role 92; definition 91; preventing fear of re-injury 99; psychological responses 91; rehabilitation 93–8; return to sport 98
intake interviews: description 15; impression management strategies 19–20; interview guide 16; listening; non-verbal strategies 19; overcoming nerves 16; purpose 16; verbal strategies 19

intrinsic motivation 61–2, 64, 78, 130–7, 141, 148–50, 153, 156, 202,
Isoard–Gautheur, S. 64–5, 106, 150
Ivarsson, A. 91, 99–100
Iwatsuki, T. 239

Jaakkola, T. 140
Jackson, B. 108
Jalleh, G. 161
Janelle, C. M. 63, 72
Jensen, J. L. 56
Johnson, D. W. 38
Johnson, M. B. 158
Johnston, L. H. 92
Jones, D. F. 62
Jones, G. 44, 186, 188–9, 191
Jones, M.V. 27, 221, 224
Jordett, G. 242–3
Jourden, F. J 201
Jowett, S. 27, 105–10, 112, 117, 164

Kamphoff, C. S. 116
Kapalka, G. M. 85
Keegan, R. J. 130, 139, 144
Keetch, K.M. 72
Kelly, G.A. 43, 50, 184, 197
Kerr, H. A. 91
Kiluk, B. D. 82
Kindermann, W. 95
Kingston, K. M. 34, 64–5
Kleitman, S. 66
Knowles, M. S. 70–2, 78
Kobasa, S. C. 184
Koedijker, J. M. 76
Koehn, S. 195
Koocher, G. P. 10
Kowalski, K. C 209
Krohne, H. W. 209
Kühn, A. A. 74
Kvist, J. 99

Lafrenière, M.-A. 108
Lam, W. K. 75–6
Lambert, J. 56
Lane, A. M. 210–11
Land, W. 244
Lang, P. J. 173
Langan, E. 152
language processing disabilities 82
Latham, G.P. 33–4, 37, 40, 95, 191
LaVoi, N. M. 112
Law, J. 75–6
Law, M. 63
Lazarus, R. S. 207–9, 211, 215

leadership 2, *50*, 113, 116–17, 152
learning 55–7, 70–8, 134, 141–2, 162, 172–3, 175–6, 187, 201–2
learning disabilities: athletes with; ADHD 79, 81–2, 84–7, 89–90; attitudes of coaches 83; behaviours of athletes 80; coaching principles 84; managing disruptive behaviour 86; peer mediated intervention 87; visual perception disabilities 82
Lee, T. D. 72–3
Lemez, S. 64–5
Leo, F. M. 116
Lepper, M. R. 143
Levrini, A. 15–16
Lewthwaite, R. 58, 74, 132
Liao, C. M. 75–6
Lindeman, E. C. 70–1
Lindqvist, A. S. 158
Lindsay, P. 100
listening 15, 19, 21, 88, 125, 128, 155
Liu, T. 56
Locke, E. A. 33–4, 37, 40, 95, 191
Lonsdale, C. 26, 242
Lorimer, R. 108
Lumia, A. R. 158
Lyle, J. 2

MacPhail, A. 58
Madan, C. R. 27, 175, 181
Madrigal, L. 91
Mageau, G. A. 109–10, 112, 150–52, 164
Mahoney, J. W. 187
Mandigo, J. L. 209
Manzaneque, J. M. 232
Marcos, F. M. L. 116
Mardon, N. 234
Marsh, H. W. 66, 143
Marshall, H. H. 143
Martin, K. A. 96, 172, 177–8, 182, 203
Martin, L. J. 34, 38, 118–19
Martin, S. B. 63
Masters, R. S.W. 75–6, 240
mastery motivational climate 132, 139–44, 147, 189
McLaren, C. D. 140–1
McNaughton, N. 185
meditation *233*–8
Meichenbaum, D. 76
mental imagery: 4 Ws 172; ability 175; concentration 173; confidence 173; content 172; definition 171; flow 173; injury 173; performance 172; perspective 174; PETTLEP 175; skill acquisition 172; theory 173–4
mental toughness: 4 Cs model 184; definition 183; development 186; goal setting; interventions 187–8; models 184–5; neuropsychological model of mentally tough behaviour 185; training 178
Merriam, S. 70
Mesagno, C. 241–2
Millar, S.–K. 57
Miller, A. 191
Miller, S. 196
mindfulness based stress reduction training: 3 axioms of mindfulness 231–2; acceptance of negative mindset 236; benefits 232–*3*; breathing ladders 236; caring thoughts 235; definition 231; meditation body scan 234–5; reperceiving 232; techniques 234; tips for effective meditation 235
Mitchell, I. 92
Moen, F. 233
Møller, M. 16
Møllerløkken, N. E. 64
Moore, L. J. 106, 220–1, 223–4, 227
Moran, A. P. 241
Morente- Sánchez, J. 162
Morgan, K. 140–1
Morgan, T. K. 124
Morozova, L. V.
motivation 2, 5, 26, 35, 37, 39–40, 45, 50, 55, 58, 61–2, 64–5, 74–5, 77, 109, 118, 126; age differences 131; amotivation 131; coach influence 132; definition 130; different types of motivation 130; extrinsic motivation 131; intrinsic motivation 130; RESISTANCE 135–6
motivational climate: climate; performance motivational climate 140; definition 139; ego involving climate 140; impact on athletes 140; manipulating 140–4; mastery motivational 139 TARGET 142–4; task involving; climate 139
Mullane-Grant, T. 241–2
Mullen, R. 241
Munroe, K. 118, 172, 182
Muris, P. 185
Murphy, S. M. 39, 174–6

neuropsychological model of mentally tough behaviour 184–5

Nicholls, A. R. 3, 9, 23, 106, 158, 161–2, 176, 185, 188–90, 207–15, 221, 226, 243,
Nicholls, J. G. 64, 131, 134, 142
Nicolas, M. 226
Nietzel, M. T. 15
Nikbin, D. 106
Nippert, A. H. 92, 96
non-verbal behaviour 203–4
Nordin, S. 173

observational learning 202, 204–5
Occhino, J. L. 148, 150
optimism 24, 161, 190, 193, 232,
Oudejans, R. R. D. 242–43
Owusu–Sekyere, F. 187

Paige Pope, J. 150
Pain, M. A. 172–3
Park, C. L. 98
Peacock, E. J. 26
peer mediated intervention 87, 88
Pelletier, L. G. 26
performance motivational climate 58, 139–41, 144, 147
performance profiling benefits 44; coach performance profile 49; completed performance profile 47; definition 43; discrepancies 46; how to use 44–6; monitoring 47; team profile 47
Perkins, A. M. 185
Perreault, M. E. 57
Perry, J. L. 226
Personal Construct Theory 43, 50, 184
pessimism 190
Petitpas, A. J. 17
Petróczi, A. 26
PETTLEP 171, 175, 177, 181–2
Philippe, R. A. 187
Pijpers, J. R. 242–43
Podlog, L. 94
Poczwardowski, A. 105–6, 108, 112, 209
Polman, R. C. J. 96–7, 208
Post, P. G. 73
Prapavessis, H. 118
pre-performance routines 242
pressure: acclimatisation training 242, 244; reframing 244
Prevatt, F. 15–16
problem-focused coping 209, 211, 215–16, 218
Proteau, L. 63
psychoneuromuscular theory 173

questionnaires: advantages 23; disadvantages 24; uses of 25

Raedeke, T. D. 65
Rahim, M. 110
Rees, T. 122–5
Reeve, J. M. 151–2
Reeves, C. 209, 211–12
referrals 9, 11, 16
Reid, G. 82–4
Reischmann, H. 70
relatedness 65, 68, 98, 132, 134, 140–1, 147, 150–4, 156, 202
reperceiving 232, 236, 238
RESISTANCE 135–8
revised reinforcement sensitivity theory
Rhind, D. J. A. 109–10, 112, 164
Richardson, A. 171, 203
Rief, S. F. 81
Rieke, M. 62
Rizzo, T. L. 82–4
Robin, N. 175
Rodgers, W. 175
Roiger, T. 92
Rosenberg, M. 66
Rosenfeld, L. B. 124–7
Ruddock-Hudson, M. 92
Ryan, R. M. 130–1, 137, 148–50
Ryska, T. A. 118

Sachse, R. 20
Sackett, R. S. 173
Sagar, S. S. 106
Sandström, E. 105
Scanlan, T. K. 58, 124
Schack, T. 191
Schmidt, R. A. 73
Schneider, W. F. 16–18, 20
Schweizer, G. 203
secondary task strategies 224–5
Self-Determination Theory: basic psychological needs 150; coach role 150–1; controlling coach behaviour 153–4; external regulation 149; identified regulation 149; importance of self-determined motivation 149; integrated regulation 149; introjected regulation 149; self-determined motivation 149; strategies to fulfil basic psychological needs 151–3
self-efficacy 194, 211–12, 218, 223–4, 227, 230

self-esteem 51, 58, 66, 69. 87, 124, 140, 154, *159*, 161, *163*, 210
self-focus hypothesis 240
Seligman, M. E. P. 161, 190
Shapiro, S. L. 231–32, 238
Sheard, M. 187–8
Sheldon, K. A. 76–77
Sheridan, D. 123
Siegenthaler, K. L. 58
Singer, R. N. 63
Singhal, A. 27, 175, 181
Shilts, M. 37
Shumaker, S. A. 122
skill acquisition 63, 172, 210
SMARTS goals 33, 36–8, 41–2, 95
Smith, A. L. 65, 123
Smith, A. M. 92, 96
Smith, C. 79–82
Smith, D. 10, 177
Smith, H. W. 36–7, 95,
Smith, M. 62
Smith, R. E. 57, 66, 140–2, 146, 210–11
Smith, W. 242–4
Smoll, F. L. 57, 66, 124, 141–2, 146
social support: adversity, overcoming 142; benefits 123–4; career transition 123; coach role 123; definition 122; emotional challenge 125; emotional support 125; listening support 125; multi-dimension 124; preferences 126; network 127; reality confirmation support 125; task appreciation support 125; task challenge support 125
Sommers–Flanagan, J. 15, 19
Spaniol, J. 82
sport confidence: benefits 195–6; definition 194; developing 200–4; feedback 201; instructional strategies 200; mental imagery 203; non-verbal behaviour 203; observational learning 202–3; profiling 197–9; reinforcing ability 203; sources 195–7; sport-confidence model 194–5; training environment 203
sports coaching: definition 2
Sport Drug Control Model 158, *159*, 161–3, 166
Staufenbiel, K. 34
Stebbings, J. 76–7
Stein, J. F. 82
Stowe, C. M. 84
stress: definition 207; neuroendocrine responses to stress 208
Strick, L. 79–82

Strong, S. R. 20
Strycharczyk, D. 183
Swain, A. 135–6
symbolic learning theory 173
sympathetic-adreno-medullary (SAM) 222

Tam, J. T. 242
Tamminen, K. A. 63
TARGET 139, 141–2, 144–7
task-involving climate 139
Taylor, J. 16–18, 93–99
Taylor, K. E. 82
Taylor, S. 93–9
Taylor, S. E. 66
team cohesion: coach behaviour 116–17; conceptual model 113–*14*; definition 113 group integration 114; importance of 115–16; individual attractions to the group 114; influencing factors 118; leadership 116; strategies 117–18
te Wierike, S. C. M. 98
Tennen, H. 66
The Guardian 235
Theeboom, M. 113, 140–1, 203
Thelwell, R. 186, 209
Treasure, D. 139–44, 146
Triple Code Model 174
Turner, M. J. 223

Udry, E. 92, 96
United Kingdom Anti Doping Agency (UKAD) 161
U.S. Department of Education 79, 84

Vallerand, R. J. 109–10, 112, 131, 134, 149–52, 164, 196
Van Raalte, J. L. 10
Vargas–Tonsing, T. M. 75, 200
Vealey, R. S. 27, 194–5, 205
Vieira, J. L. L. 106
visual perception disabilities 79, 82

Wadey, R. 98
Walters, S. R. 57–8, 173
Wandzilak, T. 57
Watson, A. 76–7
Weinberg, R. S. 184, 187, 189, 196
Weinstein, R. S. 143
Weiss, M. R. 64, 116–17, 132–5
well-being 2–3, 9, 12, 41, 57–8, 61, 66–67, 69, 77, 82, 93, 107, 122–3,

132, 149–51, 174, 181, 207, 211, 213, 215, 219–20, 230, 237
Weston, N. J. V. 44
Westre, K. R. 116–17
Whaley, D. E. 116
Widmeyer, W. N. 38
Wilde McCormick, E. 234
Wilkman, J. M. 34
Williams, A. M. 63
Williams, L. 64
Williams, S. E. 227
Wilson, R. C. 150, 194

White Paper on Sport 158
Wong, P. T. P. 26
Woodman, T. 196, 208
World Anti-Doping Agency (WADA) 157, 161
Wrisberg, C. A. 44, 47, 49, 72
Wu, W. F. W. 72–3
Wulf, G. 56, 72–4, 132

Zabala, M. 162
Zourbanos, N. 76–7, 124